Internet and Intranet Security Management: Risks and Solutions

Lech Janczewski
University of Auckland, New Zealand

IDEA GROUP PUBLISHING
Hershey USA • London UK

Senior Editor:	Mehdi Khosrowpour
Managing Editor:	Jan Travers
Copy Editor:	Brenda Zboray Klinger
Typesetter:	Tamara Gillis
Cover Design:	Connie Peltz
Printed at:	BookCrafters

Published in the United States of America by
Idea Group Publishing
1331 E. Chocolate Avenue
Hershey PA 17033-1117
Tel: 717-533-8845
Fax: 717-533-8661
E-mail: cust@idea-group.com
http://www.idea-group.com

and in the United Kingdom by
Idea Group Publishing
3 Henrietta Street
Covent Garden
London WC2E 8LU
Tel: 171-240 0856
Fax: 171-379 0609
http://www.eurospan.co.uk

Library of Congress Cataloging-in-Publication Data

Janczewski, Lech, 1943-
   Internet and intranet security management : risks and solutions / Lech Janczewski.
      p. cm.
   Includes bibliographical references and index.
   ISBN 1-878289-71-3
      1. Internet (Computer network)--Security measures. 2. Intranets (Computer networks)--Security measures. 3. Computers--Access control. 4. Cryptography. I. Title.

TK5105.875.I57 J358 2000
005.8--dc21   00-022538

British Cataloguing in Publication Data
A Cataloguing in Publication record for this book is available from the British Library.

NEW from Idea Group Publishing

Internet and Intranet Security Management: Risks and Solutions

Table of Contents

Preface

In information security, as in all areas of information technology, knowledge and practice is advancing rapidly. There is a need for up-to-date material, but the rate of change is so great that a textbook only a few years old will already be obsolete. Covering the most important changes in the field of information security to produce an updated text before it becomes obsolete is a lot to ask of one author, so we have asked several, each expert in their own speciality, to complete one chapter.

Overlaps are minimal, but chapters are substantially independent. Readers can, therefore, either follow the text from the beginning to end, or pursue only their special interests without having to read the whole text.

The book is divided into four separate parts:

Part I: State of the Art

Here major issues concerning development of Internet and intranet are discussed. To present a balanced, world perspective, two points of view have been included: from the United States (*J.Palmer et al*) and from a much smaller country, New Zealand (*J. Gutierrez*). Despite their different situations both countries face surprisingly similar information security problems.

Interestingly, system malfunctions rather than hackers and similar unwelcome characters are still considered to be the greatest security threats.

Part II: Managing Intranet and Internet Security

Three authors discuss issues related to efficient management of the security of distributed systems.

Electronic commerce requires not only technology but also people trusting this method of doing business. In his chapter *Dieter Fink* discusses the components of trust for electronic commerce and the methods of building and sustaining it.

The foundation of every security system is the information security policy (ISP). *Lech Janczewski* presents a method to allow rapid creation of an effective ISP. A variety of documents that standardise development and assessment of information security functions are discussed.

Fredj Dridi and *Gustaf Neuman* present an overview of Internet security issues with special emphasis on Web security. An architecture is presented in which security services are built to protect against threats and to achieve information security for networked systems. Basic security protocols like IPSec, SSL, Secure HTTP, and others are also presented.

Part III: Cryptography Methods and Standards

Cryptography is the major technique allowing secure transport of data through insecure environments and secure storage of data. In this part three authors discuss a number of important issues related to cryptography:

Export of cryptography is restricted by a number of national and international agreements. *Henry Wolfe* in his chapter describes and discusses these restrictions. In his opinion, it is impossible to enforce these restrictions and they should be abolished. To allow a smooth introduction to more technically challenging issues discussed later in the book, Dr. Wolfe presents a short description of the most popular types of ciphers.

Adequate security requires not only implementation of powerful cryptography (for instance the development of a DES replacement), but also an adequate solution for successful cryptography deployment. These issues are discussed by *Dieter Gollmann*.

In the final chapter of Part III, *Chris Mitchell* outlines the major standards regulating cryptographic methods. The OSI security architecture, DES, Message Authentication Codes, Digital Signatures, Hash Functions, and Key Management are presented

Part IV: Security and The Law

It is not enough to understand information security merely in terms of technology (like PKI) and psychology (trust). Understanding the law is also necessary. Technology is advancing so rapidly that law makers can't keep up and changes, which are often inconsistent, are made in haste. Issues such as the rights of an employee to keep data on his/her computer at work private, are not well understood. These issues are discussed by *Charles* and *Nicole Prysby*.

As professionals living in the USA, Charles and Nicole Prysby have an American viewpoint. To give the reader a wider perspective the last chapter of this book, written by G. Gunasekara from Auckland, presents similar issues in a New Zealand context.

Acknowledgments

The project could not have been successfully concluded without each author's contributions, and to each I give my heartfelt thanks. I feel privileged to call them my friends, a friendship that was tested by this project. The test must have been passed — they are still willing to talk to me.

Special thanks are due to Jan Travers from Idea Group Publishing for her help in advising me how to solve multiple problems and providing encouragement and to Robert Barnes for useful suggestions on how to organise the content.

There are many other people who deserve my gratitude for their inspirations, comments, and other forms of help. Professor Andrew Targowski from Western Michigan University gave me the decisive push for this project, and my employer, the University of Auckland graciously allowed me to use their facilities necessary for conducting the project. Finally, members of my family who survived my emotional stress during the life span of this work.

Lech J. Janczewski
Auckland, New Zealand

Part I

State of the Art

Chapter I

Security Risk Assessment and Electronic Commerce: A Cross-Industry Analysis

Jonathan W. Palmer
University of Maryland, USA

Jamie Kliewer and Mark Sweat
University of Oklahoma, USA

The security issue has been a compelling one for many organizations. In two separate studies completed in April 1998, Fortune 1000 companies reported more financial losses due to computer vandalism and espionage in 1997 than they ever experienced before. Several corporations said they lost $10 million or more in a single break-in. And reports of system break-ins at the Computer Emergency Response Team site are the highest they've ever been.

Management objectives for security reflect the individual organization's situation. However, there are several common themes in the objectives for security:
- Safeguarding the organization's assets and resources.
- Complying with policies, procedures, laws, and regulations.
- Utilizing resources economically and efficiently.
- Ensuring the reliability and integrity of information.

Billions of bits of information are being transferred and maintained daily throughout the world. These facts combined with trends toward a greater use of virtual organizations, electronic data interchange with trading partners, and the outsourcing of information handling have proven the effectiveness and profitability of electronic commerce. Consequently, the shift to a computer mediated business environment has opened up several new security gaps in important industrial information. Vast amounts of information can be stolen or tampered with in just a matter of seconds. In addition, companies are facing new security issues regarding sharing of information; preventing unwanted intrusions; and avoiding unintentional mistakes.

More than a million systems are now connected to the Internet, and approximately 50 million people in 100 countries from all seven continents use Internet services (U.S. Department of Commerce, 1997). Currently, the most common use of the Web is for e-mail and advertisement; however, the Internet is quickly becoming a common communication tool in business, the average businessperson is quite familiar with many of the other benefits the Internet offers. As an extension of their Internet use, many companies have implemented their own intranets and have often experienced substantial improvements in information flow, performance, collaboration, teamwork, and customer-responsiveness.

The Internet offers many potential advantages, increases the level of business with current customers, helps to find new customers, and helps to conduct business at a lower cost. However, without adequate security, the Internet involves many risks. Using the Internet for communication and advertising still necessitates isolating the corporate network to protect internal information. More firms are extending their network to include various forms of electronic commerce. Most often, electronic commerce transactions entail computer connections between known parties—various vendors, customers, and trading partners—however, without proper security in place, neither party can be certain of the transmission's authentication or content.

This chapter examines security issues across multiple organizations, focusing on the security concerns in an internetworked environment. The chapter examines current threats facing organizations including alteration, denial of service, errors and omissions, system malfunctions, fraud or theft, unauthorized disclosure, and regulatory and contractual exposure. Basic solutions necessary to minimize or control the damage are also identified. This topic is approached through three levels: Internal, Business to Consumer, and Business to Business. A survey of 35 individuals across four industries (telecommunications, energy, retail, and the public sector) provides the basis for analyzing general security perceptions, information management, and personal security activities.

OVERVIEW OF SECURITY

Information security is an important aspect of a firm that deserves adequate attention. One of the first stages in safeguarding corporate information is recognizing the importance of security. Ninety-five percent of senior management labeled data security somewhat important to extremely important in a recent Ernst & Young study. Nearly 80% of all organizations suffered information or hardware loss in 1995 and 1996. Within the same companies, lack of budget and lack of human resources were cited as major obstacles to adequately addressing security risks (Ernst & Young, 1996). Expenditures on information security are correlated with deterrence of crime. Key preventive activities include the number of hours dedicated to data security, disseminating information about penalties and acceptable usage practices by multiple means, clearly stating penalties for violations, and the proper use of security tools/solutions (Straub, 1990).

SECURITY POLICY

Primarily, a security policy should state the organization's overall information security objectives in writing. A security policy acts as a guide to the actual development and implementation of new systems and controls. Most users in an organization remain unaware of the extent of information security risks they face. Management can use written policies to clearly and definitively demonstrate the importance of information security to the organization. In addition, policies prevent managers from reallocating money in their budget originally intended for security purposes. Finally, a written policy can be used as proof that an organization has diligently addressed information security issues. This is an important piece of evidence in liability disputes.

The development of a security policy begins with an information security risk assessment. This risk assessment should indicate the value of the information in question and the risks to which this information is subjected. Once this is established, the physical, document, personal, hardware, and software securities must be aligned to protect the areas of risk. The finished product of a policy should include a definition of information security, a statement of management intention to support information security, a definition of information-security responsibilities, and finally the specific policies themselves, with any accompanying examples or explanations (Wood, 1997).

The foundation for a secure environment is the implementation of a security policy. Often, management is disappointed in the results of a new control system and becomes frustrated with the technology they have purchased. In many cases the fault is not that of the technology, but in the lack of established guidelines to the information. Before any security technology can be effective, an organization must establish what information should even be stored on a system, and who is allowed access to the different levels of information.

RISK ASSESSMENT

Risk assessment and an active security awareness program are often key elements of an organization's response to the threats posed by computer generated and managed information. Risk assessment is the process of determining if the system of internal controls is adequate. "Adequate" means the controls a prudent person would put in place, taking into account both the risks and the cost of the controls. The objective of risk assessment is to provide an analysis of threats and components to establish vulnerability lists in ranked sequence.

Threats can be generally defined as any potentially adverse occurrence or an unwanted event that could injure either the system or the organization. Threats are of many different types:

- *Alteration*. Making changes to the system without authorization.
- *Denial of service*. A facility or system is unavailable to users due to destruction or damage.
- *Errors and Omissions*. An intentional or unintentional error or omission in the system
- *System Malfunction*. Typically the result of hardware or software incompatibility or poor system design.
- *Fraud or Theft*. Theft of the system or access to the system resulting in a scheme to defraud.
- *Unauthorized Disclosure*. The system, data, or configuration is disclosed to unauthorized people or processes.
- *Regulatory and Contractual Exposure*. Failure to comply with

requirements resulting in penalties or damages

A component is one of the specific parts of the system. When assembled together, the components make up the entire processing facility. The objective is to segment all of the parts of a processing facility system into categories, allowing for a systematic review of the entire system and related threats and controls. Examples of components within an internetworked, client/server environment include:

- *Clients:* client computer hardware, system software and data.
- *Servers:* shared computer equipment, system software and data.
- *Network:* communications related equipment and software.
- *Programs*: application programs and utility software.

A risk assessment provides a systematic approach for evaluating security within an organization. Benefits of risk assessment include: agreed upon audit criteria, easily understandable picture of the system of controls, and facilitates discussion between the auditor, the auditee (client), and management, a visual cross-reference between the reasons for control tests and recommendations made, and provides the auditee with a methodology to perform self-review.

A control is a procedure or physical component that prevents a threat from occurring or mitigates its impact. The auditor's role is to identify the appropriate controls and examine them for adequacy and compliance. To facilitate communication between the client and the auditor, it is necessary to condense the thousands of potential controls into groups.

RECOVERY/CONTINUITY PLAN

Another essential element of a strong approach to information security is a recovery or continuity plan. These plans provide an organization the ability to resume and sustain operations in case disaster occurs within a system. Approaches include hotsites, warmsites, coldsites, mobile recovery, and partnering with other companies. A hotsite is a fully operational data-processing facility that is available to an organization within a few hours of a disaster declaration in order to resume operations. Warmsites and coldsites are essentially downgraded hotsites. They will provide the space and supplies needed to install a system, but will not be maintained at a fully operational status. These alternatives are less expensive and are used when recovery time is not as essential. A mobile recovery system is yet another option. It is most popular in situations where companies cannot afford to leave and restart operations in another location. Therefore, recovery trailers which house basic communication and computer facilities are brought into the vicinity in order to restore operations on site. Finally, one of the most inexpensive means of recovery is a contingency agreement between two companies. If two companies are using similar systems, a shared agreement can be drawn to allow them to rely on the other in a disaster situation. This method can be plagued by drawbacks though—especially if both companies need to enable their backup at the same time (Cain, 1997).

A recovery plan must be tested to insure its ability to function properly. Tom Garrison, business continuity planner with American Century Investments in Kansas City, Missouri suggested that, "an untested plan is only a little better than no plan since our real-world environment changes so rapidly" (Cain, 1997). Ernst & Young reported that a quarter of the companies they surveyed had no continuity plan in place. In addition, only about half of those companies with contingency plans in place have tested them (Ernst & Young, 1996). "Exercise" would be a more appropriate term to describe the process of continually improving a company's ability to maintain operations in the midst of disaster (Cain, 1997). A comprehensive and "well exercised" continuity plan is another security asset.

KEY ISSUES

The concept of threats and components for risk assessment provides a systematic way to analyze given situations. There are differing issues concerning security contingent on the types of information shared and relationships involved. This chapter examines the three basic situations: internal, business-to-consumer, and business-to-business transaction issues.

INTERNAL SECURITY

Most security breaches still occur within company walls. The FBI estimates that about 85% of all information breaches are internal

(O'Higgins, 1997). Viruses, natural disaster, and internal malicious acts were all reported as security cracks within individual companies that resulted in incidents creating losses of over $1 million (Ernst & Young, 1996).

There are multiple methods and tools to begin to reduce these internal losses. One practical and effective deterrence is to raise the awareness of security (Strassman, 1997). This is most often done through a security awareness campaign that informs employees about risks and reminds them to take precautions to prevent break-ins. This approach can eliminate some of the biggest problems which are laziness with passwords and easy access to data centers (Earls, 1997). Another problem dealt with by security awareness is the dilemma of employees with laptops taking important information away from the company without it being secured and encrypted.

A second simple means of insuring information security is the actual physical security of the hardware involved. The following list contains suggestions which help prevent losses by physically placing equipment in secure positions:

- If possible, do not locate the computer room in the first floor or basement of a building. Water damage and theft are both more apt to occur on these two floors.
- Locate kitchen facilities on floors above, but not directly over the computer hardware to minimize water, smoke, and fire damage.
- Restrict all access to computers and telecommunications devices to authorized personnel only. Visits to facilities should always be supervised by a security administrator.
- Install card or badge access systems to large central computer rooms. Isolate and intensely secure areas with highest sensitivity and criticality (servers and private information).

These are just a few examples from a long list of considerations involving site location, construction plans, equipment location, access to equipment, security guidelines, supply guidelines, electrical considerations, environment controls, emergency procedures, and even general housekeeping (Vacca, 1996) that require minimum effort to implement.

FIREWALLS

A growing security concern is the management of intranets and external networks. With more companies tying their networks into the Internet and allowing more remote access into their systems, security issues are increased. The primary solution to this dilemma has been firewalls. A firewall is a system that has the ability to control the flow of data in and out of a network. Basically, a firewall has two functions: 1) Controlling access and data coming into the network. 2) Controlling data going out of the network. There are two basic approaches to a firewall; either the firewall should permit everything to pass through except what is expressly prohibited, or it should prohibit everything to pass through except what is expressly permitted.

The main component of most firewalls is a screening router. A screening router is a device which has the capability to filter packets of information based on their source and destination IP addresses. Some firewalls are composed of only a screening router using the router as a gateway between the private network and the Internet. However, a simple screening router based firewall does not allow for much flexibility. Therefore it is usually combined with a system to increase flexibility and the ability to control information flow. With the increased functionality, a system can create a firewall configured to control data flow specifically according to an organization's security policy.

Some examples of systems implemented into firewalls are a bastion host and a proxy application gateway. A bastion host, named for the highly fortified walls of a medieval castle, is a system designed to protect critical information areas. A higher level of security and auditing capabilities surround such places on a network and are best protected by a stronger firewall such as a bastion (Vacca, 1996). A proxy application gateway is a special server used primarily to access Internet applications such as the WWW from within a secure perimeter. As opposed to communicating directly to an external WWW server, requests made by users are routed to a proxy on the firewall that is defined by the user. The proxy knows how to get out through the firewall without leaving a hole for potential hackers on the outside to get back into the private network (Kalakota and Whinston, 1996). As with any tool though, firewalls are only going to be effective if they are used properly.

Some specific attacks made by hackers on corporate networks are password sniffing, IP spoofing, and denial of service attacks. A password sniffing attack is one of simplest and most common attacks. Tools to aid a hacker in password sniffing can easily be downloaded from the Internet. In this method, a hacker finds a legitimate hole onto the network, such as an FTP port, then runs a program that searches the network for user names and passwords. Once these are acquired, the hacker has instant access to the network and can do as much damage as desired. Next, IP spoofing involves posing as a legitimate system using a fabricated IP address to trick a firewall into letting the hacker through. This kind of attack can be detected by an application firewall, but not by a packet filtering one. A third attack is the denial of service. The denial of service is achieved by multiple means, but the basic principle is to create an abundance of phony traffic that clogs the use of the network (Jackson Higgins, 1997). In addition to operating a firewall, security experts must be aware of what kind of attacks are "en vogue" so that firewalls can be strengthened to withstand these attacks.

BUSINESS-TO-CONSUMER

Inevitably, an organization must venture outside its corporate walls with information technology to relate to consumers. Whether this is done through the WWW, e-mail, payment systems, or some other form of networking, it is one more crack opened to potential security hazards. The essential security services that must be provided in this sort of transaction between two parties are non-repudiation, data integrity, authentication, and confidentiality.

1. *Nonrepudiation* is the capability to provide proof of the origin of data or proof of the delivery of data. This eliminates attempts by senders to falsely deny sending data, or recipients to falsely deny receiving data.

2. *Data integrity* detects the unauthorized modification of data whether by error or attack during transmission.

3. *Authentication* is the process used to verify the identity of the user.

4. *Confidentiality* is the process of protecting secret information from unauthorized disclosure (Ahuja, 1996).

These obstacles are currently being controlled by a multitude of developments in encryption and authentication.

ENCRYPTION

The leading trend in securing the transfer of data is encryption. Encryption is the process of mutating data so that it is unreadable until decrypted with a key. As with most security measures, there is more than one way to accomplish this task. First, there is private key cryptography. In private key cryptography, there is one shared key that will both encrypt the data for the sender and decrypt data for the recipient. The difficulty with this method is the distribution of shared keys. Insuring that both parties have knowledge of one key is a problem itself, but when the amount of messages and keys increases, key management becomes a challenge. Keeping track of which key goes with which data and is shared with which partner becomes impractical for organizations dealing with thousands of customers.

A more advanced form of cryptography which attempts to minimize the key management dilemma is public key cryptography. Public key cryptography uses a pair of keys for every user—a public key and a private key. The public key, which is available to everyone, is used to encrypt the data, while the private key, known by only the user, is used by the recipient to decrypt their message. For example, Mary wants to send a message to Joe. Mary would encrypt the message using Joe's public key and then send the data. Then, Joe is the only one able to decrypt the message with his own private key. By this method, key management is refined to maintaining a directory of public keys of users to whom an organization wants to send coded information.

In addition, public key cryptography can be used to create digital signatures that authenticate the sender of information. To continue the previous example, Mary wants Joe to know that the message she sent Joe is really from her. Therefore, she also encrypts in the message her "signature" with her private key. After Joe receives the message, the signature can only be decrypted with Mary's public key. This form of cryptography also enforces nonrepudiation. Since Mary is the only person who knows her private key, she is the only person that can leave her signature on a document. Therefore, she cannot later deny that she sent that particular document to Joe.

A similar authentication method implementing the same techniques in a broadened fashion is certificates. A certificate is the equivalent of a driver's license or a passport in the electronic world. It is a digital document that acts as a form of identification for the user and is distributed by a trusted party known as a Certification Authority (CA). Information stored in the digital document includes the version number of the certificate, serial number of the user, the algorithm used to sign the certificate, the CA that issued the certificate, expiration date, user's name, the user's public key, and their digital signature (Ahuja, 1996). Certificates have provided a foundation for enhanced security on the Internet. Rather than maintaining a lengthy list of users and passwords at each server, administrators of a system can simply configure a server to accept only certificates signed by a certain CA (Andreesen, 1996). In addition, certificates have become a standard feature in web browsers such as the Internet Explorer and Netscape Navigator.

To further increase the level of security on the Internet, protocols (languages) have been designed to handle only the encryption and decryption of data. Netscape Communications' proposed protocol is called secure sockets layer (SSL). SSL provides an entire channel of communication between two systems that is devoted solely to exchanging encrypted data. It can be used as an underlying tool for other application protocols such as HTTP, SMTP, TELNET, FTP, etc. A similar protocol designed only for HTTP security is the secure hypertext transfer protocol (S-HTTP). Because the S-HTTP is designed only for the HTTP, it has greater flexibility on that particular level of security. In addition to encrypting and decrypting, S-HTTP includes authentication and verification methods that do not require public keys like SSL. However, the two can be used simultaneously. They complement each other well, and SSL can be used as an underlying security protocol for S-HTTP (Kalakota and Whinston, 1996).

Encryption standards and security protocols are all tools that enable the security of transactions and data exchange via the Internet. Because of the increased security, some applications are already becoming more popular and new ones are constantly being created. For instance, consumers are starting to feel more comfortable giving purchasing information such as credit card numbers over the web. As long as the consumer is sure they are dealing with a reputable dealer, the risk of transferring this information over the Internet should be lower or equivalent to giving it out at a restaurant. Also, web security is enabling the use of electronic payment systems. Different forms of cybercash and netchecks are becoming safe means of payment. For those still not comfortable performing entire transactions on the web, another more tangible technology is becoming just as popular—smart cards.

Part III of this book discusses the issues of cryptography at length.

SMART CARDS

Smart cards support a large variety of applications by performing three basic functions: information storage and management, authentication, and encryption and decryption. Primarily smart cards are used as extremely portable and relatively robust data-storage devices (Shoemaker, 1997). The security advantage of a smart card is that it operates in an isolated environment. IC (integrated circuit) smart cards have the ability to hold even larger amounts of data than traditional smart cards. This creates even greater flexibility in security. IC cards have the ability to hold biometric security profiles (such as fingerprints and iris scanning) which offer a higher degree of authentication. Entire authentication profiles can be housed as well. With this feature, an IC chip card can allow a user onto different levels of security based on their level of authentication (Fenn, 1997).

BUSINESS-TO-BUSINESS

Encryption, authentication, and digital signatures are all a very important aspect of business to business relations. With more businesses moving to the Internet to exchange corporate information, security has become critical. In addition, the emergence of extranets and virtual organizations raise the need for heightened security measures. An extranet is defined as a collaborative network that brings suppliers, distributors, and customers together to achieve common goals via the web. This is much different from an ordinary web site or an Intranet which are focused on individual organizational goals (Certicom, 1997). To achieve a successful extranet, data must be able to travel securely to the different parties involved. Security policies that define what information is critical and should or should not be shared must be strictly adhered to in the cases of extranets.

Another important aspect of business to business security is electronic data interchange (EDI). EDI is the exchange of standard formatted data between computer application systems of trading partners with minimal manual intervention (Kalakota and Whinston, 1996). EDI attempts to eliminate the labor costs, supply costs, and time costs associated with the exchange of traditional paper-based business forms. The challenge faced with EDI is developing cryptographic standards and digital signatures that have the same legal status as handwritten signatures. Currently, the digital signatures that are in use are sufficient, but to be legally bound by digital contracts, trading partners often sign a paper contract in addition.

In an attempt to eliminate middlemen and flatten the supply chain, EDI has instead created a new third party intermediary. Value added networks (VANs) now often act as the "go-between" service for trading partners handling the exchange of their EDI documents. VANs are also another alternative for security measures. They take on a large portion of the security responsibility. However, the overall shift of EDI in the business community seems to be drifting away from VANs and toward the Internet. Still, the concept of outsourcing security solutions to organizations that specialize in the field is a common practice.

The question addressed by this chapter is how security issues may differ across industries and across employees (managers, auditors, operational personnel). The following section reports on findings from a cross-industry study.

A VIEW FROM THE FIELD: WHAT MATTERS TO MANAGERS

A pilot study of six firms was conducted to identify common themes in their security portfolios. Interviews and reactions to an initial questionnaire design resulted in agreement on major areas of security concerns and an amended questionnaire.

The Center for MIS Studies at the University of Oklahoma surveyed several member companies to gain a better understanding of some of the critical security issues, including user perceptions, protocols, and personal security activities. There were thirty-five respondents to the survey representing four industries: retailing, telecommunications, energy, and public sector.

RESULTS BY POSITION IN COMPANY

The results by position compare responses from those in a managerial position to those in technical, end user or systems auditing positions (See Table 1). In general, there was little difference in the responses across the two categories. However, there were some significant differences in the non-managers identification of the need for greater training on security issues. Non-managers also had a different opinion on the need for passwords for each application as they were more willing to accept multiple passwords than the managers. Non-managers also felt that there was significantly more contact between end users and systems auditors. Finally, non-managers had significantly less access to the Internet and the organization's intranet. Surprisingly, non-managers were also significantly better about changing their passwords.

RESULTS BY INDUSTRY

The survey results were analyzed by industry and by the position of the respondent in his/her company. The industry results suggest a wide variety of approaches to security, access, encryption, and protection techniques. The results on an industry basis are presented in Table 2.

Security policy responses were generally the same across the four industries. There was, again, a significant discrepancy on the amount of training, with public sector and telecom wanting more than was currently offered. There were also differences in password handling, with public sector and telecom having less stringent requirements for password protection.

Security implementation varied across the industries, with significant differences in access to the Internet, use of firewalls, virus checking, e-mail policies and data encryption. Respondents from energy suggested the strongest set of security measures including frequent contact between system auditors and end users, while the public sector seemed to have the least rigorous measures in place.

Personal security activities suggest there is high awareness of the importance of security. Public sector respondents had significantly more access to the Internet and made heavier use of encrypted information. There was also a significant difference in changing individual passwords, with telecom lagging.

Respondents were also asked to identify the areas of greatest threat to their organizations. System malfunction was identified most often as the greatest risk, followed by unauthorized disclosure and denial of service. Respondents were also asked to identify the areas in which they felt their organizations were focusing the majority of their security efforts. They identified alteration of material as the highest focus followed by unauthorized disclosure and denial of service. The unauthorized disclosure and denial of service overlap the threats and focus questions. Surprisingly, the major focus appears to be in an area these respondents did not feel was the greatest threat and the greatest threat; system malfunction was only fourth of the seven areas for focus. This may suggest some rethinking of the security issue (see Table 3).

CONCLUSIONS

The results of this study suggest that employees have a strong sense of the importance of the information asset, the need for all employees to be aware of security as an important issue, and a fairly strong general awareness of security issues.

Results suggest system level threats were of greatest concern. System malfunction was identified most often as the greatest risk, followed by unauthorized disclosure and denial of service. Fraud or theft and regulatory or contractual exposure were of the least concern. By contrast, respondents felt that the organizational focus on security was greatest in protecting against alteration and then addressing unauthorized disclosure and denial of service, with system malfunction receiving a very low priority.

Security policy responses were generally the same across the four industries. There was a significant discrepancy on the amount of training, with public sector and telecom wanting more than was currently offered. There were also differences in password handling, with public sector and telecom having less stringent requirements for password protection.

Security implementation varied across the industries, with significant differences in access to the Internet, use of firewalls, virus

Table 1. Differences between managers and other employees

Security Policy *1 = Strongly Disagree, 4 = Neutral, 7 = Strongly Agree*	Others N = 15	Managers N = 20	Significant
I am familiar with the firm's published security policy.	5.35	4.78	No
I have access to an up-to-date copy of the firm's security policy.	4.92	4.76	No
I understand what is expected of me in the firm's security policy.	5.35	4.86	No
The firm's security policy is developed with input from a myriad of employees.	4.33	3.90	No
The security policy addresses all areas that I consider to be problematic security areas.	4.81	4.00	Tend
The security policy clearly states what steps will be taken by employees in the event of a security breach.	4.42	4.29	No
Current security policies tend to interfere with my work.	3.08	3.42	No
The security policy clearly identifies an individual or group responsible for correcting security problems.	4.45	4.72	No
I have had adequate training in company security policies.	4.69	3.65	Yes
General Security Perceptions *1 = Strongly Disagree, 4 = Neutral, 7 = Strongly Agree*			
Security is the responsibility of every employee.	6.15	6.50	No
Stronger security systems cause a reduction in the performance of business processes.	3.61	4.10	No
More effective security systems tend to have a higher monetary cost.	4.92	5.05	No
Passwords are required to be changed regularly.	5.62	5.20	No
Different user passwords are required for each application.	3.64	2.62	Yes
Information is a major asset of my firm.	6.42	6.57	No
Security of Information in the Firm *1 = Strongly Disagree, 4 = Neutral, 7 = Strongly Agree.*			
The firm focuses its security budget on the areas that are the greatest threat.	4.3	4.38	No
The information that I process is of vital importance to my firm.	5.35	5.67	No
The information that I process provides a competitive advantage to my firm.	5.15	5.48	No
The information that I process would provide a competitive advantage to a competitor.	5.08	5.19	No
The information that I process would produce legal problems if it were disclosed to an unauthorized party.	5.08	4.86	No
Individuals in the firm have access to the public Internet.	6.50	6.24	No
Access to the public Internet is curbed by limiting the number of individuals with that access.	4.38	3.52	Tend
A firewall or proxy server is installed between the Intranet and the public Internet.	6.00	5.50	No
Virus checking software is installed on all clients.	6.17	5.50	Tend
The firm has an established e-mail policy.	5.00	4.95	No

Table 1 continued

Adequate physical security (i.e. locked doors, video cameras) is in place for all rooms holding storage devices.	5.00	4.78	No
The firm uses established data encryption standards.	3.71	3.88	No
The system auditors have frequent contact with users on security problems.	4.86	3.29	Yes
The most effective security systems used in this firm are the most expensive.	2.50	3.56	Tend
Personal Security Activities *1 = Never, 4 = Sometimes and 7 = Always*			
I try to keep updated on security developments.	4.46	4.80	No
I try to follow what is expected of me in the security policy.	5.53	5.75	No
I ignore the security policy if it hinders my work.	2.71	2.90	No
I use encryption schemes when sending sensitive data over a network.	2.42	3.10	No
I use encryption schemes even when sending non-sensitive data over a network.	1.57	2.29	Tend
I access the public Internet.	3.07	4.00	Yes
I access the firm's Intranet.	3.50	4.85	Yes
I send or receive financial information over a network.	2.21	2.94	No
I transmit to or receive encrypted information from a business partner.	1.43	1.85	Tend
I transmit to or receive information that has not been encrypted from a business partner.	2.14	2.60	No
I change my password frequently	4.86	3.71	Yes

checking, e-mail policies and data encryption. Respondents from energy suggested the strongest set of security measures including frequent contact between system auditors and end users, while the public sector had the least rigorous measures in place.

The discrepancies occur in the area of training and specific implementations. The expressed desire for more training may give MIS groups a ready audience for improving and enhancing current security initiatives. The implementation differences are most obvious across differing industries, so this may account for most of the difference. However, the overall lack of encryption, firewalls, and e-mail policies suggest there are at least three areas that need to be addressed more effectively in most industries. Access to the Internet and the organizational intranet also appear to differ across industries. With the continuing growth of both, this appears to be an important area as well.

Differences were found with a wide variety of approaches to

Table 2. Differences across industries

Security Policy *1 = Strongly Disagree, 4 = Neutral,* *7 = Strongly Agree*	Retail N = 10	Energy N = 10	Public Sector N = 7	Telecom N = 8	Significant
I am familiar with the firm's published security policy.	5.14	5.81	3.86	4.70	No
I have access to an up-to-date copy of the firm's security policy.	4.57	5.82	5.14	3.7	Tend
I understand what is expected of me in the firm's security policy.	5.29	5.45	4.71	4.70	No
The firm's security policy is developed with input from a myriad of employees.	3.20	4.80	4.00	3.63	No
The security policy addresses all areas that I consider to be problematic security areas.	4.25	5.00	3.40	4.00	No
The security policy clearly states what steps will be taken by employees in the event of a security breach.	5.00	4.36	3.80	4.33	No
Current security policies tend to interfere with my work.	4.60	3.63	2.83	2.5	Tend
The security policy clearly identifies an individual or group responsible for correcting security problems.	5.40	5.00	4.60	3.63	No
I have had adequate training in company security policies.	4.60	5.00	3.43	3.20	Yes
General Security Perceptions *1 = Strongly Disagree, 4 = Neutral,* *7 = Strongly Agree*					
Security is the responsibility of every employee.	6.60	6.36	6.00	6.50	No
Stronger security systems cause a reduction in the performance of business processes.	4.60	4.45	3.17	3.40	No
More effective security systems tend to have a higher monetary cost.	5.20	4.64	5.00	5.33	No
Passwords are required to be changed regularly.	5.43	5.00	2.29	3.70	Yes
Different user passwords are required for each application.	2.00	4.18	2.43	2.90	Yes
Information is a major asset of my firm.	6.86	5.91	6.71	6.80	No
Security of Information in the Firm *1 = Strongly Disagree, 4 = Neutral,* *7 = Strongly Agree.*					
The firm focuses its security budget on the areas that are the greatest threat.	4.25	4.80	3.60	4.29	No
The information that I process is of vital importance to my firm.	6.86	4.72	6.00	5.20	Yes
The information that I process provides a competitive advantage to my firm.	6.29	4.64	5.33	5.50	No

The information that I process would provide a competitive advantage to a competitor.	6.14	4.45	4.83	5.40	No
The information that I process would produce legal problems if it were disclosed to an unauthorized party.	6.42	4.27	5.33	4.40	No
Individuals in the firm have access to the public Internet.	7.00	5.45	6.71	6.6	No
Access to the public Internet is curbed by limiting the number of individuals with that access.	3.14	5.82	2.00	3.30	Yes
A firewall or proxy server is installed between the Intranet and the public Internet.	6.80	6.27	2.80	6.00	Yes
Virus checking software is installed on all clients.	5.40	6.10	4.43	6.56	Yes
The firm has an established e-mail policy.	5.50	6.10	2.43	5.30	Yes
Adequate physical security (i.e. locked doors, video cameras) is in place for all rooms holding storage devices.	5.75	5.00	3.80	4.88	No
The firm uses established data encryption standards.	1.75	4.50	3.40	4.75	Yes
The system auditors have frequent contact with users on security problems.	2.33	5.00	2.60	3.33	Yes
The most effective security systems used in this firm are the most expensive.	5.50	2.50	4.00	3.33	Yes
Personal Security Activities *1 = Never, 4 = Sometimes and 7 = Always*					
I try to keep updated on security developments.	4.40	4.91	5.00	4.30	No
I try to follow what is expected of me in the security policy.	6.20	5.81	5.29	5.50	No
I ignore the security policy if it hinders my work.	2.86	3.27	2.17	2.70	No
I use encryption schemes when sending sensitive data over a network.	2.14	3.27	4.00	2.00	Tend
I use encryption schemes even when sending non-sensitive data over a network.	1.14	1.91	3.14	1.90	Yes
I access the public Internet.	3.29	2.70	5.14	3.70	Yes
I access the firm's Intranet.	5.00	3.82	5.28	3.56	No
I send or receive financial information over a network.	3.00	2.56	2.71	2.40	No
I transmit to or receive encrypted information from a business partner.	1.29	1.30	2.43	1.80	No
I transmit to or receive information that has not been encrypted from a business partner.	1.86	2.30	4.29	1.60	Yes
I change my password frequently	6.80	5.73	5.29	4.30	Yes

Table 3. Threats and Responses

	Areas considered the greatest security threats (1= most prevalent)	Areas in which firms focus the majority of their security efforts (1= most prevalent)
	Mean	Mean
Alteration	4.34	2.77
Denial of Service	3.57	3.91
Errors & Omissions	4.11	4.60
System Malfunction	2.83	4.29
Fraud or Theft	4.97	4.43
Unauthorized Disclosure	3.40	3.37
Regulatory or Contractual Exposures	4.77	4.63

security, access, encryption and protection techniques. Security policy responses were generally the same across the four industries.

Personal security activities suggest there is high awareness of the importance of security. Public sector respondents had significantly more access to the Internet and made heavier use of encrypted information. There was also a significant difference in changing individual passwords, with telecom lagging.

The results of this study suggest that employees have a strong sense of the importance of the information asset, the need for all employees to be aware of security as an important issue, and a fairly strong general awareness of security issues. The discrepancies occur in the area of training and specific implementations. The expressed desire for more training may give those charged with security policies and procedures a ready audience for improving and enhancing current security initiatives.

Implementation differences may be industry specific. However, the overall lack of encryption, firewalls, and e-mail policies suggest there are at least three areas that need to be addressed more effectively in most industries. Access to the Internet and the organizational intranet also appear to differ across industries. With the continuing growth of both, this appears to be an area that also needs to be addressed.

In response to the multiple layers of security issues facing a firm,

Figure 1. Security Issues and Responses

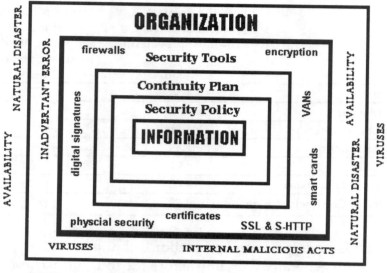

we propose a model for directing security activities within a firm. A six-level model is proposed that identifies the role of security policy, continuity planning, security tools, internal organizational management, and external impacts on the security and integrity of organizational information (see Figure 1).

REFERENCES

Ahuja, Vijay. *Network & Internet Security*. Boston, MA: AP Professional, 1996.

Andreessen, Marc. "Interoperable Security." Netscape Communications. December 1996: http://www.netscape.com:80/comprod/columns/techvision/interoperable_security.html.

Cain, Sarah L. "On the Road to Recovery." *InfoSecurity News*. 1997: http://www.infosecnews.com.

Certicom. "Overview of Security Concepts and Terminology." http://www.certicom.com/html/secqa.htm.

Earls, Alan R. "Between the Cracks." *@Computerworld* February 1997: http://www.computerworld.com.

Ernst & Young. *Information Security Survey: Analysis of Trends, Issues, & Practices* : 1996.

Fenn, Herschel, and Lett. "Smart-Card Technology and Applications." January 24, 1997, Gartner Group: Strategic Analysis Report.

Jackson Higgins, Kelly. "Under Attack." *Communications Week Interactive.* March 1997: http://techweb.cmp.com/cw/cwi.

Kalakota, Ravi, and Andrew B. Whinston. *Frontiers of Electronic Commerce.* Reading, MA: Addison-Wesley Publishing Company, Inc., 1996.

O'Higgins, Brian. "Intranet Security: Beyond Firewalls." *Electronic Commerce World* March 1997: 14.

Shoemaker, John. "Smart Cards and EDI- An Intelligent Combination." *Electronic Commerce World* February 1997: 32-37.

Straub, Detmer W., Jr., "Effective IS Security: An Empirical Study." *Management Science* September 1990: 255-275.

Strassman, Paul. "What's the Best IS Defense? Being Prepared." *@Computerworld.* February 1997: http://www.computerworld.com.

U.S. Department of Commerce, National Institute of Standards and Technology, "Keeping Your Site Comfortably Secure: An Introduction to Internet Firewalls" http://csrc.nist.gov/nistpubs/800-10

Vacca, John. *Internet Security Secrets.* Foster City, CA: IDG Books Worldwide, Inc., 1996.

Wood, Charles Cresson. "Policies From the Ground Up." *InfoSecurity News.* January 1997: http://www.infosecnews.com.

This research was supported by the Center for MIS Studies, Michael F. Price College of Business, University of Oklahoma.

Chapter II

Securing the Internet in New Zealand: Issues, Threats and Solutions

Jairo A. Gutiérrez
University of Auckland, New Zealand

The growing popularity of the Internet has taken many organisations by surprise. Established mechanisms such as fax technology, electronic data interchange (EDI), electronic messaging, and file transfers over private networks have dominated electronic commerce until now.

The advantages of the Internet are changing that technological landscape very rapidly. Those advantages include:

a) Worldwide connectivity.
b) Hardware and software independence provided by ubiquitous Web browsers.
c) User friendliness.
d) Interactive nature of Web-aware technologies.
e) Affordable technology.

However, many of those advantages are shadowed by the lack of widespread use of security and data protection mechanisms. This chapter reviews the history of the Internet in New Zealand, discusses the main problems associated with data protection on the Internet, highlights some of the solutions being implemented in New Zealand, and reviews the main issues and challenges for the future of secure Internet communications.

THE INTERNET IN NEW ZEALAND

One of the first attempts to link research organisations via computer networks was made during the early 1970s by the New Zealand Department of Scientific and Industrial Research (DSIR). The connections were made using dial-up lines and dumb terminal emulation programs.

In 1985 Victoria University of Wellington established a dial-up link to the University of Calgary in Canada for the transfer of electronic mail, and the University of Canterbury in Christchurch established a link to the University of Waterloo (also in Canada). These connections preceded any interconnection among NZ universities (Wiggin, 1996).

In 1986 Victoria University established a link with the University of Melbourne and started carrying and reselling Usenet and e-mail access to several organisations in New Zealand, including other tertiary education entities and government research institutes.

In 1989 Waikato University in Hamilton established the first Internet link to the US via a leased line running at 9600 bits per second.

In 1990 the Kawaihiko network was formed linking all seven New Zealand Universities. This network was later (1992) incorporated into TuiaNet connecting the universities to the government research units (Crown Research Institutes) and most of the remaining tertiary education organisations.

Most of the Internet traffic between New Zealand and the rest of the world passes through facilities provided at The University of Waikato by NZGate, a nonprofit activity of that university. NZGate handed over management of the international links to Netway and Clear Communications in early 1996. The Internet gate, still operating out of Waikato, was renamed the New Zealand Internet Exchange (NZIX), and it provides several 2 Mbps links to the United States, and a 128kbps link to AARNET at the University of Melbourne in Australia.

Some organisations, such as Compuserve Pacific, Telstra and AT&T, provide their own overseas connections to link their customers to the Internet. A complete reference to Internet access in New Zealand, including a list of the Internet Service Providers (ISPs), can be found in Wiggin (1999). A somewhat more detailed list of major

ISPs and their charges can also be located at (IDG Communications, 1999).

TuiaNet has handed over the responsibility for the allocation of domain names to the Internet Society of New Zealand (ISOCNZ), a group formed to promote the use of the Internet. Victoria University reports (Victoria University, 1999) that as of the first of August of 1999 the number of IP-connected organisations in NZ has grown to 22,717 with over 182,021 hosts connected to the net according to the latest Internet Domain Survey (Internet Software Consortium, 1999). Figure 1 illustrates the rapid growth of the Internet in New Zealand.

INTERNET SECURITY THREATS

A security threat may be defined as a circumstance or event with the potential to cause economic hardship to data or network resources in the form of destruction, disclosure, modification of data, denial of

Figure 1 - Growth of the Internet in New Zealand
Source: Victoria University of Wellington

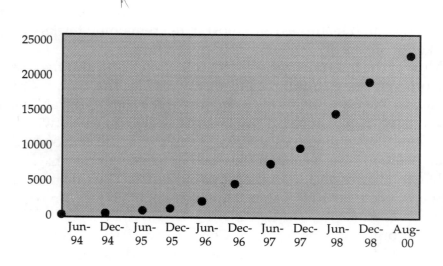

service, and / or fraud, waste, and abuse (Kalakota and Whinston, 1996). Besides those threats, Internet users need to contend with a lack of international supervision, rules and standards. Some of the main issues are discussed below:

Lack of International Supervision

Internet users can not rely on an internationally recognised set of regulations regarding data protection. There is no central mechanism or "network control centre" that supervises the flow of data. Moreover, the increasing use of web technologies can only exacerbate this situation with users downloading software and data from an increasing number of sources located anywhere in the world.

Lack of International Data Protection Standards/Legislation

The lack of a "network control centre" means the responsibility for data protection and data security is shared between millions of providers. Every message transmitted could be intercepted at any unsecured site it passes and could be modified, spoofed (falsified), cancelled or delayed. In most cases users have no control over the route a particular packet takes when it is transmitted to the Internet. Nevertheless the Internet use for business purposes is increasing exponentially, and many users are using it to transmit personal data.

Despite the increasing popularity of the Internet, an immense amount of work needs to be done at national and, especially, international levels to specify and implement data privacy regulations and laws.

Authentication/Identification Requirements

The use of Internet services does not allow for adequate anonymity nor adequate authentication. A typical Internet packet contains a header with information about the sender and the recipient (name and IP-address, host name, timestamp, etc). The header contains further information on the routing and the type of packet being transmitted. Web and e-mail users leave an electronic trace, which can be used to develop a profile of personal interests and tastes.

Although there is no central accounting of the access to news or World Wide Web sites, the information behaviour of senders and recipients can be traced and supervised at least by the Internet Service Provider (ISP) to whom the user is connected. Most ISPs will deny using this information, but the fact remains that they are technically capable of gathering it.

Although profiling users habits represents a real privacy threat, the major security risk related to the lack of proper identification and authentication features is the vulnerability of systems to hacker attacks. These attacks range from malicious pranks (such as displaying messages on particular dates), to destroying and / or compromising sensitive data. Another popular attack is to charge another user's account for Internet services.

Confidentiality Requirements

By connecting to the Internet users are exposing themselves, and their organisations, to the entire population of this very large network. Expectations of confidentiality and privacy should, but often are not, reduced by that exposure. In other words, many users tend to expect the same data protection and security features enjoyed during the times of private data networks. Having said that, it is vital for network and service providers to make sure that those expectations of confidentiality are meet. The popularity of electronic commerce transactions depends mainly on the confidentiality of sensitive data such as credit card numbers and the integrity of electronic cash mechanisms.

Interruption of Service

Recent attackers to Internet sites have used a technique called "SYN flooding". The attackers use the fact that TCP/IP protocols attempt to start data transmissions by using ACK and SYN ACK packets. The flooding takes place when the attacker's computer does not acknowledge the attacked computer's SYN ACK, and it continues to "flood" the computer with SYN packets. At the moment there are not accepted ways of combating this attack and in several cases complete sub-networks have been disconnected from the Internet in an attempt to control the problem. This is just an example of interruption or denial of service.

Masquerading

Masquerading takes place when a user pretends to be somebody else. The IP spoofing (using somebody else's IP address) attack has been used to charge another user for commercial services accessed via the Internet, or to cause damage to a remote computer while incriminating an innocent user. Some hackers use a "chain" of spoofed IP addresses to hide their location or to hinder the tracing of their original network address.

Repudiation

Repudiation occurs when a user claims that a particular message has not been sent or that the received message is different from the original. For example, a user may argue that a withdrawal message was never sent to the bank, or that the amount withdrawn was different from the amount claimed by the bank for that transaction.

EXISTING REGULATIONS AND GUIDELINES
National regulations/provisions

There are no specific laws controlling data protection on the Internet in New Zealand. The most significant legislative acts that have an impact on the communications over the Net are related to privacy concerns and to the transmission of questionable material (the Technology and Crimes Reform Bill of 1994).

The New Zealand Parliament introduced in 1994 the "Technology and Crimes Reform Bill" (NZ Technology and Crimes Reform Bill, 1994) as an attempt to legislate the use of telecommunications and networking. The emphasis of the Bill is on prohibiting and penalising the transmission of "objectionable" material[1], and provides for the Office of Film and Literature Classification to examine and classify images, sounds, and live shows "produced for pecuniary gain". The Bill also attempts to deal with "foreign" communication services carrying the same kind of objectionable material.

The Bill is basically a piece of censorship legislation, and it has been heavily criticised by several users and industry groups. The Internet Society of New Zealand (ISOCNZ) summarised its point of view in a paper (Hicks, 1996, p. 1) delivered to the Commerce Select Committee (entity in charge of reviewing such submissions). ISOCNZ argues that:

1) The Bill does not address the technologies it is attempting to legislate, thus making parts of it impossible to comply with or to enforce.
2) The Bill is not consistent with attitudes and controls on other forms of communications.

3) The Bill's contents will soon require replacement as its basic premises are overtaken by new technology and international events.

Additionally, ISOCNZ recommend a complete revision of the Bill including a public discussion of any future amendments.

International Guidelines

There is a definitive lack of international regulations regarding data protection on the Internet. Several national data protection authorities have already issued guidelines on the technical security of computer networks linked to the Internet. Such guidelines have been laid down, for example, in France, the United Kingdom and in Germany. The main topics can be summed up (International Working Group on Data Protection, 1996) as follows:

1) Providing information on the Internet is subject to the national data protection laws and regulations. In this respect the Internet is not as unregulated as often stated. National regulations might include the obligation for information providers to register at a national data protection authority.

2) Before connecting a local computer network to the Internet the risks for the security of the local network and the data stored there have to be assessed in conformity with the national law. This may include drawing up a security plan and assessing whether it is necessary to connect the entire network or only parts of it to the Internet.

3) Technical measures should be taken to secure that only the data that could be published can be accessed on the Internet.

There are also a number of international legal regulations concerning data protection on the Internet (IWG on Data Protection, 1996):

1) European Council 90/387/EEC of 28 June 1990 on the establishment of the internal market for telecommunications services through the implementation of Open Network Provision (ONP) and ensuing ONP Directives (defining data protection as "essential requirement").

2) Directive 95/46/EC of the European Parliament and of the Council of 24 October 1995 on the protection of individuals with regard

to the processing of personal data and on the free movement of such data (EU-Data Protection-Directive).

3) General Agreement on Trade in Services (GATS) stating in Article XIV that Member States are not prevented by this world-wide agreement to adopt or enforce regulations relating to the protection of privacy of individuals in relation to the processing and dissemination of personal data and the protection of confidentiality of individual records and accounts.

Internet Community Code of Practice

Recently there has been an effort from the Internet Community to implement self-regulation measures by promoting and adopting codes of practice, informally known as "Netiquette". These measures aim to make users, and in general organisations, aware of the privacy and confidentiality implications of being part of a global networking community. The Internet Service Providers Association of New Zealand is promoting the adoption of a voluntary Code of Practice that (ISPANZ, 1999, p.1) tries "to improve the standard of conduct within the Industry". The standards relate to industry members (Internet Service Providers), and commercial and public sites.

The code of practice also lays out regulations to electronic commerce (e-commerce), and encourages the adoption of Internet Standards (Request For Comments or RFCs), and other international standards such as the Platform for Internet Content Selection (PICS).

A typical e-commerce ëpractice', as encouraged by ISPANZ, is to inform customers about the availability of secure transactions mechanisms whenever they intend to purchase goods via the Internet. Another practice advises ISPs to provide customers with a schedule of all planned service outages in advance.

SECURITY SOLUTIONS

There is a common belief that lack of security is the major barrier to successful commercial use of the Internet. Businesses detest the kind of exposure provoked by attacks on the Internet. In 1996 Xtra, the largest Internet Service Provider in New Zealand, was forced to restrict access to their users to patch a security problem (Dias, 1996). It was a very simple problem. New passwords to users accounts were created disregarding normal precautions in those cases. However, users suffered from "Denial of Service" while the problem was fixed. Recent Internet-related security attacks have also taken the form of malicious code transported as e-mail attachments. Notorious among those were the Melissa virus and the Happy99 worm (Malcolm and Fusaro, 1999). Obviously, an organisation planning to base an important part of their business on the Internet would think twice about doing so given that sort of media attention.

The advent of e-commerce as an important element of the business environment adds another dimension: the web server as the weakest link in the security chain. Security holes in freely available web-server software creates a window of opportunity for hackers to get into the rest of an organisation's network before the IT department has a chance to extend the security blanket in order to include the new system.

Although a basic Internet link may be a security risk, there are several ways of addressing the potential problems discussed above. The following is a summary of the main issues:

Encryption

Using encryption can protect sensitive data travelling over the Internet. Encryption is the transformation of readable text (also called clear or plain text) into an unintelligible form called cipher text, using mathematical algorithms. Only users with a digital key, and a program based on the encrypting algorithm, can decode an encrypted message.

These are the basics of symmetric or single-key cryptography. Most commercial solutions also use asymmetric or public-key cryptography in which encryption is accomplished by using key pairs, one private, and one public. Users with private keys made available their corresponding public keys to communicating partners. Each public key will decode only those messages sent by the holder of the corresponding private key. Users maintain the confidentiality of their private keys.

There are several issues regarding the use of encryption techniques on the Internet.

Data encryption schemes are a good solution for protecting small amounts of data, such as credit card numbers or passwords, as they move from source to destination. However, encryption techniques present some practical difficulties for protecting, for instance, the contents of large computer databases from remote access by an unauthorised user. In general, encryption must be used with other techniques to provide a secure networking environment.

The United States Government has proposed a relaxation on the restrictions to export strong encryption techniques by creating a Key Recovery Infrastructure which has been considered as "overly aggressive" by, among others, the US Public Policy Office of the Association for Computing (ACM). They (Simmons, 1997) suggest that the development of a policy that serves the long term interests of both the US and the global community, should not be one based on a Key Recovery Infrastructure, but rather one that promotes the use of strong encryption (if the US does not supply this technology, other countries will). The ACM is worried about restrictions, such as the need to include Key recovery mechanisms, which would limit the research and production of innovative encryption methods in the US. The issues of exporting strong encryption techniques are discussed at length in the Chapter 7 of this book.

The lack of world-wide standards for public key encryption plus the potential problems for US-based companies attempting to export strong encryption products has created an opportunity for a New Zealand start-up company. RPK New Zealand has created an industrial-strength security and encryption standard (Raike, 1999). The security of the system, based on a cryptographic engine called a "mixture generator", is described to rest on the computational difficulty of computing discrete logarithms over large finite fields.

Back in 1996 RPK New Zealand invited scrutiny of their product by challenging Internet users to break the code and win US$3000 in the process. As of the time of this writing the company claims nobody has broken their system, and they have raised the stakes to US$10,000. The company expects to fill the market gap left by companies shackled by the export restrictions placed upon them by the US government. It is important to note that Washington is under great pressure to modify those restrictions. In the meantime RPK has patented their system and it is being commercialised under the name "RPK Encryptonite Engine". It is said to combine all the features of public key systems (authentication, digital signatures/certificates and key management) with the speed of secret key systems — in one algorithm.

Authentication and Non-repudiation

Users communicating over the Internet must be able to feel confident that they are exchanging data with the intended party. Authentication can be provided by using "digital signatures" and "certificates". With digital signatures user A prepares a message to B and encrypts it using A's private key. After that, A encrypts the message again using B's public key. B can decrypt the message using its own private key and A's public key. The use of A's private key guarantees that only A could have prepared the original message.

Nonrepudiation occurs when neither party is able to deny having participated in a transaction after the fact. Certificates bind public keys to specific entities and allow a third party (mediator) to validate this binding (Bhimani, 1996). There have been calls for the government of New Zealand to provide a national certificate infrastructure in order to promote electronic commerce. However, Ministry of Commerce officials have stated that business, not the government, should offer a public certificate service.

Secure Socket Layers and Secure HTTP

Netscape proposed in 1994 a protocol that provides security services layered above the Transport Control Protocol (TCP) and beneath any application protocol or electronic commerce application. The protocol called Secure Socket Layers (SSL) provides confidentiality, message integrity, and authentication by using a combination of encryption techniques that include public and single-key systems and digital signatures. SSL is supported in the latest versions of the Netscape Internet browser.

The Secure Hypertext Transfer Protocol is an extension to the existing HTTP protocol. S-HTTP adds message or transaction-based security at the application level. In general it provides similar functionality as SSL, but in an integrated fashion, not as a lower-layer service. Some vendors treat both approaches (SSL and S-HTTP) as complementary, however others are incorporating only one of them to their products.

Cybertech is a New Zealand company that has pioneered the use of secure technologies for electronic commerce in the Internet. One of the first secure on-line shopping sites was developed for Cybershop NZ. The site (http://www.cybershop.co.nz) uses a set of libraries and APIs linked to a SQL server, and Secure Sockets Layer technology for on-line ordering. Web pages with embedded JavaScript are used to connect the server-side software, and HTML pages are dynamically created using defined templates. Several other secure sites have been developed during the last two years.

Security Improvements for Ipv6

The Internet Engineering Task Force favours an approach that brings security into the Internet Protocol itself (Stallings, 1996). The new developments of the Internet Protocol (e.g., IPv6) offer means to improve confidentiality by encryption, classification of messages and better authentication procedures.

The IPv6 Authentication Header is an extension header that provides authentication and integrity (but without confidentiality) to IPv6 packets. For compatibility reasons it is advisable to use the MD5 message-digest authentication algorithm specified in RFC 1321 (IETF, 1992), however the IPv6 extension is algorithm-independent.

The Encapsulating Security Payload (ESP) Header provides integrity and confidentiality to IPv6 packets. The ESP mechanism can be used to encrypt either a transport-layer segment (with remaining headers as clear text) or an entire IPv6 Datagram. The new security mechanisms may be combined to provide even tighter security. Encryption can be applied before or after authentication.

ISSUES AND CHALLENGES

The discussion of the many issues related to Data Protection leads to several conclusions regarding how to best secure Internet communications:

- Given the rapid growth of the Internet, it is essential to improve end-user support in order to familiarise them with the basics of data protection and security.
- Sensitive data should only be communicated via the Internet in encrypted form.
- Security must be considered nonexistent unless it is implemented by the user or explicitly provided by an Internet systems integrator.
- An international cooperation governing data protection in the context of transborder networks and services, including an oversight mechanism, is essential.

- Software vendors should implement the new Internet Protocol (IPv6) security standards in their products, and providers should support the use of these products.
- Software vendors should support the upper-layer security solutions (SSL and S-HTTP) as complementary technologies in their products and electronic commerce outlets, and Internet Service Providers should support the use of these products.
- It is important to provide a transparent support for a certificate infrastructure, both at the national and international levels.
- Finally, it will be decisive to find out how self-regulation by way of an expanded Code of Practice might improve the implementation of national and international regulations on data protection.

CONCLUSIONS

The efforts to secure the Internet have produced a number of solutions to the main security threats. The increasing awareness of the Internet community regarding data protection is contributing to the rising utilisation of security mechanisms, and to the mounting pressure for governments to lift restrictions on the export of encryption technologies, and for software vendors to adopt interoperable security standards.

The Internet community has not yet agreed on a IPv6 Key Management protocol and there are several key management proposals available. It is very likely that by the time IPv6 is adopted the key exchange mechanisms would have been defined. In the meantime, SSL and S-HTTP will find a role to play with existing IP networks. Most e-commerce transactions over the Internet can benefit from secure transmissions of confidential data without the need for an agreed upon public-key standard.

The need for authentication and non-repudiation services should cause the adoption of certification schemes and the efforts for self-regulation of the Internet must continue. The different approaches introduced in New Zealand, and discussed here, point towards the right direction; but they will have to be combined effectively, and promoted further to arrive at a Global Information Infrastructure that provides an efficient and secure platform for the widespread use of networking technologies.

ENDNOTES

1   For the purposes of this Act, "objectionable" has the meaning given to that term by section 3 of the Films, Videos, and Publications Classification Act 1993 as if images, sounds, live shows, programmes, or foreign satellite services were publications under that Act.

REFERENCES

Bhimani, Anish (1996). "Securing the Commercial Internet", *Communications of the ACM*, 39(6), pp. 29-35

Dias, Neshan, "Call for Internet Security Body", *IT Weekly*, 9 September 1996, p. 1

Hicks, Roger (1996). "Submission to the Commerce Select Committee", Internet Society of New Zealand, July 1996, http://www.isocnz.org.nz/isocnz/submission.html.

IDG Communications (1999). http://www.idg.co.nz/magazine/pcworld/pcworld.shtml.

International Working Group on Data Protection (1996), "Data Protection on the Internet, Budapest Draft", April 1996, http://www.datenschutz-berlin.de/diskus/.

Internet Engineering Task Force (1992). "RFC1321: The MD5 Message-Digest Algorithm", April.

Internet Software Consortium (1999), http://www.isc.org/ http://www.isc.org.

ISPANZ (1999), Internet Service Providers Code of Practice, 1999, "http://www.isocnz.org.nz/".

Kalakota, R. and Whinston A.B. (1996), Frontiers of Electronic Commerce, Addison-Wesley Publishing Company, Inc.

Malcolm, A. and Fusaro R. (1999), "Not so happy virus infects firms' email", *Computerworld New Zealand*, No. 585, February 22, 1999, 1.

New Zealand Technology and Crimes Reform Bill (1994), http://iconz.co.nz/nsnz/tncrbill.html.

Raike, William (1999), RPK Public Key Cryptography, http://www.rpkusa.com/ http://www.rpkusa.com.

Simmons, B. (1997), "USACM analysis of Commerce Dept. cryptography export proposals", RRE News Service, 13 February 1997.

Stallings, W. (1996), "Building security into IP packets", *New Zealand Network World*, No. 16, Oct/Nov. 96, 53.

Victoria University (1999), http://www.comp.vuw.ac.nz/~mark/netsites.html.

Wiggin, Peter (1996), Wired Kiwis, Clear Communications.

Wiggin, Peter (1999), http://www.wiredkiwis.co.nz/isps/index.htm.

Part II

Managing Intranet
and
Internet Security

Chapter III

Developing Trust for Electronic Commerce

Dieter Fink
Edith Cowan University, Australia

While much attention is currently being devoted to solving technological challenges of the Internet, for example increasing the bandwidth on existing narrowband network platforms to overcome bottlenecks, little attention appears to be given to the nontechnical aspects. This has been a mistake in the past as human resistance to, or incompetence during, the introduction of new Information Technology (IT) often caused Information Systems (IS) to fail. By focusing on a broad range of technical and nontechnical elements early in the adoption of Internet technology, we have the opportunity to avoid the mistakes made in the past.

The Internet has given rise to electronic commerce (e-commerce) through the use of the World Wide Web (Web). E-commerce, by its nature, offers enormous possibilities but in an uncontrolled environment. Therefore, for e-commerce to be accepted, trust must be established as soon as interaction with a Web site begins. In the virtual environment of the Web trust has become even more important because the parties are not in physical proximity. There are no handshakes or body language to be observed when closing a deal. Furthermore, jurisdiction is unclear. Developments on a global scale are required that provide assurance that e-commerce can be conducted in a 'trusting' manner.

E-commerce can be defined as the process of conducting business between entities (organisations, persons) using appropriate electronic methodologies and procedures. Simply stated, e-commerce is a means of exchanging products, services and information over electronic networks that make up the Internet. The Internet can be described as a non-hierarchical, democratically structured, collaborative arrangement entered into by millions of network users. This informality and lack of overall control creates the perception in many people that the Internet is inherently insecure and cannot be trusted.

The question of trust and related concepts has occupied our minds for many decades. In 1958 Morton Deutsch wrote, "The significance of the phenomenon of trust and suspicion in human life is attested to not only by past preoccupations but also by current problems." (p. 265) Today we can categorise as a 'current problem' the trust or lack of it associated with e-commerce. In this chapter we will again examine the concept of trust and apply it to the environment and needs of e-commerce.

THE NEED FOR TRUST

Fink (1999) surveyed final year university students, the future business leaders, to capture their perceptions of e-commerce. The study hypothesised that the success or failure of e-commerce will be determined by the trust that they would show towards the use of the Internet. In other words, the students would weigh up their perceptions of the capabilities of e-commerce against perceived concerns and risks. His findings indicated that business students believed that the capabilities of e-commerce were not currently fully achieved because of the high levels of concerns and risks that exist. Fink (1999) concluded "As a consequence, the trust students currently have in e-commerce is relatively low." The students, however, were optimistic about future prospects of e-commerce, which they believed would significantly improve over the next few years.

The importance of trust has been widely acknowledged, but difficulty has consistently been encountered on how to define the concept. In the words of Hosmer (1995, p. 380), "There appears to be widespread agreement on the importance of trust in human conduct, but unfortunately there also appears to be equally widespread lack of agreement on a suitable definition of the concept." With the rapid emergence of e-commerce, and its acknowledged significance in future, the challenge once again has arisen how to determine the meaning of trust and to evaluate its contextual implications.

Early researchers analysed the concept in contexts different to the ones that now exist. For example Hirsch (1978) related trust to the physical exchange of goods and held the view that "trust was a public good, necessary for the success of economic transactions" (p. 78, cited in Hosmer, 1995). Under e-commerce, physical products and services become digital ones but the need for trust does not diminish. Trust remains "vital for the maintenance of cooperation in society and necessary as grounds for even the most routine, everyday interactions" (Zucker, 1986, p. 56, cited in Hosmer, 1995).

A closer examination of the characteristics of e-commerce readily establishes the need for trust. The following are some examples. First, there is the principle that diversity results in less reliance on interpersonal similarity, common background and experience (Mayer et al., 1995). Diversity is a key feature of e-commerce and participants can be found all over the world. With e-commerce, customers can choose from a wide range of products and services available anywhere in the world. Suppliers can form strategic alliances with other firms to overcome their deficiencies (e.g. intelligence sharing) or exploit market opportunities beyond their means (e.g. becoming a bigger virtual organisation). The diversity of e-commerce increases the need for trust.

Second, the extensive use of the supply chain relies on the existence of trust (Powell, 1996). The supply chain was conceptualised by Michael Porter (1985) as a flow of products, services and information from one participant in the chain to the next, thereby linking suppliers, manufacturers, distributors and consumers. Under e-commerce, the virtual chain replaces the physical chain. We are witnessing an increasing supply and distribution of digital products such as computer software and books on the Web. This has created the opportunity for new players to enter the supply chain, potentially disrupting established trading relationships. The trust that exists between existing participants in the chain is being threatened by new relationships.

Third, the move towards self-directed teams and the empowerment of workers in modern organisations has greatly increased the importance of trust (Mayer et al, 1995). Teams and workers demand 'any-time, any-place' computing to collaborate with each other and to carry out their responsibilities in an efficient and effective manner. The Internet provides a ready means to achieve this, but because of its perceived inherent insecurity it may not be fully exploited by the modern workforce for collaborative purposes.

ASSUMPTIONS, DEFINITIONS AND PRINCIPLES

In an attempt to provide suitable definitions for trust, one needs to establish the underlying assumptions from which they can be developed. According to Tyler and Kramer (1996), trust can be viewed from an instrumentalist and non-instrumentalist perspective. The instrumentalist model reflects rational behaviour while the non-instrumentalist model applies to social relationships. If one accepts that e-commerce is essentially about maximising one's business opportunities, then the instrumentalist model appears to best meet the requirements of e-commerce. Furthermore, people behave rationally and "people's decisions about whether to cooperate – for example, their willingness to trust others – are based on their estimates of the probability that others will reciprocate that cooperation." (Tyler and Kramer, 1996, p. 10).

The instrumentalist model focuses on the efforts of self-interested individuals to achieve optimum outcomes in interactions with others along two principles.

1. Trust is a calculation of the likelihood of future cooperation (Williamson, 1993, referenced in Tyler and Kramer, 1996). "As trust declines, people are increasingly unwilling to take risks, demand greater protection against the possibility of betrayal, and increasingly insist on costly sanction mechanisms to defend their interests." (Tyler and Kramer, 1996, p. 4) Declining trust in long-term relationships increases transaction costs because of the need for self-protective actions.

2. Trust is determined by the 'reputational' market and the 'shadow of the future' (Axelrod, 1984, referenced in Tyler and Kramer, 1996). In other words, unsatisfactory performance by a supplier will lead to a decline in the supplier's reputation and cast a shadow over future dealings between consumers and the sup-

plier. With the growth in the size of the market the effectiveness of the reputational market declines.

The instrumentalist perspective of trust can be termed essentially a 'calculative' one; it reflects "the assumption that the decision to trust is predicted primarily on the computation of risks, albeit a computation that favors trust in the near term if the 'shadow of the future' looms sufficiently large" (Tyler and Kramer, 1996, p. 5). For e-commerce three implications arise. One, risk assessment is critical to doing business on the Web and, hence, increasing attention is being given to security measures to minimise risk exposure. Two, many business dealings occurring on the Web are of a short-term, temporary nature which has given rise to 'swift trust' (Meyerson et al., 1996). Both aspects will be elaborated on in later sections. Third, e-commerce has seen a tremendous growth in market size (its spans the globe) and hence has reduced the effect of the 'reputational market'.

The strong interest in e-commerce is understandable because today's organisations and individuals cannot ignore the potential benefits of e-commerce or they risk being worse off. E-commerce provides strong advantages over traditional forms of business. The opportunity to market products and services, by reaching a global audience electronically, are substantially enhanced. Reduced physical involvement in transaction processing brings about lower costs. Banking transactions on the Internet cost substantially less than customer transactions over the counter. Advertising is now done more effectively on the Web rather than in, or additional to, the press and radio.

Hosmer (1995) offered a definition of trust that reflects a moral obligation. "*Trust* is the reliance by one person, group, or firm upon a voluntary accepted duty on the part of another person, group, or firm to recognize and protect the rights and interests of all others engaged in a joint endeavor or economic exchange." (p. 393) One can argue about how realistic in today's world the expectation of 'voluntary accepted duty' is to look after the interests of others. The anonymity offered by the Web provides scope for unethical and criminal behaviour. Techniques such as WebTrust are emerging that provide parties doing business on the Web with independent third party assurance that their interests and rights are being protected.

An even stronger moral viewpoint is apparent in the following definition of trust. Trust is "the willingness of a party to be vulnerable to the actions of another party based on the expectation that the other will perform a particular action important to the trustor, irrespective of the ability to monitor or control the other party" (Mayer et al, 1995, p. 712). The definition emphasises vulnerability and risk-taking when conducting e-commerce, both attracting much attention of those responsible for securing e-commerce. The association of trust with vulnerability, risk and security is discussed in a later section.

After a review of the literature on trust, Hosmer's (1995) arrived at the following conclusions.

1. Trust is generally expressed as an optimistic expectation on the part of an individual about the outcome of an event or the behaviour of a person. If the person expects the worst, he/she will protect him/herself by means of market contracts, hierarchical controls, legal requirements, and informal obligations.
2. Trust generally occurs under conditions of vulnerability. The loss if trust is broken will be much greater than the gain when trust is maintained.
3. Trust is generally associated with willing, not forced, cooperation and with benefits resulting from that cooperation. Trust is usually expressed as an attempt to increase or facilitate cooperation and/ or the potential for joint benefits.
4. Trust is generally difficult to enforce. Contracts and controls are expensive substitutes for trust and have the undesirable side effect of reducing innovative and cooperative behaviours.
5. Trust is generally accompanied by an assumption of an acknowledged or accepted duty to protect the rights and interests of others.

Handy (1995) reviewed the role of trust in the modern virtual organisation and offered the following 'rules' of trust.

1. Trust is not blind; it is observed in action over time. This corresponds to the stagewise evolution of trust outlined by Lewicki and Bunker (1996) in which three forms of trust can be identified, namely deterrence-based, knowledge-based and identification-based trust. These forms are discussed in a later section.
2. Trust needs boundaries and confidence in someone's competence. "Freedom within boundaries works best, however, when

the work unit itself is self-contained, having the capability within it to solve its own problems. Trust-based organizations are, as a result, reengineering their work, pulling back from the old reductionist models of organization, in which everything was divided into its components parts or functions." (Handy, 1995, p. 46)

3. Trust demands learning. Every individual has to be capable of self-renewal. E-commerce brings about significant changes in the way business is conducted and those that want to use its potential will have to adopt new practices including ones that establish adequate levels of trust.

4. Trust is tough. Organisations tend to restrict their core commitments to a smaller group of 'trusties'. This particular view seems to contradict the move towards worker empowerment.

5. Trust needs bonding. This is achieved through creating appropriate vision and mission statements for the organisation and adhering to the principles of total quality of excellence.

6. Trust needs touch and personal contact to make it real; "high tech has to be balanced by high touch to build high-trust organizations. Paradoxically, the more virtual an organization becomes, the more its people need to meet in person." (Handy, 1995, p. 46)

7. Trust requires a multicity of leaders as Handy (1998) demonstrated with the following anecdote. "I once teased an English audience by comparing a team of Englishmen to a rowing crew on the river – eight men going backward as fast as they can without talking to each other, steered by the one person who can't row! I thought it quite witty at the time, but I was corrected after the session by one of the participants, who had once been an Olympic oarsman. 'How do you think we could go backward so fast without communicating, steered by this little fellow in the stern, if we didn't know each other very well, didn't have total confidence to do our jobs and a shared commitment — almost a passion —— for the same goal?'" (p. 47) The leadership of the rowing team comprises the person who is steering the team, the captain of the crew, and the coach.

CONDITIONS AND DETERMINANTS

Although there have been numerous attempts to define and

provide meaning to trust, no 'global' definition or complete acceptance of relevant antecedents for trust exist. Butler (1991, p. 647, cited
in Hosmer, 1995) commented that "there is no agreement as to what
these trust conditions are, and there is no instrument for measuring an
exhaustive set of them." Instead, "Several terms have been used
synonymously with trust, and this has obfuscated the nature of trust"
(Mayer at al, 1995, p. 712). Below is an outline of the conditions and
determinants that have been associated with trust and how they may
be relevant to e-commerce.

Trustworthiness

Trust is most often linked with trustworthiness. According to
Deutsch (1958) trust exists when the trustworthy person is aware of
being trusted and he/she is somehow bound by the trust invested in
him/her. The person is 'responsible' to the trust of another. Motivation to be responsible, according to Deutsch (1958), can come from a
positive sentiment towards the other and wanting the other one's goal
to be realised, a fear of punishment if one is not responsible, and when
one's internalised values makes one responsible.

The first two behaviours (positive sentiments and fear of punishment) are particularly relevant to electronic business-to-business
commerce while the third (internalised values) is more pertinent to
electronic business-to-consumer interactions. Business-to-business
systems, also called Inter-Organisational Systems (IOS), have been
established for a number of years as Electronic Data Interchange (EDI)
and Electronic Funds Transfer (EFT) systems. Those linked by IOS
form a community that is trading among themselves electronically
and rely on trust to achieve shared, satisfactory outcomes in their
business dealings.

One's internalised value system has more relevance to person-to-
person and person-to-business interactions on the Web. There are a
variety of buyers, sellers and other players who communicate with
each other in different locations in no predefined manner. The forum
in which they interact is the Internet rather than physical buildings
and offices. The degree to which the interactions succeed and levels of
trust are generated are determined by the relationships that are
developed and participants' ethical and moral values.

Integrity

"The relationship between integrity and trust involves the trustor's perception that the trustee adheres to a set of principles that the trustor finds acceptable." (Mayer et al, 1995, p. 719) In e-commerce these principles are signified to others most commonly in the form of symbols and seals of trust. In the former category we have traditional brands (e.g. American Express, Mastercard) and Web-originated brands (e.g. Verisign, Cybercash). In the latter there are merchant seals (e.g. WebTrust) and technology and network seals (e.g. Telstra's Surelink in Australia). Trust of this nature will be discussed more fully in a later section.

Ability

"Ability is that group of skills, competencies, and characteristics that enable a party to have influence within some specific domain" (Mayer et al, 1995, p. 717). Hart and Saunders (1997) used the example of EDI to show how competence enhances trust between trading partners. It is reflected in the capacity of an organisation to process information efficiently and to show that they understand the business processes of their prospective EDI partners. Demonstrating competence is a strong persuasive tool. "The potential threat to drop the partner exposes, or highlights, the more powerful firm's view that the prospective EDI partner is expendable. Thus, coercive power negatively affects trust in the EDI partner. By contrast an approach that focuses on explanations of how EDI use will improve operational efficiency, reinforces the view that the partner is valued by the more powerful firm" (Hart and Saunders, 1997, p. 34).

Reliability

Hart and Saunders (1997) outlined the role of reliability, which they perceive as consistency between what a firm says and does. Reliability reinforces and strengthens cooperation and high levels of cooperation reinforce trust. Using the example of EDI, Hart and Saunders (1997) identified trust as the reliability needed to ensure accurate information is provided during transmission (e.g. correct data formatting when translating from a proprietary to a non-proprietary protocol) and when generated within the firm (e.g. providing partner with correct inventory forecasts).

Confidence

A number of researchers have equated trust and confidence or implied that trust was synonymous with confidence (Hosmer, 1995, referencing Deutsch, 1958; Zand, 1972; Golembiewski and McConkie, 1975). Some authors (e.g. Luhmann, 1988, referenced in Mayer et al, 1995) argued that a difference exists while others maintained that "The relationship between confidence and trust is amorphous in the literature on trust" (Mayer et al, 1995, p. 713).

The distinction of trust and confidence depends on perceptions. A useful approach is to link the two concepts with risk. Luhmann (1988, referenced in Mayer et al, 1995) associated trust with risk while confidence is not associated with risk. One can illustrate this distinction as follows. If a person makes payments on the Web by disclosing his/her credit card details without considering risk and therefore an alternative form of payment, one could argue that the person is in a situation of confidence. On the other hand if the person chooses one action in preference to others because of an assessment of the respective levels of risk the situation can be defined as one of trust.

Cooperation

Trust and cooperation are often used synonymously although one can cooperate with someone who is not trusted. Mayer et al (1995) identified this possibility in situations where an external control mechanism will punish the trustee for deceitful behaviour, the relationship does not involve vulnerability, the trustee and trustor have the same motives, and there is a lack of available alternatives. According to Powell (1996) trust increases in cooperative situations through routinising contact between parties, reducing errors, and allowing for adjustment in the relations. EDI systems demonstrate clearly the requirement for trust in cooperative arrangements.

Predictability

The distinction between predictability and trust is ambiguous. Mayer et al (1995) held the view that trust goes beyond predictability. "To equate the two is to suggest that a party who can be expected to consistently ignore the needs of others and act in a self-interested fashion is therefore trusted" (p. 714). They maintain that risk is associated with trust (willingness to take a risk) while predictability is not because another party's predictability is insufficient to make a person willing to take a risk. The relationship between risk and trust and its application to e-commerce is outlined in a later section.

Dependence

Trust can be viewed as the reliance on another person under conditions of dependence and risk. Dependence is experienced when outcomes are contingent on the trustworthy or untrustworthy behaviours of another while risk is determined by the experience of negative outcomes from the other person's untrustworthy behaviour (Kipnes, 1996). Zand (1972, referenced in Hosmer, 1995) exaggerated the role of dependence by suggesting that trust was the willingness of a person to increase his/her vulnerability to the actions of another person whose behaviour he/she cannot not control.

Dependence on the actions of others will vary by task, the situation and the person. E-commerce provides many good illustrations of dependence. For example, we increasingly depend on the Web for up-to-date information in areas such as travel and news. We are, however, also witnessing a decrease in our dependence on particular suppliers of goods such as books and CDs because of the many suppliers that offer these products on the Web. While some are increasingly dependent on the Web others are still reluctant to engage with it because of their lack of trust in the technology.

Openness

Hart and Saunders (1997) defined openness as the willingness to listen to new ideas and share rather than withhold information. This behaviour reinforces trust by reducing the probability that the trading partner will behave opportunistically. Inter-organisational systems, such as EDI, are excellent examples to demonstrate the need for openness in establishing trust between firms. The parties must be open in respect of the standards to be used and the synchronisation of their work. Through openness they gain an understanding of each other's work practices to make collaboration work.

Caring

Openness as outlined above is linked with the concept of caring. According to Hart and Saunders (1997) caring is demonstrated by goal compatibility, "the unequivocal representation that both firms share similar, not conflicting, goals" (p. 35). For example, in an EDI situation, the use of proprietary communication standards (as compared to using a universal protocol such as TCP/IP) demonstrates a lack of caring or worse an aim to restrict the trading partner's ability to exchange electronic messages with other firms. "Non-proprietary protocols support more seamless interconnection and, thereby, represent caring toward the trading partner's interests" (Hart and Saunders, 1997, p. 35).

Benevolence

"Benevolence is the extent to which a trustee is believed to want to do good to the *trustor*, aside from an egocentric profit motive. Benevolence suggests that the trustee has some specific attachment to the trustor" (Mayer et al, 1995, p. 718). An example of benevolence can be found in the relationship a university has with its students. A university seeks to provide educational opportunities to its students in a form that it believes is of genuine benefit to them. For example, many of the educational products are now delivered conveniently to the students through the Web. Students themselves trust that the university has their best interest at heart.

RISK AND TRUST

Risk is an essential component of trust; "one must take a risk in order to engage in trusting action" (Mayer et al, 1995, p. 724). However, "It is unclear whether risk is an antecedent to trust, is trust, or is an outcome of trust" (Mayer et al, 1995, p. 711). One could argue that risk-taking behaviour and trust behaviour "are really different sides of the same coin" (Deutsch, 1958, p. 266). What really matters is that the connection between risk and trust depends on the situation and the context of a specific, identifiable relationship.

Risk-taking takes into account the probability of the occurrence of an event between parties and the difference in the anticipated ratio of what Deutsch (1958) calls 'positive and negative emotional consequences' to the parties. The probability of negative consequences will depend on how risky the situation is and the existence of security measures that can avoid the risk from happening or reduce its impact. However, what level of security is adequate is difficult to establish as organisations and individuals vary considerably from one another in the degree of assurance they require before they will act in a situation that has the potentiality of danger or negative consequences.

Knowledge of the risk and security processes behind e-commerce appears not to be widespread. Parties trading on the Internet either take risk and security for granted or assume they are absent. An example of the latter view is that 'nothing should be sent on the Internet which one would not send by postcard since the security levels are about the same.' Before examining the security requirements for e-commerce we outline its major business and technological risks. It should be remembered that risks don't generally occur in isolation but tend to interact with each other.

Business Risks

As previously stated, e-commerce is a means of exchanging products, services and information over electronic networks that make up the Internet. The Internet is a non-hierarchical, democratically-structured, collaborative arrangement entered into by millions of users. This informality and lack of overall control creates the perception that the Internet is inherently insecure. As a consequence business risks arise as follows (Fink, 1998).

- *Products and services*. The risk exists that products and services ordered on the Internet are not of the quality promised or are not delivered even though they have been paid for. The buyer may even deny having placed the order.
- *Inadequate legal provisions*. Concern currently exists in a number of areas which have not been adequately defined or tested in law. Questions are asked as to what constitutes an offer and acceptance, how do the copyright provisions work, and where does the jurisdiction exist when trade spans the globe.
- *Reliability of trading partners*. Under e-commerce, firms often form alliances for the benefit of the group. Should the systems of a member fail, then others in the group will be affected. The Year 2000 bug, if not fixed before 1 January 2000, is predicted to have dire consequences for the operations of businesses that are part of a supply chain.
- *Behaviour of staff*. Staff need to be made aware that there exists an etiquette on the Internet (netiquette) which should be followed. Examples of unacceptable and/or illegal behaviour include slan-

dering other persons in e-mail messages, misrepresenting the firm by placing personal opinions on a Web site, and hacking into competitors' computer systems (also referred to as 'nuking').

- *Demise of Internet Service Provider (ISP)*. Firms connect to the Internet via an ISP will be affected by problems they experience. Should the provider suddenly go out of business, it would leave the firm unable to continue with e-commerce and therefore cause it to incur losses. An ISP should be carefully selected and its performance regularly evaluated to ensure continuity of service.

Technological Risks

The Internet is a network of networks which interchanges data using a set of communication standards called the Internet Protocol Suite, in particular Transmission Control Protocol/Internet Protocol (TCP/IP). The IP is used to route data packets across the network from one host computer to another and has become the de facto internetworking standard because it is simple, efficient and robust in adapting to network failures and configuration changes. TCP provides the transport frame for IP. However, TCP/IP was not designed with security in mind and can, therefore, easily be misused. This creates a number of technological risks (Fink, 1998).

- *Hacker attack*. Being connected to a global network provides the opportunity for others sharing the network to penetrate the computer system in an unauthorised manner. Once in the systems, hackers can cause damage (e.g. introducing a virus) and steal valuable information. Separating the internal network from the external network through a firewall gateway can prevent attacks.
- *Computer viruses*. This is harmful software that can be introduced through data obtained from the Internet. Once in the computer, it can cause great damage such as destroying the data stored on hard disk storage. The installation of virus scanning software can ensure that viruses are detected and eliminated before they cause harm.
- *Data interception*. All data and messages being forwarded across the Internet are potentially subject to interception and modification while being transmitted. To ensure privacy and integrity of data, it should be encrypted prior to transmission and decrypted at the destination.

- *Misrepresentation.* Business on the Internet can be conducted with a degree of anonymity and allows people to hide their true identity (e.g. by using anonymous remailers) or represent themselves as someone else (through a technique called 'IP address spoofing'). The use of authentication technology such as digital signatures and certificates overcomes this risk.

Vulnerability

Risk is closely associated with vulnerability. "Making oneself vulnerable is taking risk" (Mayer et al, 1995, p. 712) and, as discussed earlier, trust is about risk. Risk can, therefore, be defined as the choice to expose oneself to a vulnerable situation where the possible damage may be greater than the advantage that is sought.

One should clearly distinguish between vulnerability, threat and attack. A threat is anything that can have an undesirable effect on the system. For a threat to cause damage the system must be vulnerable to allow the potential threat to occur. Furthermore, for damage to occur there has to be an attack. Vulnerability is the probable extent of a successful attack on the system.

The analogy of a house is often used to illustrate the concept of threat, vulnerability and attack. Threats to a house may take many forms such as natural disasters (fire, lightning strikes and earthquakes), burglary or accidents, but this does not mean that these threats will materialise. The house's vulnerability to these threats can only be assessed in the particular circumstances. For example, it may be in an earthquake-prone zone or vulnerable to burglary because it is in an isolated area. The actual damage to the house only occurs when an attack, such as a burglary, takes place.

A good example is e-commerce to illustrate the concepts of vulnerability and risk as the mechanism for paying for purchases on the Web. The most widely available method of making payment on the Internet currently is the use of a credit card. The purchaser provides the credit card number and allows the charge to be debited against the credit card account. However, to disclose the credit card number on the Internet poses risks since the number can be intercepted and used for fraudulent purposes. The cardholder, therefore, has to decide whether or not to accept the vulnerability of the system and take the risk associated with this form of payment in return for the benefits that trading on the Web offers.

To decrease the vulnerability and, hence, the risk of credit card payments on the Web requires the development of a secure system of electronic cash (e-cash). E-cash technology and systems are currently at various stages of development and testing. Among the well-known developments are Cybercash, Digicash, Mondex and the Secure Electronic Transaction (SET) standard. However, for e-cash to become norm it has to meet the so-called ACID (atomicity, consistency, isolation, durability) security criteria.

- *Atomicity.* This ensures that e-cash cannot be split into discrete parts. For example, measures should exist to prevent e-cash, when transferred from one account to another, from disappearing or being credited to both accounts.
- *Consistency.* Under this criterion, all trading parties agree on the critical facts of the exchange. For example, when $1 passes from buyer to supplier, both agree that the buyer has $1 less and the supplier $1 more in their respective accounts.
- *Isolation.* To make e-commerce viable, it needs to be able to process large volumes of transactions. Isolation requires that transactions are kept apart and not confused. This requires that each payment transaction is uniquely identified, processed and recorded.
- *Durability.* To store e-cash requires that it is stored electronically on computers. Safeguards must exist to ensure that e-cash available to the computer before it crashed has not 'disappeared' (i.e. its electronic form is lost) by the time the computer recovers.

To develop trust in e-commerce we have to be prepared to take risks in adopting new electronic payment systems. "Without trust, risk is avoided, innovative activities dry up, only routine actions are available for retrospective sensemaking, and uncertainty remains unresolved" (Meyerson et al, 1996 p. 179). We have to be prepared to experience vulnerability "in terms of the goods or things one values and whose care one partially entrusts to someone else" (Meyerson et al, 1996, p. 170). However, vulnerability is unsettling and people try to reduce it by cultivating alternative partners, projects and networks; cultivating adaptability and the feeling of mastery that 'I can handle anything they throw at me'; and/or having the presumption of trust since this often acts like a self-fulfilling prophecy (Kipnis, 1996).

Uncertainty

Since vulnerability is contained in reciprocal trust relations, it involves being trusted or having to trust others (Kipnis, 1996). The former gives power over others. "We believe it is better to control our world than for our world to control us. The requirement that we trust others introduces unwanted uncertainty into our lives. It means that other people control outcomes that we value. It gives people power over us. And, ..., people and organizations often go to extraordinary lengths to be rid of the uncertainty that accompanies the need to trust" (Kipnis, 1996, p. 40).

Uncertainty differs from vulnerability in that it focuses on the ease with which others can disappoint our expectations. "Uncertainty on matters of trust is highest when there is a 50-50 chance ('a midpoint of uncertainty') that an unmonitored person will take advantage of our trust" (Meyerson et al, 1996, p. 177). "Faced with high uncertainty, people should be inclined either toward complete trust (1.0) or complete distrust (.0), both of which provide more certainty and use up less attention in monitoring" (Meyerson et al, 1996, p. 177).

Three conditions and/or assumptions (Barber, 1983, referenced in Hosmer, 1995) determine the outcome of an uncertain event:

- Expectation of the persistence and fulfillment of the natural and existing social order. In other words, a person would expect the world to continue without discontinuous change.
- Expectations of technically competent role performances from those involved. However, the difficulty is that most people are unable to critically evaluate the competencies of specialists.
- Expectations of morally correct role performance from those involved. This equates to the concepts of fiduciary duties and responsibilities.

E-commerce offers a reasonable degree of certainty because of the inherent robustness of the underlying technology. The Internet is widely used and has proven to be a reliable medium for conducting commerce. Furthermore, most users are 'Web-literate' in the way they exploit the functionality of the Internet and the ability to create Web pages has become easier through the use of HTML software. The concern about e-commerce participants always exhibiting morally correct behaviour, however, remains. It is not unreasonable to expect that among the millions of Web users a number of people behave destructively as can be seen from the release of damaging computer viruses from time to time.

Computer Crime

Computer crime can severely undermine trust and we should, therefore, be aware of it and be able to detect and avoid it. However, criminal behaviour is difficult to anticipate since a broad spectrum of illegal acts are carried out and the perpetrator does not necessarily have a criminal record. The impact of computer crime is generally serious since it requires the organisation to spend time catching up for lost productivity when facilities are disturbed.

It appears that most IT users are more concerned about attacks from outside their work place, particularly from hackers, than attacks from the inside. Counter measures to outside attacks have emerged in the form of firewall protection and virus detection software. However, just as great are the threats from insiders particularly from those who are familiar with the workings of the systems. They know where and when to cease opportunities to commit a crime. The danger is increasing substantially since more and more employees have access to terminals by being part of the Internet.

Among insiders, clerical staff, coworkers and computer staff have the opportunity to carry out computer crime. Clerical staff spend a large amount of their time operating business information systems and thereby gain detailed knowledge of how these systems function under different conditions. They have the opportunity to manipulate the systems for fraudulent purposes unless good security measures prevent this from happening or are able to detect it.

The most serious computer crimes are those carried out by IT-trained staff. There is a broad range in sophistication of crimes they are capable of committing. Among the easier acts are the stealing of information by placing it on a transportable format such as floppy disks, the deliberate destruction or corruption of software and data, and the suppression of activity logs or audit trails. More sophisticated acts are difficult to detect and include techniques such as data diddling, Trojan horse, sniffer attacks and IP spoofing (Fink, 1998). It is beyond the scope of this chapter to discuss these computer crime techniques in detail.

Legal Concerns

Doing business on the Internet is different from traditional forms of business and has given rise to a number of legal issues and concerns (Fink, 1998). With the acceptance of e-commerce, jurisdiction over the Internet will become more critical. Developments on a global scale are required in such areas as authorising certification, e-commerce insurance and law enforcement, to mention a few. Trust in e-commerce will increase with an effective system of enforcing warranties and prosecuting fraud. The following are some of the areas in law that have not yet been fully evaluated and resolved.

Businesses connected to the Internet become potentially subject to the laws of the country in which they do business. For example, by advertising goods under a particular trademark on a Web site, the trademark is potentially used in all countries where the Web site is accessed. If the company has not secured the trademark in a particular country or countries it could be infringing trademark registrations in that country or those countries. A suggested practical solution is to include a notice on the Web page that particular goods and services are only available to residents of specific countries and users should indicate their agreement to the condition. When the item is mailed to the purchaser, the compliance with this condition should be verified.

Most of the issues raised for Electronic Data Interchange (EDI) are relevant to e-commerce. With EDI the problem is not so much that messages are electronic but rather that they are easy to alter, deny or lose than paper-based messages. For this reason EDI systems rely on Trading Partner Agreements (TPAs) which are traditional paper-based contracts that deal with transactions that are electronic. They cover the need to send written confirmation for certain types of electronic messages. At present there appear to be no electronic contracts linked to e-commerce transactions and TPAs may, therefore, be the best legal safeguard for the moment.

A degree of uncertainty appears to exist in relation to the offer and acceptance of goods traded on the Internet. Organisations are advised to carefully consider whether the various offers contained on a Web site constitute 'offers' capable of acceptance or merely 'invitations to treat'. If they are 'offers' then the placement of an order by the purchaser constitutes a legally binding contract and the supplier is obliged to supply the good(s). If they are 'invitations to treat', the placement of an order will be an offer by the user which the supplier is free to accept or reject. With high value transactions it is recommended that certainty of the legal agreement is obtained and to display the terms of the contract online.

A problem exists on how legal agreements take effect when Web sites are accessed. For example, does clicking on the mouse to download a digital product in country 'A' constitute the commencement of a valid contract for those in country 'B' where the server containing the product is stored? Where is the contract considered valid, in country 'A' or in country 'B'? In which country should a dispute be resolved?

Under traditional systems, the party to a written contract is identified by his/her signature on the contract. Under Common Law, the signature can be a mark placed anywhere on a document. In an electronic environment, the equivalent of a mark is the digital signature. The question therefore arises whether or not a court can be persuaded, as a matter of evidence, that a digital signature is as reliable as a paper-based signature and makes a digital signature admissible.

The Internet makes it possible to cheaply, easily and quickly obtain excellent but unauthorised copies of works and distribute them widely. Many of the existing copyright laws, devised decades ago, are limited in scope and to a particular technology namely 'wireless telegraphy'. Reforms are needed to improve copyright protection for books, computer software, artworks, films, sound recording and broadcasts on the Internet. Under reforms, copyrights should be technology neutral rather than specific as in the past and should be applicable to future developments in technology and transmission methods including Web TV.

Another issue is the currency of the information presented on the Web. The Australian Financial Review reported on 3 April 1998 the news that GIO Australia was refunding $1.2 million to policyholders following a complaint by a customer to the Australian Competition and Consumer Commission. The complaint was about misleading product information publicised via the Internet. It was found that the 1997 GIO Web site was promoting benefits that had been withdrawn almost a year before. According to the article, GIO has since appointed dedicated compliance officers to ensure its product information on the Web was kept up to date, a task the GIO is reported to have described as 'mammoth'.

COST OF TRUST

Lack of trust increases the transaction costs between individuals and in and between organisations (Cummings and Bromiley, 1996). In other words, if a person or organisation perceives a lack of trust, consideration will have to be given to developing and implementing often costly control strategies and security measures to bring about the desired level of trust.

Control Strategies

In order to contain the cost of trusting, Kipnis (1996) proposed three strategies. They are: give up wanting, reduce dependence, and control the trustee. Each strategy has relevance to e-commerce. First, the nature of e-commerce has the effect opposite 'to give up wanting' since its primary aim is to increase consumer demand and the volume of trade. It does this in a number of ways. The size of the market is increased because digital products and services can be delivered to anyone, anytime and anywhere. Prior to e-commerce, the ability of the firm to reach potential customers was determined by physical factors such as the size and location of its sales force and the dealer network. Under e-commerce customers no longer have to wait for the 8-5 opening hours to have their enquiries serviced.

The second control strategy 'reducing dependence' is feasible under e-commerce because of the large number of sellers from which the consumers can choose. This has been facilitated by the use of intelligent agents. An agent is a software product that has intelligent behaviour reflected in its capacity for reasoning, communications and being adaptive. A consumer agent, therefore, supports consumers' buying activities including shopping preferences and bidding at auctions. Hence consumers are able to reduce the cost associated with having to rely on a small number of suppliers or a particular supplier.

Sellers, however, act in the opposite way in order to increase dependencies by adopting deliberate marketing techniques. Among them are pull and push marketing or a combination of the two. Under the pull strategy, sellers generate demand by attractively displaying their products and services on the Web through the use of multimedia technology. Under the push strategy, sellers 'push' their products and services by broadcasting information to a broad range of potential clients, or make available specific information to those that they believe have a particular interest. In this way they are able to increase their marketplace.

Another strategy adopted by sellers is customer tracking which has become a controversial aspect of the Web. The technique is also referred to as 'shopping carts' — a way of tallying individual items into a single order as the consumer browses or searches the Web site. When a person clicks on an item it gets added to the electronic cart and stays there until 'check out'. The use of 'cookies' allows a Web server to pass preferences (including the shopping cart) to the browser. When the browser visits the site again the server can recognise those preferences and, thereby, influence consumers' purchasing behaviours.

For the third control strategy, 'control the trustee', Kipnis (1996) offered a number of suggestions. For trustees outside the firm, reliance is needed on regulatory agencies, professional bodies of ethics, and civil laws to make untrustworthy behaviour costly for trustees. This scenario can be found in professional associations to which doctors, lawyers and accountants belong. To control trustees inside the firm, strategies applicable to what Kipnis (1996) calls 'third-stage technology' are appropriate. This technology consists of today's computers, robots and other automated machines and employees must be trusted to regulate the technology. Trust can be achieved by selecting employees from professionally and technically trained applicants whose values and ideologies of work are similar to those of management.

Meyerson et al (1996) outlined another control strategy, namely the use of hedges to reduce perceived risks and vulnerabilities and, thus, the costs of trust. Hedges have the purpose of allowing one to enter into a risky activity because the 'worst case' outcome is anticipated and covered. They require anticipatory action about things that might go wrong. The disadvantages of hedges are that they are an act of mistrust, and they can foster an exaggerated confidence. An example of a hedge in e-commerce is to restrict the credit limit of one's credit card used for purchases on the Web to a small amount so that the exposure to a loss is relatively small.

Hedges of a more permanent form are security measures that organisations can implement. Below is a discussion of security at various levels within the organisation to secure and, hence, increase the level of trust in e-commerce.

Organisational Security

This takes the form of procedures in which management signifies their expectation of behaviour of their employees towards e-commerce. Organisational measures provide practices for the acquisition, development and operation of e-commerce, including security (Fink, 1998).

- *Security strategy.* Security strategies usually exist in larger IT installations but often are not present in smaller ones or may not exist for e-commerce. Fortunately, security strategies appropriate for the e-commerce environment, such as those contained in this book, are evolving and can be adopted by organisations.
- *Security policy.* To ensure that strategy is achieved, management needs to formulate e-commerce security policies. They should form part of organisational policies and be clearly articulated throughout the organisation. Policies should be achievable and provide encouragement to employees to follow them rather than to be seen as another odious task to be performed.
- *Security coordination.* An e-commerce activity is a multifaceted phenomenon, consisting of Internet technology and various business applications. When parts of an e-commerce application are acquired, developed, changed or discontinued, changes in security will be required. Changes need to be well managed and coordinated so that no security weaknesses arise as a consequence.
- *Insurance.* Consideration should be given to supplementing e-commerce security measures with insurance to minimise risk in a cost-effective manner. Insurance policies can be obtained to cover the loss arising from attacks on the organisation, including theft, destruction of data and records, professional errors, computer crime and business interruptions.
- *Audit.* Audit not only has a deterrent effect but can also discover weaknesses in security and, thus, prevent future losses from occurring. Auditors should adopt a proactive role by identifying e-commerce security shortcomings and make recommendations on how to overcome them.
- *Security awareness.* To raise the level of e-commerce security, the right attitudes and behaviour throughout the organisation are critical. Awareness programs need to be planned and executed.

They should begin with a discussion of security procedures and policies when employees first come aboard and followed up with refresher courses to update and monitor employees' awareness.

- *Security support*. Organisations and individuals are now using the Internet in sophisticated ways. To ensure they operate safely adequate security skills and support should be present. When they are inadequate and cannot be developed on short notice, consideration should be given to supplementing them from outside sources.
- *Security training*. The release of e-commerce strategies and policies should be accompanied by appropriate training covering all aspects of e-commerce operations including security. Training may take a number of forms ranging from formal classes to informal seminars and demonstrations. Training will not only lead to a greater empowerment of users but also to their acceptance of security responsibilities.

Application Security

Under a manual system, a number of people are usually employed to carry out controls and perform internal checks. However, e-commerce systems differ from such systems in that transactions are processed electronically without or with a minimum of human intervention. Often high volumes of transactions are involved. New security approaches are required for such an environment and should include the following (Fink, 1998).

- *Application processing*. Strong application processing controls are required and should be more 'automated' than are those in a manual system. They should include computer-based edit and validation checks, record reconciliations, sequence checks, and the identification of unusual transactions.
- *Transactions in progress*. Determining the status of e-commerce processing is complex since transactions can be at various stages of processing and transmission. For example, the electronic invoice may already have been received, but the good itself has not yet arrived. The system should keep track of incomplete transactions and control measures should prevent unauthorised access to transactions still in progress.
- *Data completeness*. There are a number of methods available to verify that the data was received intact. These measures include

comparing control totals calculated by the receiving computer with totals stored in the transmitted data, checking the sequence of numbers embedded in each data record, and examining each successive record to ensure it is not a duplicate of a previously received record.

- *Audit trail.* An adequate audit trail of all system activities must be kept and regularly be reviewed. Of special interest are unauthenticated access attempts, data transmission failures and unusual system uses and transactions. They should be identified and followed-up so that necessary remedial action can be instituted and causes of errors or poor practices be investigated.

In addition to the above, the organisation will have to adopt failsafe security to safeguard against the consequences of a badly managed e-commerce disaster. It is generally estimated that among computer-dependent organisations, the majority go into liquidation within a relative short time of a disaster occurring. The required security is in the form of a disaster recovery plan and procedure. The critical objectives of disaster recovery are to reduce the time spent in catching up for lost productivity while the system is not operational, to facilitate maintaining some semblance of normal business activity, and to minimise the likelihood of errors and fraud occurring during this period of upheaval.

Disasters, however, are not easy to predict and have varying impact. A loss of system documentation, for example, may slow down e-commerce operations but does not cause them to collapse. On the other hand, extensive destruction of data will have an immediate, severe impact. The approach to disaster recovery, fortunately, is a structured one. Through planning and taking the necessary procedures, organisations as well as individual users, can ensure that a mishap does not become an irrecoverable disaster.

People Security

Trust is largely a people issue and dealing effectively with people in a security context requires a well-controlled environment and effective management practices. To deter fraudsters, the saying 'the best deterrent is the certainty of detection' should be adopted. Appropriate e-commerce security measures need to be implemented to deter, detect and prevent threats arising from the mischievous actions of people (Fink, 1997).

- *Hiring*. Management should be guided by human resource principles during the hiring process. All new staff should undergo security screening including checks on character references, employment history and criminal record. Interviews will also help to establish attitudes of potential employees towards security.
- *Leaving*. As soon as an employee indicates that he or she intends leaving, all Internet access should immediately be denied. On leaving, the person should routinely be debriefed. In this process all keycards, identification badges, keys, manuals and other materials are returned and the former employee is informed of continuing obligations regarding confidential matters that the person was privy to during the period of employment.
- *Conditions of use*. A document should be drawn up containing the expectation of the employer for the proper use of Internet facilities by employees. The conditions of use should be comprehensive and self-explanatory and put in writing. They should state that unauthorised Internet use and the sharing of confidential codes and passwords may be grounds for termination and other punitive measures.
- *Monitoring*. It is now a common practice that employees sign agreements that govern their behaviour during employment. Included are practices to monitor the performance of employees. Management should be proactive to minimise ill feeling on the part of the employee that may arise from time to time. These measures is will substantially reduce the likelihood of computer crime occurring.
- *Rotation of duties*. One of the most effective security measures in human resource management is the regular rotation of duties among employees. It has been found that employees may not take vacations or refuse a transfer because of the fear that evidence of fraud may be uncovered while other employees are handling their jobs.
- *Separation of duties*. E-commerce duties should be separated as far as possible. For example, the employee who develops the Web site should not also be the employee who operates applications. This would leave illegal activities, incorporated in the software, undetected. In smaller entities, this principle is often compromised because of the necessity that staff carry out a wide range of

functions.

- *Action*. The aggrieved employer should consider taking action in response to unauthorised or illegal actions by people. For example, if it was carried by a disgruntled employee, there could be the possibility of suing the person civilly for the time lost and expenses incurred. However, one would have to prove malice and that losses did not arise from simple negligence.

Security Technology

E-commerce involves the marketing and supply of digital products and services over the Internet and receiving payments for them. This means that data and information being transmitted across electronic networks are secured in order to ensure confidentiality and integrity. Another challenge is to identify and establish the authenticity of entities with which business is done. Further complications arise from the involvement of third parties, such as Internet Service Providers (ISPs), and people intending to use Internet technology for fraudulent purposes. A number of security domains and technologies can, therefore, be identified for e-commerce (Fink, 1998).

- *Access*. Concerns exist for the transmission of information between internal and external networks. Under a manual system, protection is achieved through physical means such as locks and keys, fences and walls. With e-commerce, networks are kept apart through the use of a firewall gateway.
- *Confidentiality*. To ensure that the content of transactions (e.g. orders and payments) and messages remain intact, manual systems limit access to them. With e-commerce all confidential and sensitive information being transmitted should be encrypted to protect content.
- *Authentication*. To establish the authenticity of the trading partner (e.g. is the party authorised to place the order?), traditional systems have relied on letterheads and written signatures. Under e-commerce, digital signatures and digital certificates achieve this.
- *Attack*. The Internet provides trading opportunities for thousands among which will be some who will seek to carry out fraudulent, unauthorised or illegal activities. They are wide ranging and include the introduction of computer viruses and various forms of computer crime, which are often difficult to detect. Under e-

commerce specialised computer auditors should be used to detect and prevent illegal acts from occurring.

Trust Building

The question of whether to rely on security or to rely on trust building in developing trust was considered by Creed and Miles (1996). They leaned towards the latter. "Indeed, it is our view that both across the firms within a network and within the various network firms, there is little choice but to consider trust building and maintenance to be essential as control system building and maintenance are viewed in the functional form" (Creed and Miles, 1996, p. 30). They maintained that trust building is more effective than control systems since "If the parties do not trust one another to perform and instead act according to this lack of trust, the form will fail" (Creed and Miles, 1996, p. 30). They recommended trust building at various levels.

At the individual level Creed and Miles (1996, p. 33) concluded that "trust is build by trusting". This is akin to approaches used in recognised professions and highest levels of skilled artisans. "When the 'master' professional treats the apprentice as a colleague from the beginning, he or she is taking a risk in the hope that such trust will both elicit greater trustworthiness and will be returned." (Creed and Miles, 1996, p. 33) Organisations should therefore provide employees with necessary knowledge, skills and guidance to enable them to operate and manage e-commerce systems in a trustworthy manner.

At the team level, trust needs to be part of modern self-managing teams. Trust is generated by putting teams through exercises to build awareness of common responsibilities and fostering the skills needed for self-governance. A good example is an audit team that works together in applying professional audit techniques when examining the client's financial accounts. Each team member has an important role to play in establishing the audit opinion on various systems and subsystems they are responsible for. In forming the overall audit opinion the team trust that the individual members have carried out their duties in a competent manner.

At the firm level, management should "begin the process of activating dormant preferences for cooperation" (Creed and Miles, 1996, p. 33). This means that organisations view employment relationships as social as well as economic exchanges. Modern 'virtual' organisations operate on this principle and, as outlined in an earlier section, Handy (1995) suggested that their vision and mission statements emphasise the need for learning, bonding and leadership to enhance trust.

At the network level, trust has been recognised as a major issue in building supplier relations. Creed and Miles (1996) discussed the trust that exists between Motorola and its suppliers. Motorola is in a strategic partnership with small but highly competent firms that develop state-of-the-art equipment. Because these firms do not always have the cash to acquire expensive new manufacturing facilities, Motorola extends their purchase orders, which can be used by the firms as collateral to obtain the necessary capital. Thus Motorola takes the risk that suppliers will ultimately be able to deliver even after they have given them the funds.

TRUST IN CONTEXT

As shown in an earlier section, the antecedents of trust (ability, integrity, etc.) are strongly affected by the situational context. More specifically, specific consequences of trust are determined by factors such as the stakes involved, the balance of power in the relationship, the perception of the level of risk, and the alternatives available to the trustor (Mayer et al, 1995). The following is an analysis of trust in various contextual situations that take these factors into account.

Individuals

According to Kipnis (1996), the following principles apply to trust at the individual level:

- Trust levels are the lowest in work settings in which diversity (gender, culture, and race) are highest.
- We trust, with cautious faith, people who have interacted reliably with us in the past.
- We try to contain the costs of trusting other people.

The above views can readily be applied in the context of electronic mail (e-mail) where text messages are delivered over a network. E-mail messages are generally created by one person and intended for one or more people. In order to develop trust in the technology, the sender of an e-mail message should take into account the characteristics of the recipient viz. his/her gender, culture and race. This is a complex area and much research still has to be done to establish similarities and differences in these domains.

The consequences of loosing trust can be severe. Within interpersonal networks trust and distrust have opposite effects, their influence is not symmetrical. Trust builds incrementally, but distrust has a more dramatic 'catastrophic' quality. Thus, while we cautiously develop trust with each other, often over a lengthy period of time, a sudden, unexpected and unpleasant development can destroy the relationship. Should one of the parties have cause to loose trust in the other party it may be impossible to reestablish it.

In order to reduce the cost of trusting other people we aim to increase the resilience of the relationship. According to Meyerson et al (1996) resilience is high when once in place, it is not easily disrupted, and once shattered, it is not easily restored. On the other hand it is low when expectations are high but so are reservations. The relationship is analogous to having one foot in the water, but bracing the other firmly on solid ground.

Organisations

The research into organisational trust has been characterised by shortcomings and problems similar to those outlined in previous sections. "Although a great deal of interest in trust has been expressed by scholars, its study in organizations has remained problematic for several reasons: problems with the definition of trust itself, lack of clarity in the relationship between risk and trust itself; confusion between trust and its antecedents and outcomes; lack of specificity of trust referents leading to the confusion in levels of analysis; and a failure to consider both the trusting party and the party to be trusted" (Mayer et al, 1995, p. 709).

Organisational trust is trust between units within organisations or between organisations. It expresses itself as "an individual's belief or a common belief among a group of individuals that another individual or group (a) make good-faith efforts to behave in accordance with any commitments both explicit or implicit, (b) is honest in whatever negotiations preceded such commitments, and (c) does not take excessive advantage of another event when the opportunity is available" (Cummings and Bromiley, 1996, p. 303).

Organisational trust is based on the rationale that "trust rests on the socially embedded, subjective, and optimistic nature of most interactions within and between organisations that involve trust" (Cummings and Bromiley, 1996, p. 303). Hosmer (1995) held a similar view when, after a review of the approaches to trust within organisational theory, he concluded that "trust seem to be based, at least in part, upon the underlying assumption of moral duty with a strong ethical component owed by the trusted person to the trusting individual. Perhaps it is the presence of this implied moral duty – an anomaly in much of organizational theory – that has made a precise definition of the concept of trust so difficult" (Hosmer, 1995, p. 381).

The views above seem to indicate an implicit acceptance of our duty to trust others. It could be argued that to develop trust for e-commerce requires a more explicit approach since e-commerce is a relative recent phenomenon. We can identify different forms of trust that are suitable for e-commerce by referring to the taxonomy provided by Shapiro et al (1992). They distinguish between deterrence-based, knowledge-based and identification-based forms of trust. All three have relevance to e-commerce and will be discussed in a later section.

Collaborative Networks

Over the last decades people working in organisations have no longer been regarded as labourers but are now treated as valued members. This changed attitude has been accompanied by the tendency to establish small groups of colleagues united by mutual trust and an increasing exchange of information, ideas and intelligence within organisations (Handy, 1995). As a result, the modern organisation is adopting collaborative, networked structures in which trust requirements are high and consequences of failing to meet them can be severe.

Collaborative networks depend on minimal transaction costs for their responsiveness and efficiency. The existence of high levels of trust allows a reduction in transaction costs (Creed and Miles, 1996). By achieving high levels of trust, costly security measures, for example to safeguard access to information, can be eliminated. Furthermore, internal structures of network firms must be highly adaptive to facilitate rapid responsiveness to external developments such as the Internet (Creed and Miles, 1996). This is only possible if a high level of trust in these new developments can be developed.

Powell (1996) identified four types of network-based collaborations for which fundamentally different types of trust are present. They are found in industrial districts, research and development partnerships, extended business groups, and strategic alliances and collaborative manufacturing.

In an industrial district, also referred to as networks of place, trust is based on ties of place and kinship. This type of collaboration consists of integrated, small-scale, decentralised production units where "networks of loosely linked but spatially clustered firms create a distinctive 'industrial atmosphere' where the 'secrets of industry are in the air'" (Powell, 1996, p. 53). Firms are commonly grouped in zones according to their products (e.g. motorcycles and shoes in Bologna, Italy), the time horizons for collaboration are long and extended kinship bonds exist. Monitoring is facilitated by social ties and constant contact facilitated by technology such as e-mail.

In a research and development partnership, there exists a common membership in a professional community. This is the glue that 'thickens' cooperation. The major activity is trading of information and people (e.g. Silicon Valley) and the sharing of different competencies to generate new ideas. It uses inhouse research and cooperative research with external parties (e.g. universities and research institutes) to achieve its aims. Internet technologies suitable for these arrangements include conferencing and groupware software.

Extended business groups share historical experiences, obligations and advantages of group membership. In Japan they are called *keiretsu* (meaning societies of business) where "the large networks of producers look like complex, extended families, organized either in a cobweb-like fashion or a vast holding company with financial institutions at the apex" (Powell, 1996, p. 58). They apply the principles of obligation and reciprocity in their business dealings to generate trust.

The major characteristic of strategic alliances and collaborative manufacturing is their mutual dependencies. This is akin to the electronic supply chain discussed in a previous section. The strategic network is a relationship between autonomous firms which allows them to be more competitive in comparison with non-affiliated 'outsiders'. "Members of a diversified group possess a shared normative foundation; partners feel they are following a common set of rules. Trust is in the air" (Powell, 1996, p. 59). Since they lack the 'natural' basis of trust that other networks possess they rely on contractual agreement and constant communication to curb potential opportunism. These requirements are reflected in EDI systems outlined below.

Interorganisational Systems

Hart and Saunders (1997) viewed the adoption of an EDI system as an opportunity to build and reinforce trust between firms. EDI technology increases information sharing by enabling the provision and retrieval of information electronically. More information is exchanged more quickly. This makes participating firms more tightly coupled and reduces the possibility of opportunism (self-interest). Firms can thereby ensure continuity in a relationship and commitment over a long period of time.

The processes of EDI can be adopted to reinforce trust in a number of ways (Hart and Saunders, 1997). For example through EDI one can influence the trading partner to invest in setting up an EDI system and management can be persuaded to allow access to information and the integration of computer systems. Under EDI, the partners work closely with each other in setting up and testing computer hardware and software. Through this interaction, opportunistic behaviour is discouraged and trust is developed.

An EDI network is an example of an electronic hierarchy (Hart and Saunders, 1997) which cuts down the number of a firm's trading partners (to streamline operations and reduce costs) thereby arriving at a 'small numbers' situation. This is usually accompanied by high switching costs, few alternatives and extended contractual time frames. As an electronic hierarchy, EDI arrangements incur elements of vulnerability and risks (Hart and Saunders, 1997). For example, under an EDI system, one partner may not know for certain what the other partner might do with the information that is being exchanged and, even worse, the information provided could be used in some way to take advantage of the firm.

Temporary Systems

Meyerson et al (1996) identified the trend under which organisations are moving away from formal hierarchical structures to more flexible and temporary groupings around particular projects. Causes can be found in the increasing use of subcontracting and emergence of more networked organisations. The group often works on tasks with a high degree of complexity but lacks formal structure for coordination and control. There is little or no time for confidence-building activities. This results in high-risk and high-stake outcomes which can impact negatively on trust.

Temporary systems such as audit teams and research and development projects are typically made up of a set of diversely skilled people working together on a complex task over a limited period of time (Goodman and Goodman, 1976). They have the following characteristics with potential relevance to trust (Meyerson et al, 1996):

- Participants with diverse skills are assembled by a contractor to enact expertise they already possess.
- Participants have limited history working together.
- Participants have limited prospects of working together again in the future.
- Participants often are part of limited labour pools and overlapping networks.
- Tasks are often complex and involve interdependent work.
- Tasks have a deadline.
- Assigned tasks are non-routine and not well understood.
- Assigned tasks are consequential.
- Continuous interrelating is required to produce an outcome.

Even though in temporary systems everything is risked, every time, they have to operate as if trust is present. They are also preoccupied with action. "To act one's way into an unknown future is to sharpen the element of risk in that projected action, which gives character to the action and substance to risk." (Meyerson et al, 1996, p. 180) Within temporary systems "people have to wade in on trust rather than wait while experience gradually shows who can be trusted and with what: Trust must be conferred presumptively or *ex ante*." (Meyerson et al, 1996, p. 170)

If membership in a temporary system is a one-shot event with little prospect for future interaction, vulnerability is low as is the need for trust. However, where trust is needed it takes on the form of 'swift trust' (Meyerson et al, 1996). To achieve swift trust people develop a series of hedges; they behave in a trusting manner but also hedge to reduce the risks of betrayal (see earlier section on control strategies). An example of a hedge is the restriction on the limit of one's credit card when making payments on the Web. With a low limit, say $200, it is still possible to make a series of small payments and at the same time reducing one's exposure to credit card fraud.

Virtual Organisations

Under e-commerce an electronic form of organisation has emerged which is referred to as the virtual organisation. Venkatraman and Hendersen (1998) envisage the virtual organisation along three strategic characteristics.

1. *Virtual expertise*. The Internet and intranets are used for identifying, creating, storing and sharing knowledge and expertise across and within organisational boundaries for improved organisational effectiveness.
2. *Virtual encounter*. This describes the relationship between the organisation and its customers (business-to-customer interaction). It allows customers to access the organisation's products and services through the Internet.
3. *Virtual sourcing*. This is the integration of the organisation in a business network (business-to-business interaction). Strategic alliances and new relationships are formed for enhancing the delivery of value to customers.

Handy (1995) examined the nature of virtual organisations from a trust perspective and wondered "whether a company is, in the future, going to be anything more than the box of contracts that some companies now seem to be" (p. 41). "They exist as activities not as buildings; their only visible sign is an E-mail address" (p. 42). For virtual organisations, "Trust is the heart of the matter." .... "Virtuality requires trust to make it work; Technology on its own is not enough." (p. 44)

What people cannot see with a virtual organisation they often cannot contemplate. However, intangible assets, also referred to as intellectual capital, are valued by the market many times higher than the tangible ones. For example, the market value of high-tech companies can be up to 20 times worth the visible assets. These organisations have become information- and knowledge-based and "feed on information, ideas and intelligence (which in turn are vested in the heads and hearts of people)" (Handy, 1995, p. 48). For them to function effectively, trust must exist in the willingness of people to give up their knowledge and ideas for the benefit of others in the organisation.

FORMS OF TRUST

Shapiro et al. (1992) found that trust develops in stages and takes on different forms which they identified as deterrence-based trust, knowledge-based trust and identification-based trust. This stagewise evolution of trust exhibits itself as follows (Lewicki and Bunker, 1996).

- When relationships first occur they are based on deterrence-based trust. They may not move past this form, particularly if the relationship does not necessitate more than 'arms-length' transactions, the interdependence is heavily bounded and regulated (e.g., through professional ethics), and violations have occurred that discourages a deepening of the relationship.
- As parties learn more about each other, they search for more information about each other. The new form of relationship is termed a knowledge-based trust relationship.
- More information may lead parties to identify with each other, thereby, creating identification-based trust. This stage may not be reached if parties lack the time or energy to invest beyond knowledge-based trust or don't have the desire for a closer relationship.

The movement between stages requires 'frame changes' (Lewicki and Bunker, 1996). First, the change from deterrence- to knowledge-based trust is accompanied by a change from contrast (differences) to assimilation (similarities). Second, the change from knowledge- to identification-based trust requires a move from knowledge about each other to identification with each other.

Deterrence-Based Trust

Lewicki and Bunker (1996) identified the existence of this form of trust when people or trading partners do what they say they would do and trust is build because of consistency in their behaviours. Consistency is sustained by threat of punishment that will occur if consistency is not maintained, for example loss of relationship. With deterrence-based trust there is a cost involved when performance fails and a reward when performance is achieved.

This form of trust works well for professional bodies and associations. Accountants, lawyers, engineers, doctors, etc. are bound by codes of conduct and ethical regulations in order to become and continue to be members of their professional bodies. Should they be found guilty of misconduct, the trust that their clients have in them is violated and their reputation is hurt not only in the eyes of the clientele but also in those of their friends and associates. The rules and procedures of the professional bodies determine the severity of the deterrence.

Knowledge-Based Trust

Lewicki and Bunker (1996) defined this trust as one where one party (the trustor) understands and predicts the behaviour of the other party (the trustee) based on information and knowledge about each other's behaviour established over a period of time. It is based on judgement of the probability of the other's likely choice of behaviour. For knowledge-based trust to occur, information is needed by one party to understand and accurately predict the likely behaviour of the other party.

Knowledge-based trust needs predictability to enhance trust, i.e. repeated interactions in multidimensional relationships (e.g. wants, preferences, problem solving approaches). 'Courtship' behaviour is used for relationship development. A good example of the occurrence of knowledge-based trust can be found in e-commerce interactions where product and service customisation takes place to satisfy a customer's desires. The seller and buyer exchange information with each other, for example to specify the size of a pair of jeans or the layout of a greeting card, until the buyer's specific wishes have been agreed upon.

Identification-Based Trust

Under this form of trust, trading partners establish common desires and intentions based on empathy and common values (Lewicki and Bunker, 1996). There is an emotional connection between them and one can act as an 'agent' for the other. Identification-based trust, by its nature, is often associated with group-based trust. Trust is linked with group membership and certain activities occur to strengthen the trust between members. This may take the form of a collective identity (joint name, logo, title), joint products and goals (a new product line or objective), and/or commonly shared values (Lewicki and Bunker, 1996).

A study by Cheskin Research and Studio Archetype/Sapient (1999) established that for trust to occur on the Internet, individuals first rely on certain forms being followed before, over time, these forms give way to reliance on experience. Consequently, the 'forms' that suggest trustworthiness are the main determinants of whether someone will trust and interact with a Web site. According to the findings of Cheskin Research and Studio Archetype/Sapient (1999), the six fundamental forms that were found to communicate trustworthiness on the Web are:

- Brand. The most trusted Web brands are those that are well known and the least trusted aren't well known.
- Navigation. Consumers rely on the quality of navigation to tell them if the site is likely to meet their needs.
- Fulfillment. The site should clearly indicate how an order will be processed and provide information on how to obtain information should problems occur.
- Presentation. The design attributes of the site should reflect quality and professionalism.
- Up-to-date technology. Consumers want to see the use of technologies understood to be important to security, such as encryption.
- Logos of security-guaranteeing firms. Even though recognised by consumers, brand names such as credit card symbols do not necessarily communicate trustworthiness. On the other hand, 'security brand' seals of approval do communicate trustworthiness.

The emergence of security-guaranteeing firms is an important development for e-commerce. These firms provided identification-based trust through symbols of trust and seals of trust. In the former category we have traditional brands. (e.g. American Express, Mastercard) and Web-originated brands (e.g. Verisign, Cybercash). In the latter there are merchant seals (e.g. WebTrust) and technology and network seals (e.g. Telstra's Surelink in Australia).

WebTrust is a good example of the types of security services being provided. It was set up by the American Institute of Certified Public Accountants and the Canadian Institute of Chartered Accountants with the aim of providing third party assurance for customers and businesses using the Web. WebTrust provides the framework and the methodology to provide assurance as to integrity and security, as well as the disclosures of business practices of a firm doing business on the Web. To get the seal of approval firms have to pass standardised criteria required by a WebTrust audit and display the seal on their Web site. The seal provides assurance in three areas (Muysken, 1998):

- Business practices. Secure and proper practices are adhered to and these are disclosed when doing business on the Web.
- Transaction integrity. To ensure integrity, appropriate procedures and controls such as verification and validation exist.
- Information protection. Information passing between customer and business remains confidential and private through the use of security mechanisms such as encryption and certification.

SUMMARY AND CONCLUSIONS

The concept of trust has occupied the minds of researchers and practitioners for many years and is again gaining prominence with the emergence of e-commerce. As was the case in the past the requirements for developing trust in this new trading environment are difficult to determine. The preferred way is to examine e-commerce trust according to previously established antecedents. A review of the literature indicated that the conditions and determinants of trust cover a wide range and include trustworthiness, integrity, ability, reliability and so on. They are relevant to e-commerce and without their existence e-commerce is unlikely to reach its full potential.

In addition to defining e-commerce trust, it should be examined in various contextual situations. This recognises the multidimensional characteristics of e-commerce. Trust is required at the individual and organisational levels and within collaborative networks and inter-organisational structures. We are also seeing new forms of trust to cater to the needs of temporary systems and virtual organisations. Essentially, however, the collective trust requirement for e-commerce can be met by one or more of three forms of trust, namely deterrence-, knowledge- and identification-based trust.

Trust evolves from deterrence- through knowledge- to identification-based trust. Over time it appears that e-commerce currently relies mostly on knowledge- and identification-based trust. Knowledge-based trust can be found in electronic business-to-business commerce, such as EDI systems, where openness and information sharing are key to establishing trust between trading partners. We are currently witnessing a surge of identification-based trust provided by security-guaranteeing organisations, such as WebTrust, whose seal of trust indicates to the consumer that the particular Web site has a high level of security and integrity.

Security measures are an obvious way to minimising e-commerce risk and thereby increase levels of trust. Generally, not much knowledge exists about e-commerce security; those that use e-commerce either take security for granted or don't have faith in it. Fortunately, a range of proven security measures and technologies exist to safeguard e-commerce at organisational, application and people levels. Security, however, comes at a cost and this can be minimised by adopting trust-building strategies.

Trust can be developed in a number of ways but in doing so the nature of trust and underlying assumptions need to be considered. Various rules and principles of trust exist and they can form useful guidelines in establishing trust for e-commerce. Over time the premise has emerged that trust is part of our moral obligation when interacting with one another. However, this premise should be challenged and we should take care to guard against opportunistic and selfish behaviour in e-commerce.

To achieve a satisfactory level of trust in e-commerce it is recommended that risk management techniques be practised. The two main forms of risk in e-commerce relate to business and technology. Under risk management we take into account the probability of these risk occurring and their possible negative consequences. Risk is an essential element to e-commerce because without it we would not innovate and e-commerce would not evolve. Risk and trust in e-commerce are closely linked because without risk there would be no need for trust.

REFERENCES

Axelrod R. (1984) *The Evolution of Cooperation*, Basic Books, New York.

Barber B. (1983) *The Logic and Limits of Trust*, Rutgers University Press, New Brunswick, NJ.

Butler J.K. (1991) "Toward Understanding and Measuring Conditions of Trust: Evolution of a Conditions of Trust Inventory", *Journal of Management*, 17(3), 643-663.

Cheskin Research and Studio Archetype/Sapient (1999), *eCommerce Trust Study*, January.

Creed W.E. and Miles R.E. (1996) "Trust in Organizations A Conceptual Framework Linking Organizational Forms, Managerial Philosophies, and the Opportunity Costs of Controls", in Kramer R.M. and Tyler T.R. (Eds.) *Trust in Organizations - Frontiers of Theory and Research*, Sage Publications, London.

Cummings L.L. and Bromiley P. (1996) "The Organizational Trust Inventory (OTI)" in Kramer R.M. and Tyler T.R. (Eds.) *Trust in Organizations - Frontiers of Theory and Research*, Sage Publications, London.

Deutsch M. (1958) "Trust and Suspicion", *Conflict Resolution*, 2(4), 265-279.

Fink D. (1997) *Information Technology Security – Managing Challenges and Creating Opportunities*, CCH Publishers, Sydney.

Fink D. (1998) *E-Commerce Security*, CCH Publishers, Sydney.

Fink D (1999), "Business Students' Perceptions of Electronic Commerce – Will they join the Revolution?" *Australian Journal of Information Systems*, 6(2), 36-43.

Golembiewski R.T. and McConkie M. (1975) "The Centrality of Interpersonal Trust in Group Processes" in Cooper C.L. (Ed.) *Theories of Group Processes*, Wiley, New York, 131-185.

Goodman L.P. and Goodman R.A. (1972) "Theater as a Temporary System", *California Management Review*, 15(2), 103-108.

Handy C. (1995) "Trust and the Virtual Organization", *Harvard Business Review*, May-June, 40-50.

Hart P. and Saunders C. (1997) "Power and Trust: Critical Factors in the Adoption and Use of Electronic Data Interchange", *Organization Science*, 8(1), 23-42.

Hirsch F. (1978) *Social Limits to Growth*, Harvard University Press, Cambridge, MA.

Hosmer L.T. (1995) "Trust: The Connecting Link between Organizational Theory and Philosophical Ethics", *Academy of Management Review*, 20(2), 379-403.

Kipnis D. (1996) "Trust and Technology" in Kramer R.M. and Tyler T.R. (Eds.) *Trust in Organizations - Frontiers of Theory and Research*, Sage Publications, London.

Lewicki R.J. and Bunker B.B. (1996) "Developing and Maintaining Trust in Work Relationships" in Kramer R.M. and Tyler T.R. (Eds.) *Trust in Organizations - Frontiers of Theory and Research*, Sage Publications, London.

Luhmann N. (1988) "Familiarity, Confidence, Trust: Problems and Alternatives" in Gambetta D.G. (Ed.) *Trust*, Basil Blackwell, New York, 94-107.

Mayer R.C., Davis J.H. and Schoorman F.D. (1995) "An Integrative Model of Organizational Trust", *Academy of Management Review*, 20(3), 709-734.

Meyerson D., Weick K.E. and Kramer R.M. (1996) "Swift Trust and Temporary Groups" in Kramer R.M. and Tyler T.R. (Eds.) *Trust in Organizations - Frontiers of Theory and Research*, Sage Publications, London.

Muysken J. (1998) "WebTrust and Electronic Commerce", *Charter*, August, 54-55.

Porter M. (1985) *Competitive Advantage*, The Free Press, New York.

Powell W.W. (1996) "Trust-Based Forms of Governance" in Kramer R.M. and Tyler T.R. (Eds.) *Trust in Organizations - Frontiers of Theory and Research*, Sage Publications, London.

Shapiro D., Sheppard B.H. and Cheraskin L. (1992) "Business on a Handshake", *Negotiation Journal*, 8(4), 365-377.

Tyler T.R. and Kramer R.M. (1996) "Whither Trust?", in Kramer R.M. and Tyler T.R. (Eds.) *Trust in Organizations - Frontiers of Theory and Research*, Sage Publications, London.

Venkatraman N. and Hendersen J.C. (1998) "Real Strategies for the Virtual Organization", *Sloan Management Review*, 40(1), 33-48.

Williamson O.E. (1993) "Calculativeness, Trust, and Economic Organization", *Journal of Law and Economics*, 34, 453-502.

Zand D.E. (1972) "Trust and Managerial Problem Solving", *Administrative Science Quarterly*, 17, 229-239.

Zucker L.G. (1986) "Production of Trust: Institutional Sources of Economic Structure, 1980-1920" in Staw B.M. and Cummings L.L. (Eds.) *Research in Organizational Behavior*, Vol 8, JAI Press, Greenwich, CT, 53-111.

Chapter IV

Managing Security Functions Using Security Standards

Lech Janczewski
University of Auckland, New Zealand

In this chapter we will discuss the issue of managing security processing in business organization with special emphasis on computer systems. Our intention is not to prove that managing information security resources is the most important issue within the information security domain but that it must deal first in a chain of activities leading to building and operating information systems in a secure way.

Before starting the discussion it is necessary to look at the historical developments leading to this issue. Most people are aware of the dramatic rate of development of information technology. However, few could attach quantitative values measuring this growth apart from a known statement that "If the auto industry had done what the computer industry has done in the last 30 years, a Rolls-Royce would cost $2.50 and get 2,000,000 miles per gallon." This is true, but a more precise measure must be introduced.

In 1976 IBM had almost a complete monopoly on the world computer market. The best illustration of this is the fact that the yearly IBM sales at that time were equivalent of the sales of the next four companies put together. The value of sales reached $1450 million USD (1976's value, being equivalent to almost double that value at the present). In 1998, IBM's revenues, despite losing the monopoly position on the IS market reached the value of $81.7 billion USD (IBM, 1999). The growth is substantial but changing structure of the revenues is significant: in 1976 most of the revenues came from the sales of mainframes costing the minimum those days—usually at least $250,000 a piece—while at present, gross revenues come from PCs priced in the hundreds or thousands of dollars range.

This illustrates the progress rate but also the shift in the typical data processing models. Officially, in September 1999, we celebrated 30 years of the Internet, but practically in 1960 and the early seventies stand-alone installations dominated the computing world. Lack of telecommunication facilities and limited multi-user and multi-tasking systems made the lives of personnel responsible for the development and maintenance of security systems relatively easy. The author remembers attending a security conference in Brussels, Belgium, in the late 1970s when the dominant issues discussed there were about protection against natural calamities (fire, flood and similar incidents) plus possible acts of frustrated staff (like damaging the content of a disk pack using a hidden magnet).

Indeed, in those days the term *computer security* was predominantly related to the physical security of the installation limited to the building housing the system.

Gradually from the early 1970s, remote terminals became an indispensable components of information systems. However, due to their limited processing capabilities all security functions were build into the central data processing unit.

Introduction of microprocessors and widespread telecommunication facilities dramatically changed the scenery. Microprocessors started offering cheap but powerful data processing capabilities. Networking provided means to quickly collect and disseminate the results. According to Lou Gerstner, IBM's Chairman and CEO, "Every day it becomes more clear that the Net is taking its place alongside the other great transformational technologies that first challenged, and then fundamentally changed, the way things are done in the world" (Gerstner, 1999).

These changes made most of the security techniques almost useless: remote users equipped with significant processing capabilities and efficient transmission media became capable of effectively penetrating resources of the central processors. The administrators were not able to comprehend the danger and to erect effective protection barriers on time. The culmination of this process was observed around the late 1980s. Only frequent reports from worried users and system administrators like Cliff Stoll (described in his book *Cuckoo's Egg*) created enough pressure to design and implement security measures adequate to the situation.

The next interesting twist of the situation happened only recently: remote terminals are capable of performing quite powerful data processing but a significant part of that processing is taken back by the major application installed in the server. This concept of "thin client" is in some sense returning to the old idea of the central processing unit exchanging data with a set of non-intelligent terminals. The concept allows new implementations of the old security techniques.

Issues of managing security on all organisational levels, like physical security, system security, etc., could broadly be divided into two domains:

- Development of methods allowing assessment of security efficiency.
- Development of techniques aimed on implementation of methods allowing setting up of efficient and effective security systems.

These techniques and methods operate on practically all levels of security systems, from pure technical details to managing security function and their incorporation in the fabric of the business organisation. The knowledge of these techniques is important as it will be proven that it could dramatically reduce efforts to set up and run a security system.

ASSESSMENT OF COMPUTER SECURITY

Assessment of security of an information system and its main component, the computer, is a very difficult task. The difficulties result from culmination of the following factors:

- Computer itself is a finite-state machine but its enormous complexity makes defining all transitional functions practically impossible. Usually we are able to predict behaviour within the typical program execution path but departures from this path usually make most of the predictions invalid.
- The data modifies the computer behaviour and that adds the next

level of complexity.

- An attack on a computer and its data resources may have many different forms and could be launched from many locations. Even the most experienced developer is unable to predict this. The overwhelming majority of reported computer crime acts exploited these weak points.
- Most of the information system users are not security experts and they are not capable of assessment if a given system is or is not safe.

Early researchers in this field recognised these facts and in the early 1970s, work started on the development such evaluation methods. The long list of these projects starts with the Trusted Computer System Evaluation Criteria (TCSEC, 1985) developed under the funding of the United States Department of Defense. The publication was presented in an orange coloured cover and since then is commonly referred to as the "Orange Book". The *Orange Book* did not address the issue of networks, so soon after this publication the National Computer Security Center presented in July 1987 the Trusted Network Interpretation (of The Trusted Computer System Evaluation Criteria). The document was sporting the red cover so the publication became the "Red Book". Later, the Department of Defense issued a series of reports presenting various aspects of security related matters. Since these publication were bound in different colours, the whole series is called the "Rainbow Series."

After publishing the *Orange Book* several other countries presented similar documents:

- Security Functional Manual, UK Department for Trade and Industry Draft Report, (SFM, 1989),
- IT-Security Criteria: Criteria for the Evaluation of Trustworthiness of IT Systems, in Germany, (ITSC, 1988),
- Canadian Trusted Computer Product Evaluation Criteria, ver 3.0e, in Canada (CTCPEC, 1993).

Since the security evaluation criteria developed in Europe were quite similar, in 1991 the Commission of the European Community sponsored a project aimed on bringing the European efforts together. The results were published as so-called ITSEC: Information Technology Security Evaluation Criteria (ITSEC, 1991).

In the response to the Europeans, the United States published "Federal Criteria for Information Technology Security" in 1992 (FCITS, 1992).

Finally in this saga, all the interested nations joined their efforts and produced a document titled "Common Criteria for Information Technology Security Evaluations." Several versions of this document were published starting from 1994, such as version 0.6 in April 1994 and version 1.0 in January 1996. An excellent summary of all these documents was presented by Charles Pfleeger in his book *Security in Computing*, (Pfleeger, 1997). The latest version 2.0 has been accepted in June 1999 as an international standard ISO IS 15408 (ISO 15408, 1999).

In this chapter we summarise the evaluation methods presented in the *Orange Book* and in the latest *Common Criteria*.

THE ORANGE BOOK

The *Orange Book* allows one to assess the status of security affairs within given computer systems. As a result of applying the described procedures, a particular system could be placed in one of seven classes of security ratings, grouped into four clusters ranging from highest class A through B (consisting of B1, B2, and B3) and C (of C1 and C2) to D (the lowest).

The authors of the *Orange Book* follow several principles in defining characteristics of systems fulfilling requirements of each class. The most important are:

- The primary object of security evaluation throughout all the classes is protection of confidentiality. It is easily understandable taking into consideration the fact that the document was developed under the auspices of the USA's Department of Defense, and military authorities usually consider secrecy as the most important parameter. Therefore, the issues of protection of integrity and availability are not formally addressed. In the literature that aspect was considered by many authors (i.e., Amoroso, 1994). Nevertheless, existence of many security controls suggested by the *Orange Book,* such as the accountability controls, directly increases integrity and availability.
- Security controls suggested by the *Orange Book* are upgradable, i.e., if a given control exists in the B1 class, it must exist in all the upper classes.

- Class D, which is labelled by several authors as "no security" is, in fact, defined as a class of systems that have been evaluated for belonging to a higher category but did not receive such allocation. Everybody having even minimal knowledge of Windows 95 would agree that package could be classified as being in the D class, nevertheless it is offering some protection of information.

All controls discussed in the *Orange Book* could be divided into four groups:
- *Security Policies*. This includes such protection mechanisms like discretionary and mandatory access control, security labels, object reuse.
- *Accountability*. Audit trail, identification and authentication, ability to set up a trusted path.
- *Assurance*. Ability to proof security of such parameters like system architecture, integrity and testing, management of trusted facilities and configuration, recovery and distribution.
- *Documentation*. Existence of security features user's guide, test and design documentation and similar.

The content of each group in defined in Table 1 (after Phleeger, 1997). In this table, group D has not been presented as no single parameters apply to this group. For the exact opposite reasons, group A was not presented either as ALL listed parameters must be positively verified for a system belonging to the A group. Some parameters may bring additional requirements with transfer from one category to the other. For instance migration from B2 to B3 class imposes additional requirements on Discretionary Access Control. For the sake of clarity these last changes have been omitted in Table 1. General characteristics of the groups are as follows:

D Group:
Systems with no defined security features.

C Group:
- Identification and authentication of the users.
- Discretionary access controls must be used.
- Basic audit controls are introduced.

B Group:

All the security requirements form the class C plus:

- Label-based mandatory access control based on Bell-LaPadula rules.
- Formal requirements in the respect of design specification, covert channels analysis, trusted recover and similar aspects.

A Group:

All the security requirements form the class B plus:

- Formal model of the system developed and security mechanism formally verified.

The procedure for obtaining a security rating is very long and costly.   Currently one of the most popular operating systems Windows NT version 3.51 in a stand-alone configuration received the C2 category. Only two systems in the world are know to have the A group security rating (Gollman, 1999).

The Orange Book's evaluation criteria deals with stand-alone systems. To address issues of network security National Computer Security Center issued their "Red Book" officially known as "Trusted Network Interpretation" (Red Book, 1987). The content of this publication is divided into two parts:

- *Interpretation of the TCSEC*
  This is an attempt to extend the evaluation principles outlined in the TCSEC document into the network domain. The specific security features, the assurance requirements, and the rating structure of the TCSEC are extended to networks of computers ranging from isolated local area networks to wide-area internetwork systems.
- *(Other) Security Services*
  This part describes a number of additional security services (e.g., communications integrity, denial of service, transmission security) that arise in conjunction with networks. Those services available in specific network offerings, while inappropriate for the rigorous evaluation applied to TCSEWC related features and assurance requirements, may receive qualitative ratings.

Generally, the Red Book discusses security issues of centralised networks with a single accreditation authority and fails to deal with a

Table 1: Definition of security groups from the Orange Book

	C1	C2	C3	B1	B2
SECURITY POLICY					
Discretionary Access Control	√	√	√	√	√
Object Rreuse		√	√	√	√
Labels			√	√	√
Labels Integrity			√	√	√
Exportation of Labeled Information			√	√	√
Labeling Human-readable Output			√	√	√
Mandatory Access Ccontrol			√	√	√
Subject Sensitivity Labels				√	√
Device Labels				√	√
ACCOUNTABILITY					
Identification and Authentication	√	√	√	√	√
Audit		√	√	√	√
Trusted Path				√	√
ASSURANCE					
System Architecture	√	√	√	√	√
System Integrity	√	√	√	√	√
Security Testing	√	√	√	√	√
Design Specification and Verification			√	√	√
Covert Channel Management				√	√
Trusted Facility Management				√	√
Configuration Management				√	√
Trusted Recovery					√
Trusted Distribution					
DOCUMENTATION					
Security Features User's Guide	√	√	√	√	√
Trusted Facility Manual	√	√	√	√	√
Test Documentation	√	√	√	√	√
Design Documentation	√	√	√	√	√

system built of fairly independent components (different environment in the wide meaning of this term).

The latest version of the Common Criteria (CC), which was elevated to the status of the international standard attempts to eliminate most of the weak point identified with all previous versions of the evaluation criteria starting from the *Orange Book*. As a result, it is a very detailed document and relatively not easy to study and under-stating. The whole length of the three parts exceeds 600 pages! An interested reader could download the document from Web (CC, 1999).

Basically, the authors claim that the Criteria covers most of the security aspects except:

- Evaluation of administrative, nor legal framework security measures.
- Evaluation of technical physical aspects of IT security like electromagnetic emanation control.
- Evaluation of the qualities of cryptographic algorithms.

CC could be used for the evaluation of security measures of hardware, firmware or software being such products like operating systems, computer networks, distributed systems and applications. During this evaluation process, such an IT product is known as a Target of Evaluation (TOE). The CC addresses protection of information from unauthorised disclosure, modification, or loss of use. CC are useful to all classes of IT users: consumers, developers, evaluators and many others.

The basic evaluation process used in CC is presented in Figure 1.

CC defines seven different aspects of security problems called Assurance Classes:

- Configuration management
- Delivery and operation
- Development
- Guidance documents
- Life cycle support
- Tests
- Vulnerability assessment

The Assurance classes are further divided in Assurance families. For instance the lifecycle support, (called Class ALC) is further divided into Assurance Families:

- Development security (ALC_DVS),
- Flaw remediation (ALC_FLR),
- Life cycle definition (ALC_LCD),
- Tools and Techniques (ALC)TAT).

Figure 1. TOE Evaluation Process (from CC)
PP : Protection Profile, ST : Security Target

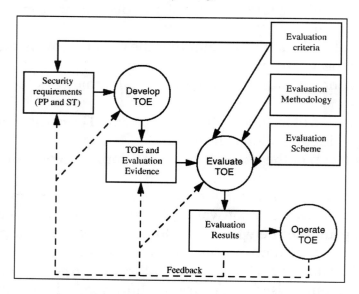

Assurance classes are then grouped into seven Evaluation Assurance Levels, being:

- EAL1 - functionally tested
- EAL2 - structurally tested
- EAL3 - methodically tested and checked
- EAL4 - methodically design, tested and reviewed
- EAL5 - semiformally design and tested
- EAL6 - semiformally verified design and tested
- EAL7 - formally verified design and tested

The reader may notice that a number of security groups from the *Orange Book* and CC's Evaluation Assurance Levels is the same and equal to seven. It is, therefore, tempting to compare functional characteristics of classification offered by these two evaluation methods. Many authors did it in the past comparing for instance the *Orange Book* classification and ITSEC (Gollmann, 1999). Definitely there are many similarities between these two classifications, especially on the top end of the scale where the *Orange Book* class A is a good equivalent of the EAL7. However, on the other levels the differences are significant, like the CC does not have an equivalent of the D group (from the *Orange Book*). Therefore, in the opinion of the author it would be counterproductive to do such a comparison.

As it has been shown the idea germinated by the Orange Book over 15 years ago resulted in a very comprehensive international standard. Following the methodology outlined in there it is possible to get a very detailed and accurate assessment of a computer system security status. This is a positive side of the story.

The negative one is that methodology is very elaborate, costly and time consuming. It is estimated, for instance, that the assessment of the Windows NT to get the C2 ratings took well over a year. Information systems are under constant development and a system today could be dramatically reshaped within a few months. This questions the usefulness of the evaluation criteria approach.

These inadequacies gave birth to a dramatically different "baseline" approach. The foundations of the baseline approach were set up by the Organization for Economic Cooperation and Development (OECD), who published in 1992 the "Guidelines for the Security of Information" (OECD, 1992). This publication details the nine principles to be adhered to in the deployment of information systems, and five strategies by which the principles may be applied. The guidelines are addressed to all information systems in both the public and private sectors. The objective of security of information systems is the protection of the interests of those relying on information systems from harm resulting from failures of availability, confidentiality and integrity. The nine principles are:

Accountability Principle

The responsibilities and accountability of owners, providers and users of information systems and other parties concerned with the security of information systems should be explicit.

Awareness Principle

In order to foster confidence in information systems, owners, providers and users of information systems and other parties should readily be able, consistent with maintaining security, to gain appropriate knowledge of, and be informed about the existence and general extent of measures, practices and procedures for the security of information systems.

Ethics Principle

Information systems and the security of information systems should be provided and used in such a manner that the rights and legitimate interests of others are respected.

Multidisciplinary Principle

Measures, practices and procedures for the security of information systems should take account of and address all relevant considerations and viewpoints, including technical, administrative, organizational, operational, commercial, educational and legal.

Proportionality Principle

Security levels, costs, measures, practices and procedures should be appropriate and proportionate to the value of and degree of reliance on the information systems and to the severity, probability and extent of potential harm, as the requirements for security vary depending upon the particular information systems.

Integration Principle

Measures, practices and procedures for the security of information systems should be coordinated and integrated with each other and with other measures, practices and procedures of the organization so as to create a coherent system of security.

Timeliness Principle

Public and private parties, at both national and international levels, should act in a timely coordinated manner to prevent and to respond to breaches of security of information systems.

Reassessment Principle

The security of information systems should be reassessed periodically, as information systems and the requirements for their security vary over time.

Democracy Principle

The security of information systems should be compatible with the legitimate use and flow of data and information in a democratic society.

Many countries adopted these principles as a basis of developing their own, more detailed guidelines or standards. The most known, perhaps, is the British Standard BS 7799, published in 1995 and titled "Code of Practice for Information Security Management" (BSC, 1995). The objectives of the Code of Practice are:

1. To provide a common basis for companies to develop, implement and measure effective security management practice
2. To provide confidence in inter-company trading

The Code of Practice is intended to be used as a reference document for managers and employees who are responsible for initiating, implementing and maintaining information security within their organisation.

The Code of Practice addresses the following groups of issues:

1. Security policy
2. Security organisation
3. Assets classification and control
4. Personnel security
5. Physical and environmental security
6. Computer and network management
7. System access control
8. System development and maintenance
9. Business contingency planning
10. Compliance

The following note to the readers of the document illustrates in the best way the authors intentions:

"A word of advice on developing corporate guidelines on information security management. There is no single best structure for security guidance. Each category of users or IT specialist in a particular environment will have a different set of requirements, problems and priorities depending on their particular function, organisation and business or computing environment. Many companies have addressed this problem by developing a portfolio of individual interpretation guides for particular groups of employees, to ensure more effective dissemination of security guidance across the Company" (PD 0003, 1993).

The value of the Code was confirmed by accepting it as a standard in several other countries like Australia and New Zealand (AS/NZS, 1996).

Code of Practice is one example of standards dealing with information security issued by international and national standard organisations. Generally these standards could be divided into three major groups:

1. General guidance or philosophy
2. Security management
3. Technical, procedural issues.

The OECD recommendations presented before belong to the first group. Code of Practice is an example of the second group. For obvious reasons most of the standards (or Request for Comments) belong to the third group. In this book Chris Mitchell in the chapter on the development of the security mechanisms presents international standards related to the cryptography and key management field. Hence more detailed discussion of these standards is beyond the framework of this chapter.

Similarly to the British Code of Practice, in 1995 the USA National Institute of Standards and Technology had prepared a publication titled "An Introduction to Computer Security: The NIST Handbook," (NIST, 1995). This handbook provides assistance in securing computer-based resources (including hardware, software and data) by explaining important concepts, cost considerations and interrelationships of security controls. It gives a broad overview of computer security to help readers understand their computer security needs and to develop a sound approach in selecting appropriate security controls. The content of the Handbook is divided into three sections on management controls, Ooperational controls and technical controls.

The security of data processing and transmission is not a simple issue. All the documents described so far confirm that. Unfortunately, in an effort to cover the issue in a complete way these documents are difficult to follow and even more difficult to implement. Besides that, especially in the case of the Common Criteria, the value of these documents is, somehow, questionable. It was said before that the investigation of a system for granting a specific security clearance could last even a year. This effort is summarised by a simple statement that a given product belongs to a specific security category like C2 or B1. Such a statement has rather commercial or marketing value then any practical meaning. What sort of practical conclusions could a typical CEO draw from receiving such information about his/her products? Besides the developments in the IS technology could render some of the paradigms of the methodologies out of date. This was suggested by several authors like (Hosmer, 1996).

The methodologies presented so far advocate performance of an extensive risk analysis. Big business organisations could afford this, but small businesses employing 5 to 20 people hardly are able to do so. As a result, a so called "baseline" approach emerged. A baseline approach can be seen as a "bottom-up" methodology, where a generic set of controls is defined for most organizations or business areas operating under normal circumstances. By installing these baselines controls, an organisation can be sure that the most common and serious risks have been addressed adequately under normal, generic circumstances. Therefore, the objectives of security baselines are to provide a minimum level of security (Solms, 1997). Cited before British Code of Practice is an example of such approach.

In conclusion of this part it can be said that major methodologies/recommendations developed for setting up and assessment of security measures could be divided into three groups:

- Common Criteria allowing assessment of security status, in the form of an international standard.
- National or international standards tracking with various aspects of security subsystems, from managerial via operational to detailed technical solutions,
- Baseline approach represented by the British Code of Practice or similar Australian/New Zealand standard.

ISSUE OF THE DEVELOPMENT OF INFORMATION SECURITY POLICIES

At this moment a very important question should be asked: in practical terms, to what extent could the above documents help an average business organisation in the development of their data security system?

The development of an efficient data security system must be done through a systematic procedure. Implementation of an "ad hoc" approach could lead to leaving serious security holes in the protection mechanism. It is very difficult to resist temptations not to use such a method: when something goes wrong, a remedy must be found quickly, usually in the form of installing a specific security measure, which, as a rule of thumb, stays for ever. After some time a number of these measures create a false image of having a protected system.

A systematic approach would reduce the probability of leaving security holes unplugged. It requires passing the following steps (Janczewski, 1999):

1. Convince management that information security is an issue and they must act now!
2. Appoint a person responsible for information security.
3. Assess your info resources and their vulnerabilities.
4. Identify the threats.
5. Perform risk analysis.
6. Design your line of defence: physical protection, hardware, software, organisation, people.
7. Develop your information security policy.
8. Implement the policy.
9. Review the policy annually.

These steps form a summary of the majority of the existing methodologies of setting up a security system. The problem is, however, that many of these methodologies could not be feasible for smaller organisations or these undergoing rapid changes. Hence, there is a need to follow the outlined procedure in a quick way.

The above procedure is focused on the development and implementation of an Information Security Policy (ISP). This is a relatively labour intensive and long lasting activity. If a business organisation is thinking seriously about securing their information resources development of an ISP is a must. Therefore, an effort should be undertaken to make the procedure leading to the ISP development feasible for a company of any size from the smallest to the biggest. In the opinion of the author, the best method of the ISP development is to concentrate on the baseline approach and to implement as much as possible the security standards described in the earlier parts of this chapter. The major advantage of such method is dramatically shortened time needed for the ISP development. Research conducted by Leung (1998) confirmed that. Let's then have the closer look at ISPs and how they can be developed.

IMPROVED METHOD OF DEVELOPING ISP

The ISP is defined as a set of mandatory rules governing an organisation's protection of information confidentiality, integrity and availability, which may be refined into lower-level, more technical sub-policies that will achieve it (Leung, 1988). An ISP usually has a life span of more than a year and can be described as a part of the organisation's strategic plan (Janczewski, 1977). Typically, an ISP should address two major areas of security:

- Managing data security, normal protection, prevention of crisis.
- Disaster recovery and contingency planning, for handling emergencies.

In the shortest version an ISP could be of one page length, in the longest form it could extend to several hundred pages, describing the practical implementations of the policy statements. For instance a short statement that everybody should do the backups of their records could be expanded to detailed information how often, on which media, where these media should be stored, how records should be recovered, administered, etc.

As a minimum an ISP should contain the following statements:

- Statement of the management intentions, supporting the goals and principles of information security
- Presentation of specific regulations, principles, standards and compliance requirements including:
  1. Basic information security procedures related to physical security, security of hardware, software, systems and staff.
  2. Business continuity procedures.
  3. Compliance with legislative and contractual requirements.
- General and specific responsibilities for all aspects of information security including outline of procedures for reporting suspected security incidents.

To be efficient, a review and maintenance procedure must be established. Nothing is more discouraging than a policy demanding specific actions, with heavy penalties for noncompliance while the action clearly does not make sense. Imagine an organisation which has a statement in their ISP demanding reporting of all the hardware faults to the specific IBM technical support while the company switched mainframe to UNISYS!

Also, the ISP must be consistent throughout the organisation. The importance of this could be seen in an example of an organisation handling backups using different schedules and procedures. Recovery from a disk crash could be a nightmare!

Leung (1998) suggested a procedure for developing an ISP based on implementation of British Standard BS 7799, "Code of practice for information security management". This standard was adopted (with few minor changes) by many other countries (like Australia and New Zealand) and is widely available. Leung proved that his methodology would render quality results in a much shorter period of time than a regular ISP development cycle.

The methodology is based on an 8-step procedure:
1. Evaluation of the firm security stance.
2. Application of ranking to the items in the BS 7799.
3. Selection of items based on Rank-Cost matrix.
4. Possible inclusion of new-technology related items.
5. Modification resulted from industry specific problems.
6. Modification resulted from the organisation specific problems.
7. Editing (plain English!).
8. Presentation.

Security stance is a result of company middle point between constrains imposed by:
- Budget (how much money the company is willing to spend on security).
- Security (risk tolerance of the firm).
- Ease of use (usually the more security measures being introduced the more cumbersome the controls become).

In practical terms the above is usually becoming a two-dimensional issue: budget v security.

Development of the company security stance should be based on such elements like:
- Evaluation of the company's current ISP and ISPs collected from similar businesses.
- Brainstorming the staff.

- Budget (IT and general).
- Company strategy.
- Evaluation of the value of company information resources.

Establishment of the company security stance would allow ranking of items from the BS 7799. A listing of major parts was presented before. A list of suggested items is presented in the Table 2 (Leung, 1998). Entries from Table 1 should receive double ranking: of controls (from "Critical/Essential" to "No benefit") and of costs (from "Cost negligible" to "Outside the budget").

After assigning ratings of controls, costs and the organisation's security stance, the next step is to select the appropriate items for inclusion in the developed ISP. The BS 7799 control item should be accepted as the base and then modified according to the company's security stance and the other parameters. The simplest way to do so is to convert these three ratings into numerical values, add them for each item and decide about positioning the cutting off point.

Information technology is undergoing rapid changes. This must be reflected in the content of the company's ISP. Currently, the most expanding part of IT is electronic commerce. Not all the business organisations are conducting their activities via e-commerce yet, but the number is growing rapidly. This must be reflected in the company ISP and adequate protection mechanisms erected. For example, all organisations must have a policy on how to deal with all the software sent by other Web sites aimed at enhancing the presentation of their own Web sites on the user desktop. ActiveX, Java Applets, Java Scripts and other similar pieces of software make web pages very user friendly but it could easily bring a disastrous consequence to an unaware user. The ISP must warn staff about the danger and suggest protection mechanisms.

Closely connected with the IT progress is the issue of the introduction of industry-specific items. The best way to present this point is to examine an information system servicing two types of companies: a software house and an electronic commerce retailer. Both companies must maintain very active and user friendly web pages. Both companies may expect some attacks on their information systems and both must introduce security mechanisms. However, it is clear that the security mechanisms in both cases are and should be slightly different: For the electronic retailer, the highest danger is the possibility of

Table 2: Suggested items for ranking

Management information security forum	EDI security
Information security co-ordination	Enforced path
Specialist information security advice	Remote diagnostic port protection
Co-operation between organisations	Segregation in networks
Security of 3rd party access	Network connection / routing control
Information classification	Automatic terminal identification
Security in job description	Duress alarm to safeguard users
Recruitment screening	Limitation of connection time
User training	Application access control
Secure areas	Monitoring system use
Equipment security	Security requirements of systems
Segregation of duties	Input data validation
External facilities management	Security of application files
System acceptance	Security in development and support environments
Fallback planning	Business continuity planning
Environment monitoring	Compliance with legal requirements
Network management	Security reviews of IT
Security of system documentation	System Audit

dispatching goods without securing the payments, while for a software house the highest priority is prevention of unauthorised access to their software resources (illegal changes or copying). Both sides must be secure but the security measures may be distributed in a different way.

Going further this way, the company itself may wish to introduce some very specific security measures.

The final point is to examine the ISP and introduce some editorial changes. ISP is a document which should be read (and followed) by all members of the staff whether computer literate or not. The text must be clear of all "computer talk", abbreviations and shortcuts.

What sort of time saving could one expect? A study conducted by Leung (1988) shows that companies usually need at least several months to develop their ISP. The survey done by the above-cited author indicates that an ISP develop on the basis of a BS 7799 or similar standard takes usually around 3 working days. Hence, savings are quite considerable.

How should an ISP look? In the Appendix is an example of such a document prepared for a New Zealand company with an extensive network of terminals.

CONCLUSIONS

In this chapter we discussed the importance of developments of an Information Security Policy. Every company, big or small, must at present develop such a document. The ISP could be a few pages or hundreds of pages, depending of the level of coverage. However, whatever length it is it must be prepared very carefully and updated frequently.

Traditional methods of development of an ISP could be very lengthy resulting from a detailed following of known standards on the evaluation of the risks and designing system security components. Such procedures are very costly and not well suited to the present, rapidly changing computer environment.

Hence the authors recommend implementation of a baseline approach with the use of such standards as BS 7799. Interesting enough, there are attempts now to completely computerised this procedure, starting from the simplified evaluation of security parameters (Solms, 1999) in the form of a so-called "Tool box".

APPENDIX

XYZ COMPUTER WORKSTATION POLICY & STANDARDS
QUICK REFERENCE GUIDE

This guide covers the use by XYZ staff of all types of XYZ's computer workstations. For a more detailed reference, refer to XYZ's security manual.

Access to Information
Users accessing systems and information will use an individually assigned user ID and password, where available.

Password Generation & Control
Where passwords protect access to information, the password

must be created as indicated by the policy document, changed if disclosed and, where necessary for high level user IDs, be sealed in an envelope for safekeeping by the users manager.

Printed and Magnetic Information

Magnetic information (tape and diskette) and printed information (paper, microfiche & microfilm) must be protected against unauthorised disclosure.

Notebook and Laptop Security

Notebooks and laptops must be secured to prevent theft and unauthorised use of data.

Viruses

Each and every diskette received by a user must be scanned for viruses. If a virus is found a call to the Support Desk must be placed immediately.

Working from Home

Users working from home, using their own workstation, must state their requirements in writing to their Chief manager, who must then have the requirements approved by the chief manager of organisation & methods.

Data Interchange with External Organisations

If information (data) is to be exchanged between the XYZ and any other organisation, users must ensure that interchange is completed as required by the XYZ (with reference to the manager of IS policy and security) in accordance with the provisions of the Privacy Act 1993.

Justification

A business case must exist for all requests to the manager of IS planning for the purchase of a workstation.

Hardware and Software Selection, Ordering and Installation

O and M only are authorised to control this process.

Software Evaluation

All software for evaluation must be approved by the manager of

IS planning (O&M) prior to being installed by IT support.

Computer Usage
- Protect workstation with standard screen saver and passwords.
- At the end of day terminate applications and logoff.
- Use only XYZ owned workstations and licensed software.
- Where security could be compromised the use of diskette locking devices, security software and security cables is recommended.
- Don't use private PCs at work.
- Don't remove non-portable workstations from XYZ premises.
- Don't eat or drink near a workstation.
- No games are permitted on workstations.
- Pornography, offensive material or non-standard screen savers are not permitted.
- Do not store artwork or embedded artwork in e-mails or documents unless there are consistent with XYZ business.
- No shareware, demonstration software, electronic pictures, whether free or chargeable may be installed by users on XYZ workstations.

Copyrights and Control
Users are not permitted to install any software or make copies of any software except for backup purposes.

Documentation
All business processes using XYZ workstations and software must be fully documented.

Backup
All XYZ information must be backed up.

Destruction of Computer & Telephony Hardware
Information Services are responsible for computer and telephony hardware assets and will determine the method of disposal for individual items.

Lost or Stolen Computer and Telephony Hardware
IT Services must be informed if any hardware items are lost or stolen to ensure inventories are kept up to date; replacements can be

ordered and insurance claims made.

Training

Management is responsible for ensuring that all users receive adequate training in the operation of all equipment and applications on the workstations they will be using.

REFERENCES

Amoroso, E. (1994). *Fundamentals of Computer Security Technology*, Prentice –Hall.

AS/NZS (1996). Information Security Management, New Zealand Standards.

Baseline (1996). *IT Protection Manual*, BSI, Germany.

CC (1999). *Standard 15408, Common Criteria*, http://csrc.ncsl.nist.gov/cc/ccv20/ccv2list.htm.

CTCPEC (1993). *Canadian Trusted Computer Product Evaluation Criteria*, ver 3.0e, January.

D. Gollman, *Computer Security*, Wiley.

FCITS (1992). *Federal Criteria for Information Technology Security*, version 1.0,

Gerstner, L. (1999). http://www.ibm.com/lvg.

Hosmer, H. (1996). *New Security Paradigms: Orthodoxy and Heresy*, in: Information Systems Security: Facing the information society of the 21st Century, Chapman & Hall.

IBM (1999). http://www.ibm.com/ibm/.

ITSC (1988). *IT-Security Criteria: Criteria for the Evaluation of Trustworthiness of IT Systems*, German Security Agency.

ITSEC (1991). *Information Technology Security Evaluation Criteria*, version 1.2, September.

Janczewski, L.(1999). *Electronic Commerce Security*, Notes for the 1st session of the short course at the University of Auckland.

Janczewski, L. *(1997).Are generic ISP Possible*, Department of MSIS Working Paper, The University of Auckland.

Leung, V. (1998). *Optimization of Information Security Policy Development*, Master Thesis, Department of MSIS, The University of Auckland.

Moisner, L.(1976). *Le hit parade des constructeurs*, Zer-o-un informatique, No 1, September.

NIST (1995). Guttman, B., Roback, E., *An Introduction to Computer Security: the NIST Handbook*, SPEC PUB 800-12.

OECD (1992). *Guidelines for the security of information systems*, OECD, publication No OECD/GD (92) 190, Paris.

Orange Book (1985). *DoD Trusted Computer System Evaluation Criteria*, US Department of Defence DoD 5200.28-M.

PD003 (1993). *A Code of Practice for Information Security Management*, BSI, 1993,

Pfleeger, C (1997). *Security in Computing*, Prentice Hall.

Red Book (1987). *Trusted Network Interpretation*, NCSC, NCSC-TG-005, Version 1.0.

SFM (1989). *Security Functional Manual*, UK Department for Trade and Industry, Draft Report, v21 version 3.9.

Solms, R. (1997). Can Security Baselines Replace Risk Analysis?, in: *Information Security in Research and Business*, Chapman & Hall.

von Solms, R. (1999). "The Information Security Toolbox", in Khosrowpour, M. , Managing Information Technology Resourcs in Organizations in the Next Millennium, IDEA, Hershey.

Chapter V

Managing Security in the World Wide Web: Architecture, Services and Techniques

Fredj Dridi and Gustaf Neumann
University of Essen, Germany

Advances in the World Wide Web technology have resulted in the proliferation of significant collaborative applications in commercial environments. However, the World Wide Web as a distributed system, which introduces new technologies (like Java applets and ActiveX) and uses a vulnerable communication infrastructure (the Internet), is subject to various security attacks. These security attacks violate the confidentiality, integrity, and availability of Web resources. To achieve a certain degree of Web security and security management, different protocols and techniques have been proposed and implemented. This is still a hot topic in the current research area and still requires more ambitious efforts.

We give an overview of the Internet security issues with special emphasis on the Web security. We describe an architecture built up by the means of security services to shield against these threats and to achieve information security for networked systems like the WWW. We focus on the authentication and access control services (like role-based access control) and their administration aspects. We discuss several elementary techniques and Internet standards which provide state-of-the-art of Web security.

The World Wide Web (WWW or Web) is a distributed, collaborative hypertext- and hypermedia-based information system and uses the Internet, a global public TCP/IP based communication architecture, as a transport mechanism. The Web is today the most significant use of the Internet. It introduces new protocols and standards (like HTTP, HTML, CGI, XML, RDF, etc.) which have the potential to be used in complex distributed applications. Since the Web technology can be used to provide uniform access to a wide variety of information managed by different organizations, enterprises are increasingly using the it to access Internet corporate information as well.

Advances in the Web technologies have resulted in the proliferation of significant collaborative applications in commercial environments. Collaborative applications is the term used to denote a class of applications which facilitate information sharing in an inter- or intra-enterprise environment. Examples of collaborative applications are: groupware, document (project) management, electronic commerce, and workflow automation, etc.

The term intranet usually refers to an internal enterprise network, that uses Web technology. In large organizations collaborative applications are relevant to a large number of users who want to share and grant access to documents in a controlled way. Typically, the documents are placed on various decentralized Web servers. Some of those documents may contain sensitive information and consequently must not be disclosed to every user. In addition, because the Web uses the Internet as its transport mechanism, it inherits all of the security vulnerabilities of the Internet. As a result, the demand for security services (like authentication, access control, non-repudiation service, etc.) has grown rapidly. The documents and the administration of access rights for a huge number of users is becoming increasingly complex.

The area of Inter-/Intranet and Web security is a very active research area where new approaches and techniques are constantly proposed. Literature references addressing this topic in more detail are, for example, Garfinkel and Spafford (1997); Lipp and Hassler (1996); and Oppliger (1998). In this chapter, we give an overview of the Internet security issues, with special emphasis on Web security. First, we give an introduction to the various types of security attacks the Web-based applications are exposed to. Next we describe a communication-based architecture, e.g. the Internet, for building collaborative applications. This architecture contains several services: communication, coordination, cooperation, and security services. We focus on the security services and their administration and management aspects. The security services (like authentication, access control, non-repudiation service, etc.) and the existing techniques for Web security which are ready to be used are described in the section "Security Services." The section "Security Management Services" refers to the management aspects of both authentication, and access control services. In these cases, we discuss the use of LDAP-enabled directory services in order to support Internet-based applications using these security services on a large scale. Finally, we offer concluding remarks.

SECURITY REQUIREMENTS AND POTENTIAL ATTACKS FOR INTERNET (WWW) BASED APPLICATIONS

The World Wide Web is a distributed, collaborative hypertext- and hypermedia-based information system and uses the Internet and its TCP/IP suite of protocols as a communication technology. The WWW is based on a client-server model using the Hypertext Transfer Protocol (HTTP (Fielding et al., 1997)) for transferring data between servers (Web servers) and clients (Web clients, Web browsers).

Figure 1 displays the most common usage of the Web, where a Web client retrieves data from a Web server through a Web transaction. A Web transaction is an HTTP interaction sequence, starting with a request from the client followed by a response from the server. The transferred data of the request and the response consists of header information and an entity representing the data.

Because the Web uses a vulnerable communication infrastructure (the Internet), it is subject to various security attacks. A security attack

Figure 1. Basic Web Client-Server Model

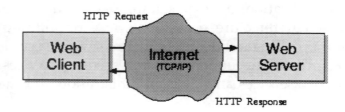

Figure 2. Areas of Information Security (in analogy to Oppliger, 1997)

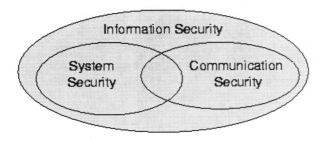

is an action which could be used to exploit a client, server, and/or network vulnerability (weakness). In addition, the use and wide deployment of executable content, such as Java applets, ActiveX, and CGI scripts provides new opportunities for attack.

Web security has to deal with the secure storage and transmission of information and is part of the more general question of information security. The main aspects of information security are system security and communication security (see Figure 2). System security refers to the protection of information within a computer against unauthorized use and abuse. Communication security refers to the protection of information during its transmission in a network. These three issues are discussed in the following sections.

Information Security

In general, the area of information security is concerned with the following security objectives:

- *Confidentiality.* Information must be only disclosed or revealed for authorized users. Therefore, sensitive information needs to be protected when it is stored or when it is transmitted over the network. This objective is concerned about both, the content of data and its existence (e.g. an URL of a sensitive Web document).
- *Integrity.* Information must not be modified by unauthorized users. This means that information must be protected from malicious or accidental alteration, including insertion of false data, contamination or destruction of data.
- *Legitimate Use.* Information must be only used by authorized users and in authorized ways. Data with different security requirements is made available to users with different privileges.

Figure 3. Potential Attacks

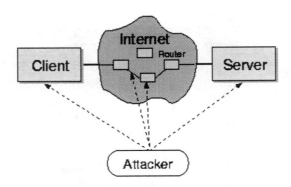

- *Availability.* Information must be available to authorized users in a timely fashion. Authorized users must get access the information when they need it.

Pfleeger (1997) discusses these information security objectives in more detail. In the following, we give an introduction to the various security attacks which can be exploited in a communication architecture in general and the attacks on a single computer system. Figure 3 depicts several targets of security attacks: single computer system, communication link, and router systems. In the sequel we describe an architecture built up by the means of security services to shield against these threats and to achieve information security for networked systems like the WWW.

Attacks Against Communication Security

Communication or network security involves the measures to ensure information security in networked systems and channels. If an application is connected to a network (e.g., Internet) without appropriate attention paid to communication security, several network-based security attacks may take place. These security attacks can be divided into two categories (Stallings, 1995):

Passive Attacks

Passive attacks can take place by intercepting the communication stream between the client and the server. The transmitted data can be eavesdropped or monitored. Passive attacks are attacks on confidentiality. We can distinguish between two types of passive attacks:

- *Release of message content*. The opponent obtains information transmitted over the communication stream. Examples are eavesdropping of passwords or the theft of confidential information.
- *Traffic analysis*. The opponent observes the message patterns in order to infer information about the profile of the communicating parties and/or about the frequency and size of the data. For example, if a large communication between two companies (one financially strong, the other financially weak) is observed, one may infer that they are discussing a merger.

Passive attacks are very difficult to detect since they do not involve any alteration of the transmitted data. Therefore, the emphasis in dealing with passive attacks is on prevention rather than on detection.

Active Attacks

Active attacks can take place by interrupting or modifying the communication stream between the communicating parties. Another kind of active attacks can occur when the opponent initiates a communication stream to the server. An active attack threatens the availability and integrity of data being transmitted. An active attack may also threaten the confidentiality of identity (masquerading). Four types of active attacks can be identified:

- *Masquerading*. These attacks can be used to enable one communicating party to masquerade as another party (someone pretends to be a different party).
- *Replaying*. These attacks involve playing back messages of another party recorded in a prior passive attack in order to a accomplish the same or similar results achieved earlier. For example, the opponent can capture authentication sequences of an authorized party and replay it to obtain access to the target system.
- *Message tampering*. These attacks can be used to intercept messages and to alter their content before passing them to the intended recipient.
- *Denial of service*. These attacks render the system unusable for legitimate users. For example, the opponent can send a large sequence of messages (e.g. HTTP requests) to the target system to overflow the available server.

One common attack in the Internet is the "Men in the middle Attack", where an attacker inserts itself between two communicating parties in order to exploit the above active attacks. In general, active attacks are difficult to prevent. The emphasis in dealing with active attacks is on detection, for example using auditing services.

Attacks Against System Security

System security refers to the protection of the hardware, operating system, and software used on both client and server machines. The system hardware can be protected by physical means, i.e., the system may be placed in a locked room and disconnected from all networks. Potential attacks against system security usually exploit weaknesses in the operating system and in the application software. There is a variety of malicious software that can attack computer systems. A malicious software may intentionally contain, for example, an undocumented entry point (trapdoor), which can be used to obtain unauthorised access to a system. Another example of malicious software is a Trojan horse, which includes malicious instructions hidden inside otherwise useful software. In order to reduce the risk concerning system security, the following aspects have to be considered:

- *Software Installation Management.* The software must be carefully configured and installed in order to limit potential damage. Typically, software running on a server machine should be granted "least privileges". For example, a Web server or a CGI application may be configured so that it runs with higher access privileges (e.g. as root) than it needs, which entails a higher security exposure than necessary. In addition, software must be checked against malicious behavior such as viruses, worms, and Trojan horses before installation. Rubin et al. (1997) give a practical guide on how to improve the security of Web clients, servers, and CGI scripts.
- *User Management.* In a multi-user system several user accounts are supported. User accounts must be kept current. That is, unused accounts must be determined and deleted. Some attackers may look for infrequently-used accounts to breach in the system. In this case, any activity done by the attackers will escape user notice. In addition, users must be educated or forced to chose proper (hard to guess) passwords, because passwords are the primary

means of user and system protection.

- *Auditing.* The operating system and application software must keep a log, e.g. in log files, of their activities. These log files must be examined regularly. Often, the log files are used to check, whether a security attack has occurred and even to determine who the attacker is. In addition, the log files may be used to link an individual to their interactivity with the system (accountability). In general, log files must be protected against attackers.

A system administrator of a machine connected to the Internet has to update the system software and its configuration regularly to protect the system against new security threats. The Computer Emergency Response Team Coordination Center (CERT-CC) acts as an information center storing known system and network vulnerabilities. This information is distributed by means of mailing lists and newsgroups as "CERT-CC Advisories". An archive of the advisories is kept at *ftp://info.cert.org/pub/cert_advisories/*.

AN ARCHITECTURE FOR SECURE INTERNET-BASED APPLICATIONS

The goal of an architecture for secure Internet-based applications is to facilitate the construction of distributed (Web-based) applications in a systematic manner. Figure 4 identifies the building blocks of an Internet-based architecture for collaborative applications, where

Figure 4. An Architecture for Internet/Web-based collaborative applications

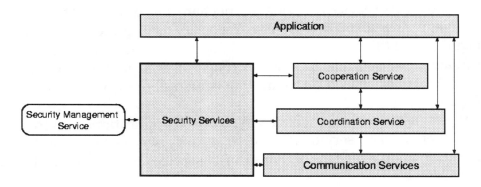

multiple users can work together in a controlled way. The basic services required for such applications are coordination, cooperation, and communication services. For example, e-commerce applications coordinate a large number of users which cooperate and share services and resources in a secure manner. The communication service is used to provide basic communication mechanisms using the TCP/IP interface to exchange data. The cooperation and coordination services are needed to create a basic platform for groupware and cooperative information systems. Cooperation mechanisms allow document and resource sharing. Coordination mechanisms allow the locking and sequencing of multiple activities.

In this chapter we concentrate on the security services, in particular on the security services for the WWW; the same principles apply to the Internet or to communication architecture in general. As discussed previously, a communication architecture is vulnerable to several security attacks. Therefore, in the design of collaborative applications security issues must be taken into account. We distinguish between two kinds of services needed to provide security in a manageable way:

- The *Security Services* provide the mechanisms to reduce or eliminate the potential damage which may be produced when security attacks are exploited.
- The *Security Management Services* provide general administration and management functions which are needed to administer the users and resources of the applications using these security services.

SECURITY SERVICES

The security services provide the mechanisms to achieve security objectives of an information system. A security service is a function or a technique that reduces or eliminates the potential damage of security attacks. For example, the use of strong authentication techniques eliminates attacks based on identity masquerading or on password eavesdropping.

We divide security services for Web-based applications into core and higher security services. The core security services represent a foundation upon which the higher security services are deployed. The

Figure 5. Dependencies of Security Services

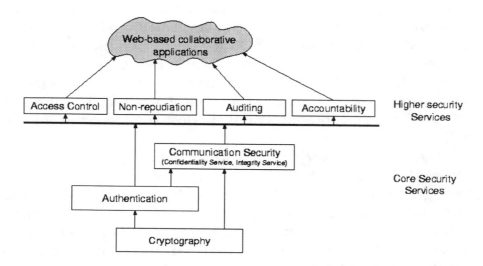

core security services include cryptography, authentication, and communication security services. The cryptography service, in turn, provides the basis for the implementation of the core security services. For example, the cryptography service is needed for the implementation of both the authentication and the communication security service which should provide data confidentiality and integrity. The authentication and the communication security services are required in order to realize the higher security services, such as access control, non-repudiation, audit, and accountability.

Figure 5 depicts the dependencies between the security services. A detailed description of the mentioned security services is given in the following sections.

Cryptography Service

Cryptography services are required for all higher security services. Cryptography services are provided by a cryptographic system that provides two complementary tasks: encryption and decryption. The algorithms for encryption and decryption are divided into symmetric and asymmetric key algorithms (Schneier, 1996). These have distinct characteristics and are used in different ways to provide security services.

The *symmetric key algorithms* use the same secret key to encrypt and decrypt the data. Symmetric key algorithms are considered to be the most efficient way to encrypt/decrypt data so that its confidentiality and integrity are preserved. That is, the data remains secret to those who do not possess the secret key, and a modification to the encrypted text can be detected during decryption (Schneier, 1996). However, such schemes have the disadvantage of requiring large-scale distribution of the shared keys. Everyone who possesses the key can encrypt/decrypt the data. Therefore symmetric algorithms are not suited for authentication. If the key is lost, confidentiality is lost as well.

Asymmetric key algorithms (also called public key algorithms) use two mathematically linked keys: if one key is used to encrypt a message, the other key must be used to decrypt it. One key is kept secret and is referred to as the private key. The second key is made publicly available and is referred to as the public key of a principal. The secrecy of the private key is considered crucial, since the private key can be thought of as representing the identity of its owner. The ability to bind the public key to its owner is crucial to the proper function of public key systems. For this reason, public key certificates, such as those defined within X.509 (ITU-T, 1997). The binding of the public key to its owner can be validated by any third party by the use of certificates.

One common application of public key cryptography is the digital signature. A digital signature should perform a function in the digital environment similar to the function of paper signature in the real word. A digital signature may be considered as a piece of data (unique string of bits) that is attached with a document to uniquely identify the originator (authentication) and to verify that the message has not been altered (integrity).

Figure 6. The use of a digital signature to provide integrity and authentication (in analogy to Bhimani, 1996)

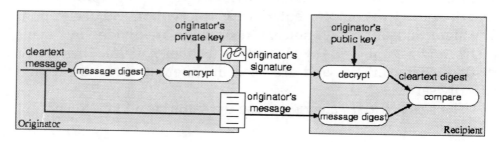

Message digest functions are also an important part of many public key systems. A message digest function (also called one-way hash function) is used to generate a unique pattern of bits (hash code) for a given input. Such functions are very hard to invert. Message digests are the basis of most digital signature standards. As depicted in Figure 6, instead of signing the entire document, simply sign the message digest of the document.

In general, public key systems are not as computationally efficient as symmetric key systems. In many applications both approaches can be used in conjunction to combine their advantages (e.g. in SSL).

A detailed discussion of several cryptographic techniques is presented in the "Cryptography and technical security standards" of this book. Also, the cryptographic techniques and their usage in the World Wide Web context can be found in Garfinkel and Spafford (1997).

Authentication Service

Authentication is a means of identifying (remote) users, that is to verify that the users are who or what they claim to be. An attack against the authentication service is a masquerade attack. Authentication is the most essential security service because reliable authentication is needed to enforce all higher security services. For example, for an access control service permissions are always granted to individuals who must be identified. The authentication service consists of two services:

- *User authentication.* The users who communicate have to verify their identity. This is particularly important for e-commerce transactions when a merchant wants to ensure that a customer is indeed the authorized user of a credit card.
- *Data origin authentication.* When a user A receives a message from a user B, then user A has to ensure that the received message is from user B and vice versa (originality).

Many methods are used to provide authentication services. Some are based on cryptographic techniques and others are based on biological characteristics such as fingerprints. The most important techniques based on cryptographic techniques are digital signatures (certificates) and user-name/password schemes.

The HTTP/1.1 provides two simple user-name/password-based

Figure 7. HTTP challenge-response authentication mechanism

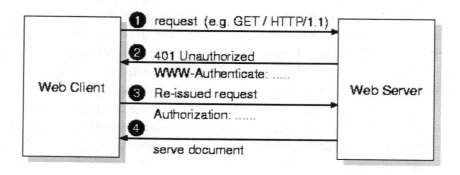

mechanisms for user authentication and for access control: Basic authentication access scheme and digest access authentication scheme. The Web server provides access to protected and unprotected resources. For protected resources, the server requires clients to authenticate themselves and replies to a client's HTTP request with a "401 Unauthorized" status code and an authentication challenge included in a "WWW-Authenticate" header field. The client may then resubmit the request including the authentication information in an "Authorization" header field (see Figure 7).

This header field contains at least an indication of the required authentication method (Basic or Digest) and a server specified realm. On the server side the realms are used to identify the resources to be protected. On the client side a realm is displayed to users so they know which user-name and password to use when the client prompts the user for the user-name and password.

Basic Access Authentication

The basic access authentication scheme is defined in the HTTP/1.0 specification (Fielding et al., 1996) and is, therefore, most widely supported by Web browsers and servers. Upon receipt of an unauthorized request for a protected resource, the server may send a 401 response with a challenge entry in the header fields like:

WWW-Authenticate: Basic realm="Stock Database"

where "Stock Database" the name of the protected space (the so called realm) on the server. In order to gain access, the client sends the user-name and password, separated by a single colon (":") character, within a base64 encoded string in the "Authorization" header field. For example, the Web client uses the following header field to send the user-name "XXX" and the password "YYY":

Authorization: Basic WFhYYOllZWQo=

If the user has supplied the correct user-name and password then the access to the document is given.

Digest Access Authentication

The digest access authentication scheme is mentioned in HTTP/1.1 (Fielding et al., 1996) and defined in Franks et al. (1997) as an alternative to the basic access authentication scheme. Basic access authentication suffers from the problem of passing the user's password unencrypted (base64 encoded) across the network. This is an easy target for an attack. Using the digest access authentication scheme, the password is never sent across the network but instead, a hash value is sent. Upon receipt of an unauthorized request for a protected resource, the server constructs a nonce value, which is server-specified data string and should be uniquely generated each time a 401 response is made. This nonce value is then sent within the a WWW-Authenticate header field to the Web client. The client constructs a digest in a predefined way (using MD5 (Rivest, 1992) per default) from the user-name, the password, the realm, the given nonce value, the HTTP method, and the request URI. The client resubmits the request including the digest in the "Authorization" header field. The server recalculates the digest based on the information it holds and makes an authentication and access decision based on whether it matches the user's digest. To prevent a replaying attack, the server may re-challenge the client with a new nonce at any time.

Communication Security Service

In a communication network (such as the WWW) the communication is typically performed over an insecure channel. Communication security provides the protection for information during the transfer over the network. It contains the following services:

- *Confidentiality services.* These protect against the disclosure or revelation of information to users who are not authorized to have that information.
- *Data integrity services.* These protect against changes to a data item.

Cryptographic techniques, such as encryption/decryption, message digest functions, and digital signatures (also used as an authentication mechanism), are important building blocks in implementing communication security services.

Communication security services may be provided at various layers of the TCP/IP-based network, e.g., the Internet layer (IP), the transport layer (TCP), and the application layer (see Figure 8). In general, adding security services at lower layers (like IP or TCP) provides transparency and at the application layer may provide flexibility. The choice of a layer for adding security depends on the security services required and the application environment in which the services must be deployed (Bhimani, 1996; Nusser, 1998; Oppliger, 1998).

Adding security at the IP layer (e.g. AH and ESP) means that the entire host-to-host connection stream will be protected. By this way, any application can make use of these added security services in a transparent way. But, at this layer it is not possible to satisfy individual security requirements of communication channels between processes or to satisfy security requirements at the application level (e.g., per document). Adding security at the transport layer (e.g., SSL) protects the connection stream between processes. As above, any application

Figure 8. Relationship between various security initiatives at the protocol stack

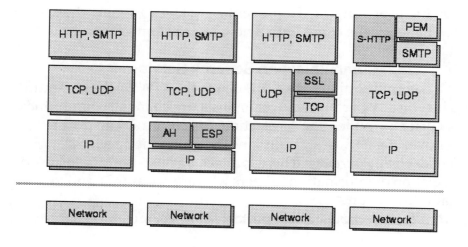

at higher protocol level (e.g., telnet, ftp, etc.) can make use of it. Even at this layer, it is not possible to satisfy security requirements at the application level. If security services are provided at the application layer (e.g., S-HTTP), then only the application protocol stream will be protected. For example, individual documents can be signed and/or encrypted. Adding security at the application layer does not require any modification of the TCP/IP software module and the network programming interface.

In the following we give a short description of the most important protocols providing communication security services for Web-based applications.

IP Security Protocol

The IETF (Internet Engineering Task Force) workgroup for IP security (IPsec) defines a security architecture which provides a set of cryptographically-based authentication (for hosts), integrity, and confidentiality services at the IP layer (Kent and Atkinson, 1998). It is intentionally neutral on what encryption algorithms should be used and allows several different protocols to be applied.

IPsec defines two security services for the IPv4 and IPv6 protocol (a detailed description can be found in Oppliger (1998)):

- *IP Authentication Header (AH).* AH provides data origin authentication and data integrity. This means the recipient of an IP packet is able to verify that the originator is authentic and that the packet has not been altered during transmission.
- *IP Encapsulated Security Payload (ESP).* ESP provides data confidentiality. This means, only legitimate recipients of an IP packet (hosts) are able to read its content.

Secure Sockets Layer

The Secure Sockets Layer protocol (SSL) (Bhimani, 1996) is a protocol layer developed by Netscape Communications Corporation which may be placed between a reliable connection-oriented network layer protocol (e.g. TCP) and the application protocol layer (e.g. HTTP). SSL protects the communication stream between client and server by providing mutual authentication, integrity and privacy. One common use of SSL is to secure HTTP communication between a Web client and a Web server. In this case, SSL connections are initiated from a Web client through the use of special URL prefix. For example,

Table 9. SSL runs above TCP/IP and below application protocols (e.g. HTTP)

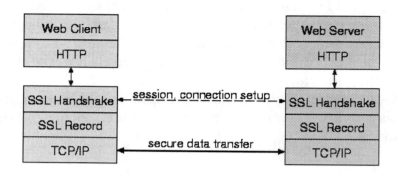

the prefix "https:" is used to indicate an HTTP connection over SSL (see Figure 9).

SSL provides a range of security services for client/server sessions. The SSL protocol includes two sub-protocols: the SSL record protocol and the SSL handshake protocol. The SSL record protocol is layered on top of some reliable transport protocol (e.g., TCP) and deals with data fragmentation, compression, authentication, and encryption/decryption. The SSL record protocol provides:

- *Integrity.* Data items transferred in the session are protected against modification with an integrity check-value.
- *Confidentiality.* Data items transferred in the session are transparently encrypted after an initial handshake and session key determination.

The SSL handshake protocol is layered on top of the SSL record protocol and is used to exchange a series of messages between the communicating peers when they first establish an SSL connection. During the SSL handshake protocol the server and the client are able to authenticate each other:

- *Server authentication.* The server is authenticated to the client by presenting a public key certificate (confirming to the X.509 v3 standard (ITU-T, 1997)). The client has to check that the server's certificate is valid and has been issued by a certificate authority (CA) trusted by him. This confirmation might be important if the user, for example, is sending a credit card number over the

network and wants to check the identity of the receiving server.
- *Client authentication.* Similarly, the server can optionally authenticate the client by requiring the client's public key certificate. This optional service may protect the server from fraudulent users and non-repudiation problems.

In addition, during the SSL handshake protocol the server and the client are able to negotiate several parameters (e.g. compression, encryption algorithm, etc.). After negotiation, a master key is created. This master key is used to determine session keys which can be used for further symmetric encryption/decryption.

The use of public key certificates assumes the existence of a public key infrastructure (PKI), including both certifying authorities to issue, revoke and distribute certificates. Since client authentication is optional, server certificates are widely used today.

Secure HTTP

The secure HTTP (S-HTTP) protocol was initially developed by Enterprise Integration Technologies in 1994 and shortly thereafter was taken under consideration by the IETF Web Transaction Security working group which submitted an RFC in August 1999 (Rescorla and Schiffman, 1999). S-HTTP is essentially a security-enhanced version of HTTP, that can be used to provide security services at the application layer: confidentiality, authentication, message integrity and non-repudiation of origin. In fact, this means that it is possible to differentiate among the security requirements of individual documents that are transmitted on a secure HTTP channel. For example, a Web application using S-HTTP can mark an individual document as private or digitally signed, in contrast, SSL encrypts the entire communication stream. One conceptual difference between SSL and S-HTTP is that, SSL establishes a secure TCP/IP connection between a client and a server, which can be used for HTTP traffic. Unlike SSL, S-HTTP uses TCP/IP connections to transmit data.

S-HTTP is also more flexible than SSL in terms of the choice of key management mechanisms and cryptographic algorithms which are negotiated between the communicating peers. S-HTTP uses private key and public key cryptography. The shared keys can be manually distributed and configured. S-HTTP can also use Kerberos tickets instead of public key certificates. This makes the deployment of S-

HTTP independent of the existence of a PKI.

Although the specifications of S-HTTP and SSL were published at about the same time, SSL got much wider acceptance by the major browser vendors because it was relatively simple to implement and does not interfere with the HTTP implementation. This resulted in the lack of a widely available reference implementation of S-HTTP (for example, neither Netscape nor Microsoft have implemented S-HTTP in their browsers and servers so far).

Access Control Service

The access control service offers the protection of resources against unauthorized access. Access control services are based on reliable authentication services. The access control function decides whether a subject (human user or system entity) is allowed to perform an operation (read, write, execute, control, etc.) on an object (data, program, port, etc.). The access control function is defined in terms of subjects, objects, operations, and access rights (see Figure 10). Access rights (also known as access control information) are defined for each subject, object, and operation triple in order to specify the level of authority for a subject to invoke the operation on an object.

The access control function is the core component of an access control scheme. Within a system, three common access control schemes can be applied: DAC (National Computer Security Center, 1987); MAC (Pleeger, 1997); RBAC (Sandhu et al., 1996). These access control schemes differ on how the access rights are organized and specified.

- *Discretionary Access Control (DAC).* The owner of an object may specify the access rights for an object at his discretion. That is, the owner has to define who may access an object with which opera-

Figure 10. A Subject performs an Operation on an Object

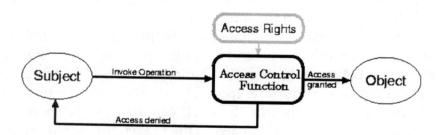

tion. A DAC scheme allows users (subjects) to grant or revoke access to any of the objects they own. The specification of the access rights is based entirely on the identities of users/groups, objects, and operations. The access rights may be specified using an access control matrix, which is basically a cartesian product of the subjects and objects. Access is permitted if the right is in the matrix cell denoted by the claiming subject and the target object. The access control matrix easily becomes very large when a significant number of users and objects are to be managed. Therefore, the access rights are usually specified using access control lists (ACL, a column in the matrix), which are rights associated to the objects, or capabilities (a row in the matrix), which are rights associated with the subjects.

- *Mandatory Access Control (MAC)*. In this access control scheme the access control decision is made beyond the control of the individual owner of the target object. The objects are classified with respect to their sensitivity level (e.g. top secret, confidential, etc.). The users are labeled with clearances according to their trust level. The access rights are defined using rules which define a dominance relation between these security labels (e.g. everyone who has the right to read a confidential document may read a public document as well). The access control function applies these rules to the given user clearance and object classification in order to determine the access. One such access control scheme is the Bell-La Padula model (Bell and LaPadula, 1976) developed for military security applications.
- *Role-based Access Control (RBAC)*. The central element of RBAC are roles, which are created according to the job functions performed in a company or organization. The access rights (permissions) are assigned to roles rather than to individuals. Users obtain these access rights if they are assigned to an appropriate role. Users are assigned to the roles on the basis of their specific job responsibilities and qualifications. By this way, RBAC reduces the complexity and cost of security administration in large networked applications.

The implementation of such access control schemes in a large corporate network requires the management of the access rights. Later, we give a directory-based approach addressing the management aspect of the access rights for Web documents.

Example: The National Institute of Standards and Technology (NIST) has implemented RBAC for the World Wide Web (RBAC/Web (Barkley et al., 1998)). The implementation of MAC in the Web context requires a labeling system for both users and documents. An implementation of DAC in the Web context requires that the administrator of a Web server owns all documents stored on it. Most Web servers are maintained by a small number of administrators. These administrators may specify the access rights for the Web documents at their discretion; therefore, a DAC scheme is used.

A typical Web document is composed of several components (e.g. mark-up text, images, or other content types) which are linked together. Therefore, a Web document may be considered as a logical document, which is defined as the set of document components connected through navigational links. The components of this set represent a single logical content. A logical document can be implemented for example using XML (Bray, 1998) and XLink (Maler and DeRose, 1998) which are recommendations of the W3 Consortium. Dridi et al. (1998) have defined a lattice-based security model that defines access control for logical document structures. Users are assigned to different roles. The document components may be assigned different security labels (classifications) to express the level of the sensitivity of the content. Roles obtain permissions in the form of clearances (security labels), that form a lattice structure with a partially ordered dominance relation. This dominance relation is used to determine the access control decision. This model reduces the security management of a system: Roles are used to abstract from subjects; classifications are used to abstract from objects.

Non-Repudiation Service

Repudiation is defined as the situation where a sender/receiver of a message later falsely denies that he sent/received the message. The non-repudiation service is used to provide proof of the origin of messages (non-repudiation of origin) or prove the delivery of messages (non-repudiation of delivery). It prevents either the sender or receiver from denying a transmitted message. Thus, when a message is sent, the receiver can prove that the message was in fact sent by the alleged sender. Similarly, when a message is received, the sender can prove that the message was in fact received by the alleged receiver.

The non-repudiation service can be achieved by utilization of a digital signature, where a trusted third party acting as an arbitrator must be involved. For example, non-repudiation of origin is given if the originator digitally signs his messages. In order to support non-repudiation of delivery, the recipient has to send to the originator, for example, a digitally signed acknowledgment containing a copy or digest of the communication contents (Ford and Baum, 1997).

Example: The non-repudiation service is often required in e-commerce transactions, where the evidence of actions is strongly required. For example a supplier may wish to have irrefutable proof that an order was placed, while the customer will require proof that it was accepted.

Audit and Accountability Service

All security relevant actions should be logged and kept in a safe place (audit trail, logging files) in order to make users accountable for their security related operations. Audit trails also are good for finding program bugs and abnormal use patterns, which are often a sign of compromise or attempted compromise. Audit data needs protection from modification by an intruder. The audit and accountability service usually requires authentication and communication security as prerequisite.

Example: Most Web servers (e.g.,The Apache Software Foundation, 1999) keep a log of successful and unsuccessful HTTP requests. Web servers can be configured to collect more or less detailed information. By default, log entries usually identify the remote host (IP address or hostname), a time stamp, the HTTP request (HTTP Method, URL, and the HTTP protocol version), etc. However, log files typically do not include the identity (user login name) of the user who initiated a request. A Web server may use the identification protocol (St. Johns, 1993) in order to determine the remote user name for each incoming connection. However, this can cause additional overhead since every request requires user name lookups to be performed. Furthermore, a Web client does not have to support the identification protocol, therefore, the identity information may not be obtained at all.

SECURITY MANAGEMENT SERVICES

In this section we concentrate on management services concerning the authentication and access control services. These security services often require a variety of security relevant information. For example, an authentication service may require security relevant information concerning the users, such as public key certificates. An access control service requires security relevant information (access rights) concerning subjects, operations, and objects.

Consider a situation where cooperative work is carried out by people working in an organization. For example, thousands of Web documents are shared among hundreds of people or projects in an Inter- or Intranet context (the Web server of our department contains about 9000 documents, all Web servers of the university together offer at least ten times more documents). The documents are typically placed on various decentralized Web servers that are owned and maintained by fairly independent parts of the organization. The number of individual access rights to be managed (granted and revoked) in the case of DAC administration based on an access control matrix is determined by the number of users times the number of documents times the number of operations (e.g. (20000 students + 1000 staff) * 90 000 documents * 2 operations (GET and PUT) equals 3.78 billion entries).

When authentication is implemented via public key certificates, a large number of public key certificates must be issued and distributed in a controlled way. Security management services are a means of addressing these problems of scale (huge number of access rights and certificates). That is, security management services are used to maintain and to set up Internet-based applications using the authentication and access control services. In general, a security management service provides administration and management functions, such as creating, deleting, updating, and/or distribution of the security relevant information.

For the authentication and access control services we identify two important security management services: certificate and access rights management. These services are described in detail in the upcoming sections.

The certificate and access rights management services typically require a database, where certificates and access rights information

Figure 11. Directory-based Security Management Services

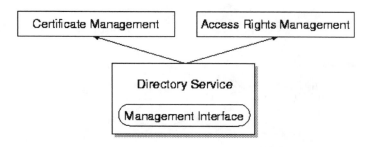

can be stored. For Internet-based applications a directory service is one promising approach to use in order to support these security management services (see Figure 11). A directory service eases the integration of a variety of Internet-based applications using these security services. In addition, a directory service simplifies the administration and management tasks. The next section describes the directory service in more detail.

Directory Service

A directory server is a kind of a database system developed to publish information to a wide variety of applications in a flexible and scalable manner. A telephone book is a typical application for a directory server. A directory server is typically optimized for a high ratio of read/search accesses to write accesses. The X.500 series of standards (ITU-T, 1993) defines the protocols and information model for a global directory service. X.500 defines the Directory Access Protocol (DAP) which specifies how user applications access the directory information. DAP is designed to operate on a full OSI stack of the ANSI protocols. Thus, the DAP protocol has a significant overhead. Furthermore, the victory of TCP/IP over the ANSI protocol suite resulted in a lack of full DAP clients and applications. Therefore, more recently a simplified version of the X.500 access protocol, named Lightweight Directory Access Protocol, LDAP version 2 (Yoeng et al., 1995); version 3 (Wahl et al., 1997) was developed, offering access to directory services supporting the X.500 directory standard over TCP/IP. LDAP is gaining wider acceptance, the number of products using LDAP increases (as the Netscape Directory Server 3.0 (Netscape

Figure 12. Directory Entry Structure

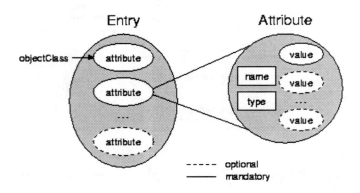

Communications Corporation, 1999; Microsoft Corporation, 1999, etc.).

LDAP defines four models to describe its data and operations (Howes et al., 1999):

- The *LDAP Information Model* defines the types of data and basic units (entries) of information that can be stored in a directory. Every entry consists of a set of attributes. Some attributes are mandatory, others are optional. Every attribute has a unique name, a type, and one or more values (see Figure 12). The type of the attribute specifies the syntax of the attribute values.

Each entry belongs to one or more object classes. In LDAP, object classes are used to model real-world objects such as a person, an organization, etc. An object class determines the set of the mandatory and optional attributes to be included in an entry. The names of the object classes of an entry are listed as values for a multi-valued attribute called objectClass. The directory schema defines the valid attributes and object classes.

In an LDAP directory entries are arranged in a hierarchical structure that reflects application specific, geographic, or organizational boundaries. The topmost node, the root entry, is a special entry which contains server-specific information. For example, entries representing countries appear at the top of the tree after the root entry

(Figure 13). One level deeper are entries representing organizations, then there might be entries representing organizational units, like departments, etc. The leaf nodes represent individuals.

- The *LDAP Naming Model* is derived from the X.500 naming model which provides unique identifiers for entries. An entry is referenced by a distinguished name (DN), which is a unique name that unambiguously identifies a single entry. An entry DN is composed of a sequence of relative distinguished names (RDNs) of the ancestor entries separated by commas. Each RDN consists of one or more attribute=value pairs joined by "+". However, a RDN typically consists of one attribute=value pair. The RDN of an entry must be unique among all entries sharing the same parent entry. For example, the RDN of the entry representing the country "de" is c=de (see Figure 13).

- The *LDAP Functional Model* describes the operations that can be performed on the directory using the LDAP protocol. These operations enable clients to authenticate, to search, and to update the directory. In addition, the LDAP protocol (version 3) defines a framework for adding new operations to the protocol to meet new application needs.

- The *LDAP Security Model* provides a framework for protecting the information (the entries) in the directory from unauthorized access. LDAP version 2 only offers a simple clear text password authentication mechanism. LDAP version 3 defines an extensible model based on the Simple Authentication and Security Layer (SASL) framework (Myers, 1997). SASL provides a standard way for adding authentication support to connection-based protocols. In addition to SASL, LDAP version 3 also supports secure connec-

Figure 13. Part of a typical directory

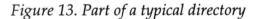

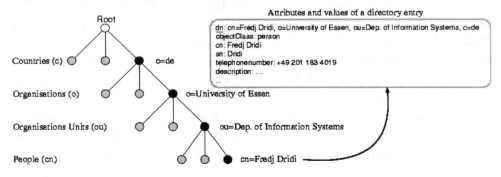

tions using the SSL protocol.

Since LDAP has become an important protocol on the World Wide Web, an URL format for accessing LDAP resources has been defined (Howes and Smith, 1997). The LDAP URL begins with the prefix ldap:// (or ldaps:// for communication with the LDAP server using SSL). An LDAP URL can simply name an LDAP server, or can specify a complex directory search. Using this URL, a Web browser can retrieve and display LDAP resources.

Example: Applications can use directory services for different purposes. Within a large organization many Web servers are typically installed. These Web servers can use a centrally managed LDAP directory server in order to locate and share user public key certificates and/or to make access control decisions.

Access Rights Management Service

As mentioned above, access control functions are defined in terms of subjects, objects, operations, and access rights. For each subject, access rights (also known as access control information) define what kind of operations it is permitted to apply to which object.

The access control function requires an interface to retrieve the access rights. In the following we describe such an interface using the LDAP protocol in the context of a role-based access control scheme (RBAC). Similar or other interfaces may be used to support the access rights management for DAC or MAC as well.

Sandhu et al. (1996) define a family of role-based access control models. We will concentrate on the base model, $RBAC_0$, which defines the minimal set of characteristics required for role-based access control. The main constructs of $RBAC_0$ are users, sessions, roles and permissions. Permissions are attached to roles and specify the approval of a set of operations to one object in a system. A permission can be described as a tuple: (object, list of allowed operations) Users establish sessions during which they may activate a subset of roles they belong to. Each session maps one user to one or more roles. During a session, users gain the access to the objects through the permissions attached to their roles.

A major benefit from RBAC is that a role serves as a grouping mechanism of users. Since the rights are attached to roles rather than to users, the number of access rights is determined by the number of

Figure 14. User-Role and Role Permissions Assignment

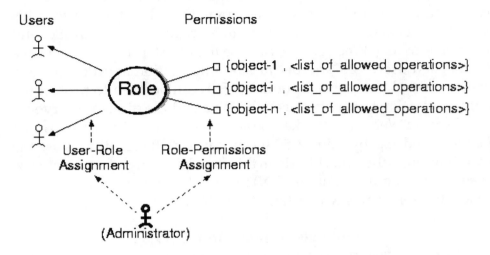

roles and not by the number of users (#roles * #objects * #operations). This improves the security management of a system, when RBAC is used.

The administrative tasks of RBAC are user-role and role-permissions assignment (see Figure 14). The management of the roles and the related permissions are often highly centralized and delegated to a small number of administrators (Sandhu et al., 1996) The information concerning the roles, user-role and role-permissions assignment may be stored in a central or distributed database which can provide support for a wide range of applications using role-based access control.

For Internet-based applications using RBAC, an LDAP directory service can be used as a database for roles, role-permissions, and user-role assignments. RBAC-enabled applications may use the LDAP services to retrieve such information in order to perform the access control decision for a given user requesting access to an object.

The LDAP standard schema (Wahl, 1997) defines several object classes (e.g., "Person", "organizationalPerson", "organizationalRole", etc.). These object classes are used to define directory entries representing users and roles within an organization. In order to represent additional information about the user-role and role-permissions assignment new object classes and attributes can be defined. A new object class defining new attributes can be defined as a subclass of the existing one.

Example: Figure 15 depicts an infrastructure where information concerning users and roles is stored in an LDAP directory server. This way, the user and role information can be managed centrally. Several applications, e.g. Web servers, can use the LDAP protocol to retrieve the needed user, role, and permission information in order to make access control decisions. Optionally, SSL can be used to protect the communication stream between the Web and the directory server.

Before a Web server makes the access control decision, users must be identified, e.g. by using X.509 certificates. X.509 certificates use the same naming scheme as LDAP. In this case, it is straightforward to use the user distinguished name (DN) included in the certificate in order to locate user entries within the LDAP directory.

Certificate Management Service

Certificates improve public key management by giving users the means to validate a public key. In short, certificates bind a public key to an individual, server, or other entity (subject). Therefore, certificates provide a suitable foundation for authentication and all services depending on it, such as, non-repudiation, communication security, and access control services. For example, a recipient of a digitally signed document can use the public key listed in the sender's certifi-

Figure 15. A directory-based users, roles, and permisions lookup

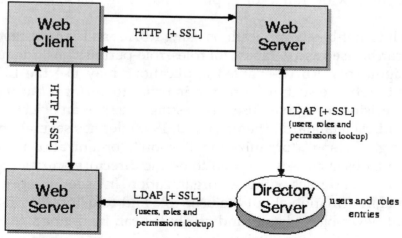

cate to verify that the digital signature was created with the corresponding private key and that the document has not been modified.

The common format of certificates is X.509 (version 3) (ITU-T, 1997). Within a large corporate network the number of certificates in use is increasing. New certificates must be issued and distributed. The certificate management service is used to provide the infrastructure to maintain the overall process of certification tasks.

The core functions of the certificate management service include:
- certificate issuance,
- certificate revocation,
- certificate distribution, and
- trust management.

Figure 16 depicts a simple directory-based architecture which implements these functions. This architecture is usually part of a public key infrastructure (PKI) involving certification authorities. A certification authority (CA) is considered as a trusted third party whose purpose is to issue and sign certificates for network entities (e.g. client, server, etc.). In general, a certificate authority creates and issues certificates based on the following steps:
- The CA receives a certification request containing the public key to be certified and information about the owner (PKCS#10 (RSA Laboratories, 1993) describes a syntax and the required fields for certification requests).
- Prior to issuing a certificate, the CA should confirm the identity of the public key owner and the accuracy of the certification request data. This step is considered as the most significant process while issuing certificates. How the accuracy is tested depends upon the practice (certification policy) of the certification authority. Such

Figure 16. Internet-based Certificate Management Service Architecture

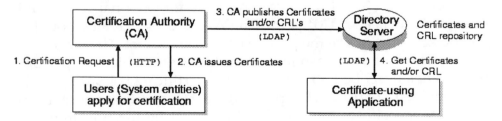

policies are typically published by the CA.

- After the correctness of the presented data is verified, the certificate is created and signed using the private key of the CA.
- A copy of the certificate is forwarded to the requester.
- For publication (distribution), a copy of the certificate may be submitted to a certificate repository, such as a directory service (e.g. an LDAP-enabled directory).
- The CA records appropriate details of the certificate generation process in an audit trail.

For large organizations, multiple CAs controlled by a trust model are required. In this case, a CA can also certify other CAs, transferring by this means trust to other authority's signature. By this way, a chain of trust can be created and managed according to different trust models. A trust model addresses the relationship between the individual certification authorities (for a detailed description of such trust models see Maley, 1996; Neumann and Nusser, 1997).

A certificate is expected to be usable for its entire validity period. This period of time is determined by the CA and indicated in the issued certificate. However, under some circumstances, a certificate may lose its validity prior to the expiration date. This is the case, for example, if the corresponding private key is compromised. Under such circumstances, the certification authority can revoke the certificate. In order to make potential users of the certificate aware of the revocation, the CA periodically publishes a signed certificate revocation list (CRL). A CRL has a predefined format (ITU-T, 1997) and is a time-stamped list of revoked certificates that have already been issued but are no longer valid. Within a CRL, a revoked certificate is identified by its serial number. A CRL might be published, for example, in a directory service (see Figure 16).

Example: In the World Wide Web context, a certification authority with a minimal certification policy can be realized via a CGI script. The user using a Web browser is prompted for personal and organizational data via an HTML form. The Web browser creates a public/private key pair, where the private key is kept secret. The public key and the user data are transmitted to the CGI script which can perform all the steps described above. When the certificate is issued the CA may send an (LDAP) URL pointing to the certificate within the certificate repository. The issued certificate can be also transmitted to the Web browser using an appropriate MIME content type ("application/x-x509-user-cert").

CONCLUSION

This chapter addressed the topic of Internet security with special emphasis on Web security. Several elementary techniques and Internet standards which form the state-of-the-art of Web security have been introduced throughout the chapter, where it is needed. First, we described potential security attacks. Next, several security services have been discussed. These security services are mechanisms that reduce or eliminate the potential damage, which may be produced when security attacks are exploited. We focused on the authentication and access control service in the Web context. The management and administration issues of these two important security services have been discussed. We have described the use of an LDAP-enabled directory service as database, where security relevant information can be stored. Two LDAP-based infrastructures were presented. The first one can be used to manage the public key certificates of the users needed by the authentication service. The second one can be used to administer Internet-based applications (e.g., Web server) using role-based access control. In this case, information concerning roles, role-permissions, and user-role assignment are stored in the directory. A major benefit of LDAP, as an Internet standard, is that it eases the integration of a wide variety of Internet-based applications using these security services.

REFERENCES

The Apache software foundation (1999). http://www.apache.org.

Barkley, J.F., D. R. Kuhn, L. S. Rosenthal, M. W. Skall, and A. V. Cincotta (1998). Role-based access control for the Web. *CALS Expo International & 21st Century Commerce: Global Business Solutions for the New Millennium.*

Bell, D. and L. LaPadula (1976). *Secure Computer System: Unified Exposition and Multics Interpretation.* In Technical Report MTR-2997. MITRE Corp., USA, July.

Bhimani, A. (1996). Securing the commercial Internet. *Communication of the ACM,* 39(6):29–35.

Bray, T., J. Paoli, and C. M. Sperberg-McQueen(1998). Extensible markup language (XML) 1.0. *World Wide Web Consortium Recommendation*. http://w3c.org/TR/1998/REC-xml-19980210.

Dridi, F. and G. Neumann (1998). Towards access control for logical document structure. In *Proc. of the Ninth International Workshop of Database and Expert Systems Applications*, 322–327, Vienna, Austria.

Fielding, R., T. Berners-Lee, and H. Frystyck (1996). Hypertext transfer protocol - HTTP/1.0. *RFC 1945*, May .

Fielding, R., J. Gettys, J. Mogul, H. Nielsen, and T. Berners-Lee. (1997). Hypertext transfer protocol – HTTP/1.1. *RFC 2068, Standards Track*, January 1997.

Ford, W. and M. S. Baum (1997). *Secure Electronic Commerce: Building the infrastructure for digital signature & encryption*. Prentice-Hall.

Franks, J., P. Hallam-Baker, J. Hostetler, P. Leach, A. Luotonen, E. Sink, and L. Stewart (1997). An extension to HTTP: Digest Access Authentication. *RFC 2069, Standards Track*, January.

Freier, A., P. Karlton, and P. Kocher (1996). The SSL protocol version 3.0. *Netscape*, http://netscape.com/eng/ssl3/.

Garfinkel, S. and G. Spafford (1997). *Web Security & Commerce*. O'Reilly & Associates, Inc.

Howes, T. and M. Smith (1997). An LDAP URL format. *RFC 2255, Standards Track*, December.

Howes, T., M. Smith, and G. Good (1999). *Understanding and Deploying LDAP Directory Services*. Macmillan Network Architecture and Development Series. Macmillan Technical Publishing USA.

ITU-T (1993). *Recomendation X.500: Information Technology – Open Systems Interaction - The Directory: Overview of Concepts, Models, and Services.*

ITU-T (1997). *Recomendation X.509: Information Technology – Open Systems Interaction -The Directory: Authentication framework*. 1997. http://www.nexor.com/info/directory.htm.

Kent, S. and R. Atkinson (1998). Security architecture for the internet protocol. *RFC 2401*, November. Obsoletes: RFC 1825.

Lipp, P. and V. Hassler (1996). Security concepts for the WWW. In *Proceedings of Communications and Multimedia Security, Joint Working Conference IFIP TC-6 and TC-11*, 84–95, Essen, Germany, September.

Maler, E. and S. DeRose. (1998). XML linking language (XLink). *World Wide Web Consortium Working Draft*, http://w3c.org/TR/1998/WD-xlink-19980303.

Maley, J.G. (1996). Enterprise security infrastructure. In *Proceedings of WET-ICE 96, IEEE 5th Intl. Workshops on Enabling Technologies: Infrastructure for Collaborative Enterprises*, 92–99, Stanford, CA, June 19–21.

Microsoft Corporation (1999). Active directory service interfaces. http://www.microsoft.com/windows/server/overview/features/ataglance.asp.

Myers, J. (1997). Simple authentication and security layer (SASL). *RFC 2222, Standards Track*.

National Computer Security Center. (1987). A guide to understanding discrentionary access control in trusted systems. NCSC-TG-003 Version-1. http://www.radium.ncsc.mil/tpep/library/rainbow/NCSC-TG-003.html.

Netscape Communications Corporation (1999). Directory deployment and installation.http://home.netscape.com/eng/server/directory/3.0/ deploycontents.html.

Neumann, G. and S. Nusser (1997). A framework and prototyping environment for W3 security architecture. In *Proceedings of Communications and Multimedia Security, Joint Working Conference IFIP TC-6 and TC-11*, 47–58, Athens, Greece.

Nusser, S. (1998). *Sicherheitskonzepte im WWW*. Springer-Verlag Berlin Heidelberg.

Oppliger, R. (1997). *IT-Sicherheit - Grundlagen und Umsetzung in der Praxis*. DuD Fachbeiträge. Vieweg-Verlag, Wiesbaden, Germany.

Oppliger, R. (1998). *Internet and Intranet Security*. Artech House Publishers, 1998.

Pfleeger, C. (1997). *Security in Computing*. Prentice-Hall, Second edition, 1997.

Rescorla, E. and A. Schiffman (1999). The secure hypertext transfer protocol. *RFC 2660*, August.

Rivest, R. (1992).. The MD5 message-digest algorithm. *RFC 1321*, April.

RSA Laboratories. (1993). PKCS#10: Certification request syntax standard. *Version 1.0*, November .

Rubin, A.D., D. E. Geer, and M. Ranum (1997). *Web Security Sourcebook*. John Wiley & Sons, Inc.

St. Johns, M. (1993). Identification protocol. *RFC 1413*, February.

Sandhu, R.S., E. J. Coyne, H. L. Feinstein, and C. E. Youman (1996). Role-based access control models. *IEEE Computer*, 29(2):38–47, February.

Schneier, B. (1996). *Applied Cryptography*. John Wiley & Sons, Second edition.

Stallings, W. (1995). *Network and Internetwork Security Principles and Practice*. Prentice-Hall.

Wahl, M. (1997). A summary of the X.500(96) user schema for use with LDAPv3. *RFC 2256, Standards Track*, December.

Wahl, M., T. Howes, and S. Kille (1997). Lightweight directory access protocol (v3). *RFC 2251, Standards Track*, December .

Yoeng, W., T. Howes, and S. Kille (1995). Lightweight directory access protocol. *RFC 1777, Standards Track*, March.

Part III

Cryptography and Technical Security Standards

Chapter VI

Cryptography: Protecting Confidentiality, Integrity and Availability of Data

Henry B. Wolfe
University of Otago, New Zealand

The protection of information for business or private purposes can be achieved through the careful selection and use of cryptographic tools. Throughout recorded history the art and science of cryptography has been the exclusive domain of government in the form of military and diplomatic use. For the most part the many and varied techniques were used for protecting strategic communications. With the advent of the microcomputer the tools to incorporate some of the complex mathematical tools necessary to provide strong encryption[1] became readily available to the public at large. That availability has contributed to the proliferation and use of cryptographic tools that are capable of providing strong encryption to anyone who would care to use them. This important security technique has become the main tool for protecting communications of all kinds and is used throughout the business community. The banking community, for example, is probably one of the largest users of data encryption for the protection of their clients' financial transactions.

INTERNATIONAL ISSUES - IMPORT, EXPORT AND USAGE

The Rationale for Cryptographic Restrictions

The use of data encryption is controlled, regulated or outlawed in some nations. The reason for this approach to the use of cryptography is to prevent the citizens of these nations from having the ability to communicate privately and/or from having the ability to store private information in a way that cannot easily be inspected in real time and without the knowledge of the originator. Nations who take this approach tend to be dictatorial in nature, however, many of the so-called free world nations are beginning to be concerned with the use of data encryption by their citizens.

Much of the concern in the "free" world is centered around the notion that the "bad" guys will use this tool to help them accomplish bad things. Emotional issues like child pornography, terrorism, drug dealing, etc are used to justify the proposition that no one (except government) should be able to communicate in a totally secure way. Further that government, specifically law enforcement and/or intelligence, should be able not only to intercept any communications but also be able to decode any encrypted communications as well. The important part of this proposition is that they declare that they need to be able to do all this without notification or cooperation from the parties to the communication in order to "protect" or "defend" their citizens or for "national security".

The one issue that those who would take the restrictive position on cryptography have consistently failed to address adequately is that of some sort of proven linkage between being a "bad" guy and being stupid. No matter what restrictions may be put in place to prevent the use of strong encryption, it is inevitable that the "bad" guys will not obey them. No thinking person should be hoodwinked into believing that the "bad" guys would be stupid enough not to use freely available strong encryption to protect their privacy. The realities are that they will and do use strong encryption.

The advent of the Internet has changed the way we look at national boundaries. In fact in cyberspace there are no enforceable national boundaries (other than being cut off from the Internet completely). This means that Internet users can transmit all sorts of information across national borders without, for the most part, any scrutiny. Furthermore, this facilitates the movement of goods and money in ways that avoid attracting taxation methods currently employed throughout the world. In addition, it also makes surveillance activities, whether legal or otherwise, much more difficult and perhaps in some cases impossible.

Just about everything resolves down to issues of money. When sovereign nations are or perceive that they will be thwarted in their pursuit of their money gathering activities they will react in whatever way they must to solve their perceived problem. The US, for example, has a number of organisations set up for that exclusive purpose. FinCEN[2], FATF[3], and OFAC[4] are but three examples of such organisations. All of them are expressly devoted to money matters.

Considering the various government agendas prevalent in today's world, one would have to conclude that the restricting of cryptographic usage would increase in the future. If we are to learn anything from history it is that prohibitions of just about any kind do not and have not worked. In all probability, cryptographic prohibition will work like the alcohol Prohibitions of the 1920s and the so-called war on drugs—a war that is not a war and that certainly appears to be unwinnable.

What Can Be Freely Traded

The Internet provides plenty of opportunity when it comes to cryptography. There appears to be a couple of agendas at work. In the first instance, there are those who believe that privacy is a basic human right and not some privilege arbitrarily granted or denied to citizens by their government. To that end, these folks make encryption software of all types, both strong and others, available to anyone who can and wants to download them. There are many sites located in a variety of national settings. Strong encryption is freely available on a world-wide basis. According to Network Associates, Inc.[5], there are more than sixteen hundred cryptographic products currently available throughout the world.

Another agenda is based on the notion that strong encryption should only be able to be used by governments and then only by "accepted" governments. Those with this point of view continue to push for legislation and formal international agreements that inhibit or make illegal the international sale of strong encryption. But sale, legal or otherwise, is really only one method for the proliferation of strong encryption.

There are cryptographic communities of interest in many friendly and unfriendly nations. In fact there are three separate specialised cryptographic conferences[6] amongst the many others that are held annually at various locations around the world. Each of these three serves the cryptographic community of interest based on geographic regions. Each conference fosters the discussion, dissemination, and exchange of cryptographic advances without censorship. The important issue to consider here is that cryptographic techniques and advances cannot be contained merely by some isolated legislation. To repeat an old phrase, "the genie is out of the bottle and not about to be returned".

Where Do We Obtain "Appropriate" Tools?

Obtaining cryptographic tools depends on what algorithms are of interest and where the person is (in which nation and their citizenship may also be relevant as well) who is trying to obtain them. At the time of writing this chapter, there were no use restrictions on cryptographic software or hardware within the US for US citizens. However, export of cryptographic products from the US is regulated by the BXA[7] which restricts such exports to certain levels of perceived security (often described by the maximum number of bits required for the encryption/decryption key - this is, however, only one of several attributes of any encryption algorithm which must be considered when assessing relative strength/security).

There are also international agreements that constrain signatories in their respective export of cryptographic products of various types. The Wassenaar[8] Arrangement is an example of such an agreement. This arrangement consists of 33 nations that have agreed (sort of - but it is in no way binding on the signatories—that's probably why it's called an "Arrangement" rather than an agreement or treaty) to restrict their exports of conventional weapons and dual-use goods and technologies. The Arrangement was revised on the third of December 1998. The Dual-Use-List - Category 5, Part 2 (*Information Security*) of this arrangement addresses security equipment and software and specifically describes the cryptographic attributes - maximum key length in bits as tied to particular algorithm types. For example, the Agreement controls: "a 'symmetric algorithm' employing a key in excess of 56 bits; or an 'asymmetric algorithm' where the security of the algorithm is based on any of the following: factorisation of integers in excess of 512 bits; computation of discrete logarithms in a multiplicative group of a finite field size greater than 512 bits..."[9] etc.

While the Arrangement allows the export of strong encryption products to "accepted" recipient nations only, it is not clear how the lists of "acceptable" and "unacceptable" nations was drawn up. There may be stated objectives but it is not clear what exactly is meant to be achieved by the Arrangement in light of the fact the strong encryption is readily available on a worldwide basis. America appears to be the moving force in the drive to restrict the freedom to use strong encryption possibly based on the myth[10] that American-invented and produced cryptographic products are somehow superior to cryptographic products invented and produced elsewhere.

The US is not the only nation that is pushing the notion of restricting strong encryption. In 1996 a study was conducted by Gerard Walsh, a former deputy director-general of the Australian Security Intelligence Organisation (ASIO). The Report was released in January 1997 but hurriedly withdrawn. The Walsh Report titled *Review of Policy Relating to Encryption Technologies* was subsequently released in which a number of paragraphs were deleted. All of the missing paragraphs have been retrieved in spite of specific Freedom of Information Act (FOI) denials.

In Chapter 1—Conclusions and findings paragraph 1.1.2 the Report states:

"Individuals living in community cede certain rights and privileges to ensure order, equity and good government, even if sometimes reluctantly. To this end, a lawful right to conduct intrusive investigations has been given to law enforcement and national security agencies and to ensure the exercise of those intrusive powers is properly controlled, various forms of oversight and a package of administrative law measures have been instituted. These have produced a significant increase in public accountability, but our time is characterised by mistrust of all powerful institutions which seek to limit the freedoms of ordinary citizens".

The question has to be asked: when were you consulted about ceding any of your God given and natural human rights to privacy?

Everyone should mistrust those that would seek to limit the freedoms of ordinary citizens. Where people have not been vigilant freedom has been lost.

One interesting paragraph that was denied under the many FOI requests follows:

> "It has to be said the continuing validity of export controls as a defensive strategy is open to question when import controls do not exist in most countries, where firms in countries covered by multilateral agreements on the proliferation of cryptography are able to circumvent United States' or Australia's export controls and buy software of their choice in Asia or Europe and when easy access to the Internet is available to all".

Export control of cryptographic products does not work. It is unlikely that it will ever work as long as there is free will and people believe that they are entitled to the basic human right to privacy.

INTERNATIONAL PRIVACY ISSUES

Universal Declaration of Human Rights - What Does It Mean?

The *Universal Declaration of Human Rights* was adopted and proclaimed by United Nations General Assembly *Resolution 217 A (III) of 10 December 1948*. More than one hundred member states have endorsed and ratified this important declaration. That not with standing, signatory states, pretty much as a matter of routine violate their responsibilities as stated in the Declaration.

For example, Kevin Mitnik[11] had been held for more than four years before reaching a plea bargain without ever receiving a trial and without the option of making bail. Just as a matter of interest, that violates **Article 9** of the *Declaration*: "*No one shall be subjected to arbitrary arrest, detention or exile*" and probably **Article 10** as well: "*Everyone is entitled in full equality to a <u>fair and public hearing by independent and impartial tribunal</u>, in the determination of his rights and obligations and of <u>any criminal charge against him</u>.*" This case is interesting because it deals with hacking and those in power have vilified Kevin Mitnik to the extent that it has been said that he is the world's most dangerous computer criminal. It probably should be pointed out that Mitnik never assaulted, murdered or otherwise physically harmed any individual. He is not a terrorist. He is not a drug dealer. He is not a child pornographer. He has not committed treason or any other capital crime.

The Article that is of most interest for our discussion here is **Article 12**: *"No one shall be subjected to <u>arbitrary interference with his privacy</u>, family, home or <u>correspondence</u>, nor to attacks upon his honour and reputation. Everyone has the right to the protection of the law against such interference or attacks"*. This Article purports to protect the individual's privacy against unreasonable interference. It is interesting to note that many signatory states as a matter of course interfere with the individual's privacy and correspondence. The FBI and NSA[12] (and probably others as well) monitors Internet traffic in the US (and it is reasonable to conclude that they also monitor this activity outside the US as well[13]). The US is a signatory of the *Declaration*. This behaviour also flies in the face of **Article IV** of the US *Bill of Rights*[14] which guarantees that *"The right of the people to be secure in their persons, houses, papers, and effects, against unreasonable searches and seizures, shall not be violated, and no warrants shall issue but upon probable cause, supported by oath or affirmation, and particularly describing the place to be searched and the persons or things to be seized"*.

Mr. Justice Brandeis in a dissenting opinion regarding Olmstead v. United States, U.S. 438 (1928) very eloquently wrote *"To protect that right (the right to be let alone), every unjustifiable intrusion by the Government upon the privacy of the individual, whatever the means employed, must be deemed a violation of the Fourth Amendment"*. Any way you look at it, random monitoring is an unreasonable invasion of peoples' privacy. Mr Brandeis' opinion was ignored then (in 1928) as it is ignored now and as is Fourth Amendment to the US Constitution, and **Article 12** of the Universal Declaration of Human Rights all of which apply to random monitoring of private communications of individuals.

Why Is This Important?

The important fact to understand is that there is no guarantee of privacy for the individual. Not in America, and not in any other country either. Governments as a matter of course violate their own laws and international treaties whenever it suits their agendas. They are always able to disguise or justify their violations as "matters of national security" or in other terms that make them palatable to their citizens. Besides, what can any individual do once their privacy has been violated? There are only a few nations where there are forums where proceedings can be brought when privacy has been violated. Many of those nations have enshrined in their privacy legislation exemptions available to law enforcement/intelligence under certain circumstances. Therefore, the only method of protecting individual privacy when communicating is the use of strong encryption technology.

CRYPTOGRAPHY: WHAT'S IT ALL ABOUT?

A Short Primer in Cryptography

Cryptography is the art and/or science of secret writing—changing readable understandable information (plain text) into unreadable random data (cipher text) and then being able to translate the ciphered text back into plain text by the same process (the algorithm) which itself is configured by a unique and secret piece of information (the key). When information is in cipher text form it ideally should be safe from being translated back into plain text by anyone but the holder of the key used for that purpose in conjunction with the proper algorithm.

Data encryption can be used to protect information in a number of ways. It can be used to facilitate secure communications. These communications can be carried out using many different mediums - from phone to microwave, from e-mail to fax. Much of the electronic commerce being done over the Internet today makes use of data encryption in conjunction with communications protocols to secure transactions against the improper use of the contents of intercepted messages. Carrying out a secure voice communication can be achieved by the use of encryption technology. Secure storage of confidential, proprietary or sensitive information can also be achieved using cryptographic techniques. An important use is with notebook computers. Since they are portable they are also more easily lost or stolen. In a recent US study several hundred thousand notebook computers were stolen in a single year. That in and of itself is not surprising but the interesting fact that emerges from that study is that a significant portion of those were targeted for the information thought to reside on the notebook. Cryptographic techniques can be used to protect the safety of information on stolen machines if only it is used.

While the methods have varied over the years in their respective levels of sophistication and security, they have been in use since Caesar's time in one form or another. In earlier times information was encrypted or decrypted by hand or through the use of mechanical or electromechanical devices. Computers, because of their inherent speed, facilitate the use of complex mathematics and intractable mathematical problems to increase the level of security offered by any given algorithm.

For the average user, cryptographic algorithms can be divided into in two distinctive families. The first is symmetric (meaning that you use the **same** key to encrypt as you do to decrypt) and is sometimes referred to as "private" or "secret" key encryption. In symmetric cryptography the single key is closely held - kept secret. If it is being used to communicate with another party, the key must be exchanged and both parties must keep the single key secret (see an example in Figure 1).

The second family is asymmetric (meaning that you have **two** keys - one for encrypting and a different but related key for decrypting) and is also known as "public" key. In asymmetric cryptography the key normally used for encrypting information can be or is published or is made available through some public method. Anyone who can obtain that public key using the proper algorithm can encrypt and

Figure 1

Figure 2.

send a secure message to the party who has published their public key. Only the person who has the "private" key, however, is able to decrypt a message encrypted with the corresponding public key. Thus, the private key is closely held by its owner and never disclosed to anyone else (see an example in Figure 2).

Symmetric Cryptography

Symmetric systems are the older of the two and vendors often use the key size (in bits—an example: DES uses 56 bit[15] keys) to describe the strength of the algorithm. This is but one dimension that describes that strength and should not be misinterpreted to be the only important attribute. The Data Encryption Standard (commonly used in the banking industry) when it was adopted as the US standard in the mid-1970s was thought to be extremely secure. In fact, Dr. Ruth Davis, Director of the National Bureau of Standard's Institute for Computer Science and Technology has stated, "that while no code is 'theoretically unbreakable,' 2500 years of computer time on a general-purpose computer 'significantly' faster than a CDC 7600 would be required to derive a key."

The U.S. Data Encryption Standard, offering a 56-bit key, has been publicly defeated by at least three separate groups. In the first instance, it took 78,000 computers working in concert for 96 days. In the second instance, it took 50,000 computers working in concert for 39 days. On the 17th of July 1998, the DES was solved for a third time. This time, the code-cracker found the key using *one* custom-built computer[16] in only *56 hours* (at a total cost of $210,000). The same group further improved on their performance when on the 19th of January

1999 when they achieve the same result in 22 hours and 15 minutes. The DES can no longer be considered adequate cryptographic protection. The plans and technical specifications for the custom-built machine are available around the world both in printed form and on the Internet. At this point it is worth mentioning that *two individuals with limited resources created DES Crack*. Imagine, if you will, what could be (and has probably been) accomplished by an organization such as the NSA which not only has pretty much unlimited funding, but which also has significant technical, mathematical and scientific talent available to it. It is very likely that a device with superior performance, compared to *DES Crack*, has been developed, used and continuously improved over the years since the adoption of the DES.

Asymmetric Cryptography

Public key systems provide the very important advantage of not requiring the secure exchange of keys in order to communicate securely. Each user's "public" key can be kept by a trusted third party that certifies its authenticity or exchanged much more easily than can be done using the symmetric system. The RSA public key cryptosystem was introduced in 1978 (created by Ron Rivest, Adi Shamir and Ken Adleman). At the time it was thought that it would take "40 quadrillion years to factor"—this system's security is based on the difficulty associated with factoring large prime numbers. The creators issued a challenge in 1977 to defeat a key pair consisting of a 129-digit number. On the 27th of April 1994, after 100 quadrillion calculations coordinated using the CPU's of some 600 participants, the RSA-129 was defeated.

The important lesson to be learned from the material described above is that there is really no 100% solution. With larger keys, either system can approach a level of computational security that would be acceptable in today's business community. However, these two examples have addressed brute force attacks only (brute force attacks try every possible key or attempt to factor every combination of prime numbers within the key range). The field of cryptanalysis is prolific and there are other attack strategies that can be successful with various encryption algorithms.

Some examples are differential cryptanalysis, linear cryptanalysis, plain text attacks, and differential fault analysis. To use this tool effectively, the user needs to consult an expert or spend the time necessary to achieve an in depth understanding of the discipline.

Differential cryptanalysis was introduced by Eli Biham and Adi Shamir in 1990. This technique looks at ciphertext pairs that have particular differences. This technique has been shown to be more efficient than a brute force attack in some circumstances[17]. Linear cryptanalysis was invented by Mitsuru Matsui and uses approximations to describe the action of a block cipher[18]. This technique is the newer of the two and there are others (see Bruce Schneier's book for more details). The interesting thing to note here is that it is likely that new techniques will evolve and that here-to-fore secure algorithms will be made insecure as a result.

The Building Blocks

The major cryptographic systems use one or a combination of two or more main building blocks or techniques. These building blocks consist of substitution, transposition and algebraic manipulation of data to be encrypted or decrypted.

Substitution refers to the replacement of one character with another—not necessarily an alphabetic character. In modern cryptography almost any of the 256 characters within the computer's character set can be used to replace any given character within the plain text message. Normally there is a single key and it is a rearrangement of one or more character sets. The standard alphabet is positioned adjacent to the key and characters from the plain text message are used to point to the desired ciphered text that will replace them (see an example in Figure 3).

Transposition is the second building block. This refers to the sequence that the characters of any given message may take. For information to make any sense to us, it must be in the proper sequence such that each word is clearly spelled out and immediately readable. Transposition makes use of various schemes of sequence changes of information. By rearranging the letters of a message that message can be made to appear to be just random characters with no apparent meaning. An historical example of this is the skytale. This was invented and used by the Greeks as early as the fifth century B.C. and is thought to be the first system of military cryptography. The device "consists of a staff of wood around which a strip of papyrus or leather

Figure 3

or parchment is wrapped close-packed. The secret message is written on the parchment down the length of the staff; the parchment is then unwound and sent on its way."[19] Thereafter, the random characters on the parchment made no sense at all until received at the desired destination where it was, once again, wrapped around a staff of identical diameter. Transposition is commonly used in symmetric crypto-systems and referred to in the DES as its S-boxes (see an example in Figure 4).

The third building block is referred to as algebraic and makes use

Figure 4

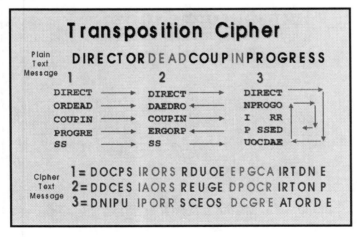

of exclusive OR a mathematics term that describes the way binary digits can be added together. This technique is extremely easy to implement in computing and is also an extremely fast computer operation. The ease of use and speed of this operation makes its use in encryption and decrypt very desirable. The way it works is two sets of binary numbers are lined up for addition in the normal way. One set represents the message - plain or ciphered text. The other represents the secret key. When the two numbers are added together, in the normal way—column by column, there is no value to carry to the next column. When 1 plus 1 make 0 carry the 1—the 1 is not carried. This technique works in both directions and facilitates a translation from plain text to ciphered text and vice versa. However, with modern cryptanalysis techniques this technique alone does not provide enough security and must be combined with other techniques (see an example in Figure 5).

Algorithms Readily Available

IDEA (International Data Encryption Algorithm) was developed by Xuejia Lao and James Massey around 1990. This algorithm has been studied and attacked by many and, thus far, has remained in tact - with no successful practical attacks revealed to date. IDEA is a symmetric

Figure 5

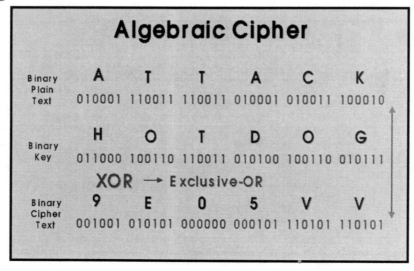

algorithm with a key space of 128 bits. This algorithm is very popular due to its perceived robustness and may be found as an option in many cryptographic products available throughout the world. IDEA is not an American product and, therefore, is not restricted from within America. Ascom Syntec, a Swiss company, owns and licenses it. At this time brute force attacks on IDEA are not possible. For example, if you could create a massively parallel machine with one billion CPU's each capable of testing one billion different keys per second simultaneously it would still take 10^{13} years of processing using such a machine to derive the key. Another way of putting it is that the key space for IDEA and other 128 bit algorithms equates to a number larger than that representing all of the atoms in the universe OR **340,282,366,920,938,000,000,000,000,000,000,000,000** different keys.

Blowfish was developed by Bruce Schneier and is a symmetric algorithm that uses a variable key up to 448 bits in length - a key space so huge that the number is too large to contemplate. Blowfish is not patented and is in the public domain. This has been around for a while and so far no cryptologic attacks have been successful. That leaves only the brute force attack. It is not computationally practical using this method on Blowfish when it is being used at its maximum strength. This algorithm is commonly found as an option in many products today available around the world.

These are only two examples of the many strong encryption algorithms available on a worldwide basis. There really is no reason to use anything less than strong encryption to protect valuable information and data.

Cryptographic Products

There are a number of cryptographic products available around the world, however, cryptographic products created in the US cannot legally be exported unless they have in some way been significantly weakened in their level of security. Coincidentally, we have a community of interest in New Zealand and there are several products that have been created here. There is a firm in Christchurch that produces hardware cryptographic devices (SignalGuard by CES[20]). This system is useful for secure communications between branches of organisations and does not require any computing resources (for the encryption/decryption process) for its use. The unique feature of SignalGuard is that encryption does not take place on data but rather on the analogue signal instead. This fact neutralises many attack strategies. Two crypto systems have been developed independently in Auckland. The first by Peter Smith is called LUC and is a public key system. The second is produced by William Raike and is called RPK and is also a public key system. Each of these is based on difficult to solve problems associated with elliptic curve mathematics. Internationally, the most commonly used crypto system used in the world is called PGP (Pretty Good Privacy – a public key hybrid system) and was initially produced by Phil Zimmermann, however, there have been several others who have assisted with this project. PGP can easily be obtained from the Internet (free) as long as you don't try to download it from the US.

There are a couple of products from Finland that hold a great deal of promise due to their very user friendly interface and the choice offered to users of a range of strong encryption algorithms. The first is *TeamWare Crypto*. The second is *F-Secure Desktop* produced by DataFellows. Each of these is based on a symmetric key system and the user can choose from a small selection of well known and proven symmetric algorithms. These products are a sample of what can be acquired easily and at a reasonable expense, however, the list should not be misconstrued as complete (as mentioned earlier there are more than 800 different cryptographic products that are currently available in the marketplace) nor as an endorsement of any product. Each, however, can provide strong encryption to users.

The most cost-effective security measure is probably the use of good backup procedures. Everyone talks about backup and many actually do something about it. However, many do not. Backup systems like ZIP drives, Jaz drives and optical drives, CD writers and the Pereos tape, are inexpensive and pretty non-intrusive. The tapes for the Pereos System, for example, are small and easy to store and not really very expensive ($30) for storing a gigabyte of data.

Secrecy vs. Privacy

A discussion of this sort would not be complete without considering the notions of privacy and secrecy. Sissela Bok wrote an excellent book several years ago; however, the issues raised are still relevant today[21]. It is often the perception that secrecy equates to guilt or is somehow threatening. The term secret merely describes the nature of the data or information being discussed and further that whatever is secret is being intentionally concealed. There is no rational way that any other attribute can be ascribed to data or information simply because it is deemed to be secret nor should it be considered awesome or worthy of respect.

Privacy on the other hand deals with one's personal domain. Since that domain is proscribed by each of us it will differ. Nevertheless we each, to a greater or lessor degree, determine and control the flow of information about us. The kinds of information we are sensitive to are the natural elements of human autonomy: identity, plans, action, and property.

Everyone has heard the phrase "if you're not doing anything wrong, you shouldn't have anything to hide". That's really Big Brother's DoubleSpeak for "if you're hiding something, then we can't watch you and protect everybody from everything". Privacy also includes being left alone - freedom from interference. Cryptography can offer a dimension of both privacy and secrecy. How it is used will dictate whether the USER is good or bad, not whether cryptography is good or bad.

CONCLUSIONS

The use of cryptography offers the opportunity to have real privacy of information and communications. It can be used to protect stored information (ideal for notebook computers and for files stored on any computer) as well as live or Internet communications. It can be used to protect business transactions that are communicated over the Internet (including the protection of credit card information). But only if it is available and only if it is "strong encryption".

The First Amendment to the United States Constitution guarantees the right to communicate without government interference: *"Congress shall make no law respecting an establishment of religion, or prohibiting the free exercise thereof; or **abridging the freedom of speech**, or of the press; or the right of the people peaceably to assemble, and to petition the government for a redress of grievances."* Encryption software and hardware simply enables one to speak in a language unknown to the government. The Constitution gives the government no blanket power to demand that we provide a translation. Speech in the dialect of IDEA should be free around the world.

The important issue to remember is that there is a continuous assault on our privacy and that new techniques are being developed all the time. Technology using strong cryptographic algorithms properly implemented can provide real privacy - as long as we are allowed to use them.

Legislation

In the bad old days of ITAR, export of cryptographic products was treated the same way as munitions and there were very specific restrictions imposed. In the first instance the relative strength of the algorithm as measured by only one of its attributes[22] was the deciding factor. Keys of forty bits or less were permitted to be exported, those greater than forty bits were not. With modern computing power this level of security is trivial to defeat and arguments came from all quarters to relax this deciding factor. Some movements were made and restrictions were relaxed to the point where products based on fifty-six bit, sixty-four bit and one hundred and twenty-eight bit algorithms could be exported but only under license and only to approved parties.

There have been several Bills proposed, however, the two that appear to have some support are languishing in Congress. These would change the export regulations currently in force (sort of). The first is in the House of Representatives (H.R. 850[23]) and was submitted on 25 February 1999 and it is called the "Security And Freedom through Encryption (SAFE) Act." It guarantees several important freedoms such as the unfettered use of encryption, prohibition of mandatory key escrow, freedom to sell encryption but also penalises the unlawful use of encryption to further a criminal act. Exporting requires a "one-time, 15-day technical review." It is not specific about what kinds of encryption can be exported, but rather leaves that to the discretion of the Secretary of Commerce. Since it is not specific, one could assume that key length would be treated as before.

The second Bill is in the Senate (S. 798[24]) and was submitted on 14 April 1999 and is called "Promote Reliable On-Line Transactions to Encourage Commerce and Trade (PROTECT) Act of 1999." It also prohibits mandatory government access to plain text (key escrow) and limits export without license to 64-bits or less and would require a one-time technical review requiring a 15-day processing period. It establishes an Encryption Export Advisory Board which determines what can be exported.

The intention to relax cryptographic policy regarding US export has recently (16 September 1999) been reported, or at least we are expected to believe that it is to be relaxed. However, as they say "the devil's in the details". The draft proposed regulatory language changes for the Commerce Department Export Regulations have been released in November[25]. In the press release of 16 September we are told that "any encryption commodity or software of any key length may be exported under license exception (i.e., without a license), after a technical review". On the other hand, in the draft regulation changes we find in Part 774 that *"d. does not contain a 'symmetric algorithm' employing a key length exceeding 64-bits"*.

This policy will be augmented by a newly (16 September 1999) proposed law (the Cyberspace Electronic Security Act of 1999 - CESA[26]). This on the surface sounds reasonable and it probably is but before export is allowed the one-time technical review must be completed. Section 207 authorises appropriations for the Technical Support Center in the Federal Bureau of Investigation ($80 million over the next four years) who serve as a centralised resource to law enforcement in cases where encryption is used by criminals. Section 203 contains clauses that would protect government methods of access to information protected by encryption or other security techniques or devices from disclosure, examination or discovery in a court proceeding.

The destination of the exported product may not be any of the seven state supporters of terrorism (Cuba, Iran, Iraq, Libya, North Korea, Sudan and Syria). There will be some post export reporting requirements for all products using algorithms greater than sixty-four bits.

It is not clear as to exactly what is meant by a "technical review". Moreover, once a product has been "certified" by review, it is not clear how it will be possible to distinguish a "reviewed" product from one that has not been "reviewed". Perhaps the reviewing entity (the Bureau of Export Administration - BXA) will return a "certified" copy of the original object code containing some additional mark that cannot be counterfeited but yet allow some way to assure product review. Only the certified object code version would then presumably be legally exportable. If code were added to the original object code submitted by the vendor/exporter and that additional code must forever after (during the export life of the specific product reviewed) remain a part of the ultimate product to be exported, then questions must be raised. The first would be: exactly what additional instructions have been added? Then the second would be: exactly which original product instructions have been modified and in exactly what way - for what purpose? But this is all conjecture since none of these issues are clearly described in the current version of the bill.

Trust is an important issue when it involves security. Historically, the US track record is not very good and I could not in all fairness recommend trusting that the "review" process in some way has not compromised the original product's security.

The reader would be correct to suggest that the notion of "added code" is supposition. However, without a mechanism to be able to distinguish between a product that has been "reviewed" and one that has not, the whole system lacks any control and, therefore, any reason for existing.

In light of the Bernstein v USDOJ case (No. 97-16686) decision, which holds that the *"prepublication licensing regime challenged by Bernstein applies directly to scientific expression, vests boundless discretion in government officials, and lacks adequate procedural safeguards, we hold that it constitutes an impermissible prior restraint on speech"*[27] . It would seem that the new laws, should any of them be passed, could be challenged successfully in the same way.

ENDNOTES

1 *Strong Encryption* refers to cryptographic techniques that provide security to a level that would require that an attacker expend resources and time beyond the current and forecasted capabilities of all of mankind in order to solve the targeted message and that the resulting solution would not be available in a timeframe that would make that solution useful.

2 *FinCEN* - **Fin**ancial **C**rimes **E**nforcement **N**etwork interestingly has exempted itself from the Privacy Act, the Right to Financial Privacy Act, and the Freedom of Information Act. FinCEN is a division of the US Treasury Department. Most other US government agencies are governed by the three Acts listed above. For anyone unfamiliar with *FinCEN*, it is instructive to read their *1997 - 2002 Strategic Plan*.

3 *FATF* - **F**inancial **A**ction **T**ask **F**orce on Money Laundering - a group of 26 member nations encompassing territories and two regional organisations that co-operate and collaborate on issues of "money laundering". Established by the G-7 Summit in Paris in 1989. FATF is primarily a confiscatory entity.

4 *OFAC* - **O**ffice of **F**oreign **A**ssets **C**ontrol - administers a series of laws that impose economic sanctions against hostile targets to further US foreign policy. OFAC

is an agency of the US Treasury Department.

5 *Network Associates, Inc.* - 3965 Freedom Circle, Santa Clara, CA 95054, Phone: 408-988-3832, Fax: 408-970-9727, **http://www.nai.com/nai_labs/asp_set/crypto/ crypt_surv.asp**

6 *Crypto, EuroCrypt* and *AsiaCrypt* - each is run in their respective geographic regions, under the banner of the International Association of Cryptologic Research, and draws participants and cryptographic experts not only from that region but also from around the world.

7 *BXA* - Bureau of Export Administration - is an agency of the US Department of Commerce.

8 *Wassenaar Arrangement* - This arrangement was initially reached on the 19th of December 1995 in Wassenaar, The Netherlands, and the Arrangement was named after that city.

9 *Wassenaar Arrangement* - quoted from the Arrangement - Dual-Use-List, pp75, paragraph 5.A.2.a.1.

10 *The Myth of Superiority of American Encryption Products* - A Cato Institute *Briefing Paper No. 42*, by Dr. Henry B. Wolfe, 12 November 1998.

11 *Kevin Mitnik* - the subject of the book *Takedown* by Tsutomu Shimomura and John Markoff - ISBN: 0786889136. Alleged to have hacked into many computer systems and alleged to have stolen software worth millions (never proven in any duly constituted Court of Law).

12 *NSA* - The National Security Agency - chartered to intercept and analyse electronic signals intelligence on a worldwide basis.

13 *Secret Power* - A book by Nicky Hagar, ISBN 0-908802-35-8, describes in detail NSA's international surveillance networks and data gathering relationships between NSA and other sovereign states.

14 *Bill of Rights* - The first ten Amendments to the US Constitution (also known as the Bill of Rights) were adopted in 1791.

15 *56 bits* - equates to a key space described as having **72,057,594,037,927,900** different keys possible.

16 *Cracking DES: Secrets of Encryption Research, Wiretap Politics & Chip Design* - Electronic Frontier Foundation, O'Reilly & Associates, Sebastopol, California, 1998, **ISBN: 1-56592-520-3**.

17 *Applied Cryptography* - by Bruce Schneier, Second Edition, John Wiley & Sons, Inc., New York, N.Y., 1996, pp-285, **ISBN: 0-471-11709-9**.

18 *Ibid* - pp-290

19 *The Code-Breakers* - by David Kahn, Second Edition, Scribner, New York, N.Y., 1996, pp 82, **ISBN: 0-68483130-9**.

20 *SignalGuard* - CES Communication, Ltd., P.O. Box 21-323, Christchurch, Nea Zealand.

21 *SECRETS: Concealment & Revelation*, by Sissela Bok, Oxford University Press, 1986, **ISBN: 019-286072-0**.

22 *Key size in bits* - which dictates the total possible key space, the maximum number of unique keys as described by 2 to the nth power.

23 http://thomas.loc.gov/cgi-bin/query/D?c106:1:./temp/~c106yIYgy4:: http://thomas.loc.gov/cgi-bin/query/D?c106:2:./temp/~c106yIYgy4::

24 http://thomas.loc.gov/cgi-bin/query/D?c106:1:./temp/~c1068qiHkj::
    http://thomas.loc.gov/cgi-bin/query/D?c106:2:./temp/~c1068qiHkj::
25 http://www.epic.org/crypto/export_controls/draft_regs_11_99.html
26 http://www.epic.org/crypto/legislation/cesa/bill_text.html
27 http://www.epic.org/crypto/export_controls/bernstein_decision_9_cir.html

Chapter VII

Foundations
for Cryptography

Dieter Gollmann
Microsoft Research, United Kingdom

Products promising to secure electronic commerce and other Internet applications tend to rely heavily on cryptography. On occasion, it seems that constraints on the deployment of 'strong' cryptography remain the only obstacle on the path to achieving security. This chapter will point to other aspects of security that are fundamental prerequisites for the successful deployment of cryptography, viz computer security and security policy. To achieve the security their systems are striving for, researchers and developers alike will have to provide adequate solutions in these areas. Otherwise, the value of strong cryptography will be greatly diminished.

Today, the Internet and electronic commerce are seen as the major driving forces for creating widespread awareness of the importance of information security, and an equally widespread demand for the deployment of security solutions. The IT sector is reacting to this demand and the market for information security products is dominated by systems using cryptography as their main protection mechanism. Some years ago, secure e-mail systems were seen in force at relevant trade exhibitions. Nowadays, visitors to those events will find that Public Key Infrastructures (PKIs) have taken over as the fashionable remedy for current security problems.

This development is underpinned by a genuine belief that cryptography is the best tool for solving the security challenges emerging in the new communications infrastructures, which offer world wide access to information, support new computing paradigms like mobile code, and offer new possibilities for conducting business. Public key cryptography is seen to provide just the right protection mechanisms for applications with large and open user communities, which demand guarantees for the authenticity and non-repudiability of transactions. Hence, a reader scanning publications on security will not have to wait too long to come across claims like the following:

- Cryptography secures electronic commerce.
- Digital signatures provide non-repudiation.
- Electronic commerce needs PKIs.

Statements of this nature can be found at all levels, from company white papers to trade magazines and to research publications. Taken at face value, all three statements are wrong. At best, they oversimplify the role of cryptography in e-commerce or overextend the meaning of technical concepts. When set in the right context, they may be true. This essay will attempt to dispel some of the misunderstandings associated with cryptography and stress those aspects of security that are necessary to supplement cryptography, and whose absence would nullify the security promised by cryptography.

We will start with a brief introduction to public key cryptography commenting on some unfortunate and often misleading aspects of terminology. We will then turn our attention to non-repudiation, which is regarded as an important security service within electronic commerce. We will use this example to highlight the limitations of cryptography when designing a 'true' e-commerce service, and to point to other security areas that have to be addressed before one can argue that parties cannot plausibly deny the actions they had performed. This example will lead to discussions of the role of cryptography in today's security applications where we note some important paradigm shifts. We continue by examining the administrative infrastructure required to connect the parties involved in distributed security services and question the role of PKIs, and conclude by investigating the role of computer security in providing the foundations for cryptographic services.

A BRIEF INTRODUCTION TO PUBLIC KEY CRYPTOGRAPHY

Public key cryptography is lumbered by two burdens, its name and a very special property of the RSA cryptosystem. Public key cryptosystems, also called asymmetric cryptosystems, split keys into two parts, a 'public key' and a 'private key'. Only the private key has to be kept secret, but there is no requirement to make the public key public. Admittedly, one of the original motivations for public key cryptography was an open communications system where public keys would be published in something resembling a telephone directory. However, public key cryptography can render useful services also in the absence of such a public directory, or any other 'public' key infrastructure. In this respect, the term 'non-secret encryption' coined in work (Ellis, 1970) predating the landmark paper by Diffie and Hellman (1976) gives a much better intuition.

Public key cryptography can be used for encryption, and for creating digital signatures. In the first case, the public key is used for encrypting documents, the private key for decrypting ciphertext. In a digital signature scheme, the private key is used for creating signatures, the public key is used for verification.

A milestone in public key cryptography is the RSA cryptosystem (Rivest et al. 1978). In this familiar scheme, a user A picks two prime numbers p and q, and a private decryption key d with $\gcd(d,p\text{-}1) = 1$ and $\gcd(d,q\text{-}1) = 1$. The public encryption key consists of the product $n = pq$ and an exponent e with

$$ed \equiv 1 \mod \operatorname{lcm}(p\text{-}1,q\text{-}1).$$

Documents have to be divided into blocks so that each block is an integer less than n. To send a message block m to A, the sender computes

$$c = m^e \mod n.$$

The receiver A uses the private decryption key d to obtain

$$c^d = m^{ed} = m \mod n.$$

The same scheme can be used for digital signatures. Then, d serves as the private signature key while the public verification key consists of the modulus n and the public exponent e. The document to be signed is an integer m, $1 \leq m < n$. To sign m, A forms the signature

$$s = m^d \bmod n.$$

The verifier needs A's verification key (n,e) and checks whether $s^e = m \bmod n$. For a correct signature, this equation holds because of

$$s^e = m^{de} = m \bmod n.$$

Encrypting and signing are essentially the same operation, only the role of the private key and the public key are interchanged. This very unique property of RSA suggests misleading claims like 'a document is signed by encryption with the private key'. We give three reasons to advance the claim that such statements should be avoided:

1. As a description of the RSA signature scheme, such a statement is incomplete. A signed document m to be verified has to contain sufficient redundancy so that it is not possible to create a valid signed document by picking a signature s and computing the corresponding document $m = s^e \bmod n$ using public information. Checking redundancy in the document is an integral part of the verification algorithm.

2. The above assertion is only true for RSA. In schemes that build on the ElGamal signature algorithm (ElGamal, 1985) like DSA (National Institute of Standards and Technology, 1994), signatures are not created by encryption.

3. Encryption algorithms are fundamentally different from digital signature algorithms. Encryption is reversible. There has to be a way to retrieve the cleartext from the ciphertext. Decryption returns a document. Digital signatures have to be verifiable. The verification algorithm takes as its input a document, a signature, and a public verification key, and returns a yes/no answer (Figure 1). Digital signatures giving message recovery are only a special case. In such a scheme, verification takes as its input the signature and the public verification key and returns the document together with a yes/no answer.

NON-REPUDIATION

For our purposes, non-repudiation is a particularly interesting security service as it provides a link between electronic documents

Figure 1. The difference between decryption and signature verification in public key cryptography

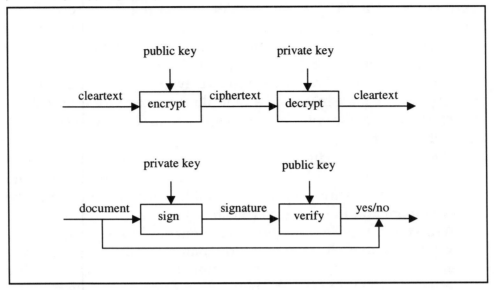

and material facts that may be disputed and submitted for arbitration in some forum, ultimately in a court of law. Non-repudiation is among the communications security services listed in the ISO/OSI Security Architecture (International Organisation for Standardization, 1988), which distinguishes between non-repudiation with proof of origin and non-repudiation with proof of delivery. However, the scope of non-repudiation is not limited to communications security. The purpose of a non-repudiation service is to collect, maintain, and make available irrefutable evidence about messages exchanged, or more generally about actions performed.

Non repudiation supports the accountability objective to trace all security-relevant events to individual users.[1] Non-repudiation services are usually implemented using digital signatures, bolstered by arguments like the following:

The essential characteristic of the signature mechanism is that the signature can only be produced using the signer's private information. Thus, when the signature is verified, it can be subsequently proven to a third party (e.g. a judge or arbitrator) at any time that only the unique holder of the private information could have produced the signature.

Can it really be true that a mathematical argument on its own (verification of a digitally signed document) may be proof that a person performed a certain action? In Figure 2 we have dissected the process of linking a signed document to *the unique holder of the private information* (signature key). The entities in this figure are a document, a person, a public verification key, and a private signature key. On top of each link, we have indicated a typical mechanism for establishing that connection, at the bottom the general field in which we can reason about that mechanism.

1. Verification of a digital signature takes as its input a signed document and a public verification key and returns a yes/no answer. Successful verification establishes a link between the document and the public verification key.

2. A digital certificate is a signed document binding a cryptographic key to a person, or in general to a name. Verifying a certificate amounts to verifying a signed document. In this respect we are still in the domain of mathematics. Creating a certificate relies on administrative measures like agreement on naming or agreement on the checks to be performed on persons requesting certificates for their public keys. There is, furthermore, the issue of distributing authentic certificate verification keys to the parties using certificates while verifying other documents. Successful verification of digital signature and certificate establishes a link between the document and the entity named in the certificate. There is no evidence yet that the holder of the private signature key is unique.

3. Finally, we need evidence that the private key can only be accessed by the entity named in the certificate. If that key is held on a device like a PC, a secure operating system has to guarantee that only a legitimate entity can access the key. If the private key is held on a special purpose device like a smart card, we still need to check that the device communicating with the card transmits the document the key holder intended to sign. An attacker who has physical access to the device holding the private key will be able to bypass the logical controls effected by the operating system, be it on the PC or on the smart card, so there has to be adequate physical security to support the argument that the key holder is unique.

As we have seen, non-repudiation relies on mathematical argu-

Figure 2. Aspects of non-repudiation

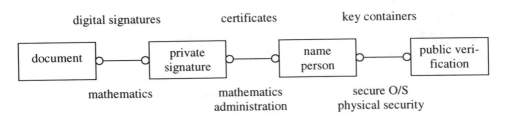

ments, administrative measures, computer security, and ultimately on physical security. On its own, cryptography can only link mathematical concepts like documents and verification keys. The link between a person and a key ultimately relies on administrative measures. Someone has to pronounce that a given key belongs to a given person. For your own purposes, you can make such a statement yourself. Of course, this statement can be encoded as a certificate and protected by cryptography. To be able to reason that a key is not only meant to belong to a unique entity, but can be used only by that entity, we have to assume that the device holding the key can perform the required access control functions.

Finally, yet another comment on terminology is due. Expressions like proof of submission and proof of delivery, combined with the mathematical nature of digital signatures and verification algorithms, may suggest that non-repudiation mechanisms can establish irrefutable proof about the occurrence of some event, and that this proof is of a precise mathematical nature. This view is misleading. First one may note that hardly any of the popular cryptographic algorithms has a proper mathematical proof that it cannot be broken. Usually, and despite many ill-advised claims to the contrary, there is not even a proof that their security is equivalent to some well-loved hard problem like factoring or discrete logarithms, whose difficulty is unknown but seems to be considerable. Secondly, as pointed out above, digital signatures are only one element in a chain of evidence.

Although cryptography may well be the strongest element in this chain, it is at its weakest element where a chain of evidence can be broken. Hence, we should approach non-repudiation as a service that provides evidence for resolving disputes, rather than proofs that cannot be refuted under any circumstances.

CHANGING CRYPTOGRAPHY

Cryptography has its origins in communications security, migrated into computer security with the advent of distributed systems[2] and now finds itself as the major security tool for the protection of electronic commerce. On this journey, cryptography has not only found new fields of application, but also some very important assumptions about the parties involved and the environment they are operating in have changed. These changes have to be properly understood to reap full advantage from the benefits cryptography can offer.

Paradigm Shifts

Communications security is traditionally explained in the setting of Figure 3. This is a black-and-white world. Alice and Bob are 'good' and want to communicate in a hostile environment. Eve is the 'evil' intruder who can intercept messages, modify messages, insert messages, and delete messages. Cryptography provides Alice and Bob with the means to establish secure logical channels in an insecure communications network. Confidentiality services prevent Eve from reading Alice and Bob's messages. Integrity services allow Alice and Bob to detect any interference with their communications.

It is customary to describe the attacker Eve as 'all powerful', but this is actually not the case. In the attack model we have sketched, the attacker cannot corrupt Alice or Bob. If we strip away the anthropomorphic metaphors, we are stating the fundamental assumption that the end systems used for communications cannot be compromised by the attacker and will always work as intended. When the end system

Figure 3. The old paradigm of communications security

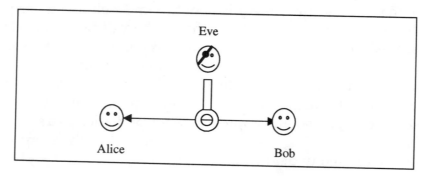

performs a very limited number of functions, consider for example a telephone handset, then it is not beyond hope to obtain the assurances to justify this assumption.

Computer systems authenticate their users through passwords. This approach worked reasonably well in systems where users logged in on devices (terminals) that were connected by a dedicated line to the host. Physical security would prevent an attacker from tapping one of those dedicated lines to obtain passwords or to take over a session. Once the terminals were connected through a local area network, parties at one terminal could potentially observe traffic from other terminals and password spoofing became an all too feasible form of attack. New strategies had to be employed to authenticate users, and cryptography made its way into computer security.

A major milestone on this road was the Kerberos authentication system (Miller et al., 1987), now also adopted for the Internet (RFC 1510). In Kerberos, a user A and the authentication server share a secret key K_a that is derived from the user's password. The user requests a ticket from the server and gets a response encrypted under the secret key K_a. The user has to type in the password at the terminal so that the terminal can compute the key K_a and deal with the server's response. The password is never transmitted on the insecure link between terminal and host. However, as noted by Bellovin and Merritt (1990), passwords and keys can also be compromised in the end systems. If the end system is a dumb terminal, i.e. a system with limited function-ality, one can hope to obtain assurances that such a compromise cannot be effected, but not so when the end system is a PC offering a

Figure 4. Security assumptions in different system configurations

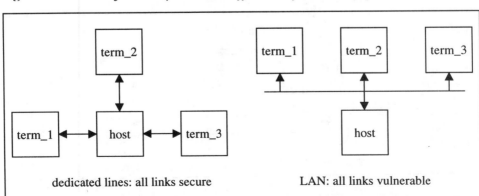

wide range of functions to its users.

A paradigm shift occurred between communications systems using simple end systems and those using complex end systems. In the latter case, a security analysis has to address end system security explicitly. (Here, simplicity is an attribute of the user's options for using the end system.)

In electronic commerce, the old black-and-white threat model is no longer valid. Customers and merchants engage in business transactions, but neither do they trust nor mistrust each other. Instead, both parties need to gather evidence so that eventually arising disputes about a transaction can be resolved efficiently. Hence, cryptography no longer protects against attacks from outsiders, but from cheating insiders (Gollmann, 1999). Of course, most transactions will not end in a dispute. Naturally, the parties also want to protect themselves against outsiders interfering in a transaction, and both parties may have privacy or business reasons for not divulging too many details to outsiders or to the other party.

In this new paradigm, Alice and Bob are replaced by customer and merchant, the end systems may potentially deviate from their expected behaviour, and the third parties provide services that help dispute resolution. Figure 5 illustrates the new paradigm in the example of a credit card transaction. A transaction entails the following steps.

- Customer and merchant agree on the details of the transaction. Messages may be signed to detect interference from outsiders.

Figure 5. Electronic commerce - a new security paradigm

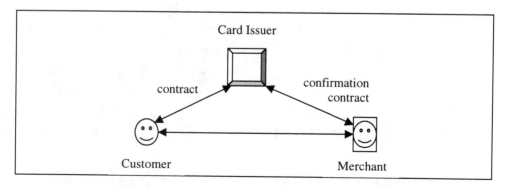

- The transaction is submitted to the card issuer for approval.
- If approval is received, both parties may commit to the transaction. It is part of the specific agreement between the three parties at which point of the protocol they become committed to the transaction.

There is no prior 'trust' between customer and merchant. One could argue that the third party acts as an introducer who facilitates the creation of trust between customer and merchant. A more sober analysis, however, would refer to the contractual relationships between the parties involved and explain that the relationships between customer and card issuer, and merchant and card issuer are already a sufficient basis for a transaction between customer and merchant.

A second paradigm shift occurred between security systems that protect against attacks from outsiders and those that can deal with the actions of misbehaving insiders.

Such paradigm shifts not only bring along a demand for new security services, they also change some of the fundamental assumptions that had been the basis for analyzing the security of cryptographic protocols. The following case study will illustrate how the second paradigm shift affects the analysis of security protocols.

A case study

The object of our investigations is the Needham-Schroeder public key protocol (Needham and Schroeder, 1978). This mutual authentication protocol uses a public key encryption algorithm to encrypt challenges with the receiver's public key. Thus, the intended receiver must process the challenge before it can become available to anyone else. In the full version of this protocol the principals obtain certified public keys from an authentication server. For our argument we only need a simplified version that omits these steps. In our presentation, the symbol P_X denotes the public encryption key of a party X; n_X stands for a nonce[3] generated by party X; encryption of m under key K is written as $eK(m)$.

1. $A \rightarrow B: eP_B(n_A, A)$
2. $B \rightarrow A: eP_A(n_A, n_B)$
3. $A \rightarrow B: eP_B(n_B)$

In the first step, the initiator A sends a nonce n_A and A's name encrypted under B's public key. Only B can decrypt this message. In the second step, B replies with A's nonce n_A and a new nonce n_B encrypted under the public key P_A of the party indicated in the first message. In the final step, A acknowledges B's challenge by replying with $eP_B(n_B)$. This protocol has been analyzed in the framework of the BAN logic (Burrows et al., 1990). To discuss the results of this analysis, we need the symbols

- A *secret(Y) B*, to denote a secret Y shared between A and B,
- $\langle X \rangle_Y$ to denote a message X combined with a formula Y.

Using the BAN axiom for shared secrets,

$$\frac{A \; believes \; A \; secret(Y) \; B, \; A \; sees \; \langle X \rangle_Y}{A \; \textbf{believes} \; B \; \textbf{said} \; X}$$

security properties like

$$A \; \textbf{believes} \; B \; \textbf{believes} \; A \; \textbf{secret}(n_B) \; B$$

can be derived for the Needham-Schroeder public key protocol, i.e. n_B is a secret key shared by A and B. Similar properties can be proven for n_A. Both Needham and Schroeder (1978) and Wobber et al. (1994) treat the two nonces n_A and n_B as shared secrets and use them to initiate a secure session between A and B. Despite these formal security proofs, Lowe (1995, 1996) found an attack on the Needham-Schroeder public key protocol. Figure 6 shows how party E can use a protocol run A has started to authenticate E to impersonate A in another protocol run with B.[4]

In this attack, the nonces n_A and n_B become known to three parties, but only E is aware of this fact. Hence it is definitely not true that they are secrets shared between two parties only, although we have just

Figure 6. Lowe's attack against the Needham-Schroeder public key protocol

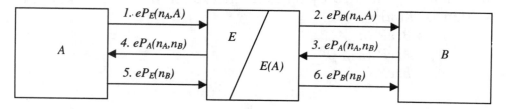

referred to proofs that suggest otherwise. How can this apparent paradox be explained? The answer lies in the assumptions made.

The BAN logic captures the spirit of the old communications security paradigm. Burrows et al. (1990) state explicitly that proofs apply only to protocol runs where the intended participants follow the protocol rules. In particular, they do not divulge secrets to third parties. So, if Y is a secret shared between A and B and if X is a message constructed using the secret Y, then the above axiom justifiably allows A to conclude that B sent X. The axiom relies on Y being a secret known only to A and B during the entire protocol run. If Y were revealed, there would be no justification to attribute message X to principal B. However, in Lowe's attack E is a party engaged in a protocol run by A, i.e. an insider.

> We assume that the intruder is a user of the computer network, and so can take part in normal runs of the protocol, and other agents may initiate runs of the protocol with him (Lowe, 1996).

In the attack, the insider E discloses the 'secret' n_A to B. We have left the old paradigm, the assumptions underlying the BAN proof no longer hold, and it is no surprise that an analysis under different assumptions reaches different conclusions.

When parties have little to lose from disclosing a secret, this should be reflected in the security model. Temporary shared secrets, i.e. secrets that are protected during message transmission through cryptographic means but may be disclosed by the recipient, can play a useful role in security protocols. They allow to identify the recipient of a message but do not identify the sender of a response to that message. For example, a valid response to a challenge that was encrypted under the receiver's public key implies that the receiver's private key was used during the protocol run to obtain the challenge. The response may arrive in a message sent via some other entity or even in a broadcast. This feature of temporary shared secrets is captured by axiom like

$$\frac{A \textbf{ believes } A \textbf{ secret}(Y) \, B, \, A \textbf{ sees } \langle X \rangle_Y}{A \textbf{ believes } B \textbf{ said } Y}$$

(see e.g., Gollmann, 1996). If Y is a secret initially shared between A

and B and if A sees a message constructed using the secret Y, then A can conclude that B must have done something with Y. B can reveal the secret to other parties without invalidating this conclusion.

Concluding the discussion of the Needham-Schroeder public key protocol, one could take the view that the BAN proofs made the 'mistake' of using an axiom for permanent and prearranged secrets to reason about temporary shared secrets established during a protocol run. However, there is also a general paradigm shift from a world where attackers are outsiders while insiders follow the rules to a world where this distinction between good insiders and evil outsiders no longer applies. The new paradigm happens to capture the realities of electronic commerce quite nicely. Where there is dealing there is also the danger of insider fraud. However, it is interesting to note that in most instances, take the security proofs of Bellare and Rogaway (1994) as a prominent example, verification of security protocols still adheres to the old paradigm.

ADMINISTRATIVE MEASURES

In the world of cryptographic protocols, *identities* are cryptographic keys. A signed document can be attributed directly just to a public verification key. In practice, we want to verify a signed document because there is something we want to do with that document.

- In a communications system, we may want to address a reply to a message received.
- A reference monitor in a computer system may decide whether to grant an access request contained in the document.

Typically, we do not send messages to cryptographic keys or maintain access control lists populated with cryptographic keys. Rather, we use *names* that are meaningful at the level of the given application. In a World Wide Web application, addresses are DNS names. In an operating system, access control lists contain user names. We, therefore, require means to link cryptographic keys to names relevant for the application (Figure 7). When we use public key cryptography, the term *Public Key Infrastructure* (PKI) stands for the system that associates names with public keys.[5]

What is the precise function of a Public Key Infrastructure? Do we

Figure 7. A layered model for security protocols

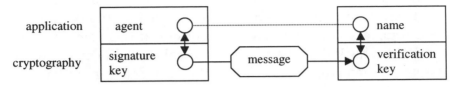

need Trusted Third Parties (TTPs) for their implementation? Consider the following three cases.

1. In a computer system, the names used by a reference monitor in access decisions are inherently local parameters. In distributed systems, users can be issued with private signature keys while the operating system keeps a local list of user names and corresponding verification keys. The integrity of this list has to be protected by the operating system, but protection need not be effected by cryptographic means. In this example, we need neither certificates nor any third party to build a 'local PKI'.

2. In an electronic commerce application such as the credit card transaction of Figure 5, customer and merchant need the public verification key of the card issuer. Both parties can receive this key out of band at the time of entering into a contract with the card issuer.[6] To verify signed documents sent by the other party, they need certificates issued by the card issuer. This example uses certificates, but the entity creating the certificates is one of the parties involved in the transaction rather than an independent TTP. We may describe this set-up as a 'private PKI'.

3. In a global communications infrastructure as envisaged in the X.509 recommendations (International Organization for Standardization, 1994), names are addresses that have to be globally unique. Keys can be bound to addresses by certificates, and in the same way as there has to be global agreement on how to allocate addresses, there may be global agreement on how to associate keys with addresses. Only now is there a case for a network of *certification agencies* (CAs) that issue certificates and provide for cross-references between different CAs, i.e. a 'public PKI'.

In the process of this discussion, another question has been answered. Is it necessary for the parties in an e-commerce transaction to verify the identity of their counterparts? In the example of Figure 5, does a certificate for the merchant issued by the card issuer vouch for the merchant's identity to the customer? As customer in a real life credit card transaction, we hardly check the identity of merchants in trade registers and merchants rarely check our identities. Rather, merchants check that customers have valid credit cards, and in turn customers may want to check that they are dealing with a merchant approved by the card issuer.

Observe that in all examples given, users request access to a service. The service may be a communications service, an e-commerce service, or access to a computer resource controlled by the operating system. The entity controlling access to the service has a set of rules to follow.[7] These rules refer to names relevant to the access control policy implemented. Thus, certificates bind names, not identities to crypto-graphic keys.[8] The primary purpose of *authentication* is to check entitlement to a service, not to verify identities. This view resolves the apparent paradox of authenticating anonymous users. Users can remain anonymous and still demonstrate that they are entitled to obtain a service by presenting an appropriate token.

This section has examined the link between names and public keys. The creation of such a link is an administrative decision. It is most natural for names to be given and links to be created by the entity that refers to the names and links during some access decision. When there is only one entity using those links, there is no need for a PKI proper. When more parties refer in their actions to the link between names and public keys, and if some contractual relationship exists between those parties, then a PKI maps the contractual relations into cryptographic protocols. PKIs do not create contractual relations by magic.

Conversely, if we start from a global PKI, users of certificates (links) have to express their policies in names defined by someone else, have to enforce their policies based on certificates issued by someone else, and may have to resolve disputes about transactions involving certificates they had not created themselves. They may not even have a contractual relationship with the CA. In particular for electronic commerce, such an arrangement does not look promising. Moreover, the more services there are that use certificates from a single CA, the more this CA and its certificates become a single point of failure. The more damage, or at least the more inconvenience can be caused to individual users whose private key has become compromised or who find that a certificate has been issued in their name to someone else. In this way, a global PKI makes electronic commerce less secure.

ASSURANCE

Mathematical arguments link public keys to private keys, and signed documents to public keys. Administrative decisions link public keys to names. Such links can be expressed as certificates. More complex organisational relationships lead to situations where a chain of certificates has to be evaluated to verify the link between a name and a public key. To complete the arrangements of Figure 7, we have to establish a unique connection between an agent and the private signature key.

We need assurance that the private key can only be accessed by agents that are entitled to use it. We consider two cases.

- The private key is held on a general purpose computer. Imagine a user's key managed by a web browser on a PC. It has to be shown that the private key cannot be copied to memory locations where it can be read out by an attacker, and that the key will only be used to sign documents the user actually wants to sign.
- The private key is held on a special purpose device like a smart card or a key module. It still has to be shown that the key cannot be read out from the card and that it will only be used to sign documents the user wants to sign.

The first line of defence is the operating system. On a simple key module, there will not be an operating system worth its name, but even then do we have to check that users cannot misuse the operations available to them to compromise keys. The analysis of a design for a key management module where just such a problem was detected has been reported in (Longley and Rigby, 1992).

Card operating systems have been evaluated to the highest ITSEC (Commission of the European Communities, 1991) assurance level E6, which requires that the security enforcing functions and the architectural design shall be specified in a formal style, consistent with the specified underlying formal model of security policy. A smart card operating system and an electronic purse have recently been evaluated to level E6 (UK ITSEC Scheme, 1999).

The future has to show to which degree the new generation of operating systems for Java cards and the like that permit code to be downloaded to the card will be able to combine more flexibility with a high degree of assurance. In any case, the assurance provided by a smart card, or any other token without its own display or keyboard, is limited by the fact that it is difficult for a user to verify that the private key is used to process the right document.

A general purpose operating system will hardly ever be evaluated to the same level of assurance as a smart card operating system, nor will a complex piece of software like a web browser. At this end of the spectrum, the assurance security evaluation can afford for the unique connection between agent and private key weakens. There is another weak link in the chain when private keys are held on a general purpose device, viz the user. Computer users are typically authenticated by password, so an attacker is much better off trying to guess that password than to guess, say, a 128-bit key.

Our second line of defence is physical security. Even if we had the most wonderful operating system and were the most security conscious users, we still have to take precautions for the eventuality of an attacker getting physical access to the device holding the private key. When the private key is stored in a PC, we may rely on the physical security of our private home, or of the office where the PC is located. When the private key is held on a smaller and mobile security token, we rely on tamper resistance. A token need not be unbreakable, but we should be given sufficient time to detect the loss of the token and to take steps to revoke its validity.

Without protection through the operating system and through physical security, cryptography rests on weak foundations. We cannot hope to secure a complex and open network of insecure devices simply by applying a healthy dose of cryptography. Cryptography is really a mechanism for transforming security problems. Typically, a communications security problem is transformed into a problem of key management and key storage. To protect keys, we have to solve a computer security problem. If we were running away from computer security, we are back to our starting point. Of course, we can hope that cryptography has transformed the original problem into something more simple. Indeed, the very reason given in (Lampson et al., 1992) to explain why cryptography was used in an authentication scheme for distributed system was that cryptography added less to the Trusted Computing Base[9] (TCB) than other alternatives. Cryptography can help to keep the TCB of a computer system small, but it does not abolish the necessity of having a TCB.

CONCLUSION

Cryptography is a convenient tool for linking security requirements specific to an application and computer security mechanisms. Today, much attention is being paid to strengthening that link itself. For example, there seems to be a widely held view that replacing 40-bit keys by 128-bit keys in symmetric encryption algorithms would in itself provide the strong security desired for electronic commerce and the Internet. Export controls and other regulations appear as the only barrier on the path towards this goal.

However, such a view is misguided. Concentrating on cryptography alone while losing sight of other aspects like application requirements and computer security, will negate the protection cryptography could deliver. Almost inevitably, cryptography implies the use of keys. We have to decide how to protect these keys and how to use these keys.

Protecting access to keys is a computer security problem. In a typical e-commerce scenario, this problem can be particularly awkward. Customers are the system managers of their own PC, potentially running the operating system of one manufacturer, the Web browser of another, and the application software of a third. If a key gets misused, can responsibility be established? Operating systems with good access control, good in particular with respect to assurance, would be a welcome addition to the armory of the security practitioner. A general purpose high assurance operating system is not likely to come cheap and, therefore, not likely to find a ready market. Smart cards are a convenient place for keeping private information, in particular if the private key belongs to the card holder and not the card issuer. High assurance smart card operating systems are being promised, but one must not forget that even then additional steps are necessary to make sure that a private key is only applied to documents in a way intended by its owner. Ultimately, one needs a trusted path from a keyboard to the device holding the key.

All these considerations on computer security apply very much also to certification agencies. Indeed, a great deal of attention is being paid to the trustworthiness of CAs and of the computer systems they employ, but the buck does not stop there. For a PKI to work, end users have to be trustworthy too. This points to a noteworthy analogy between secure e-mail systems and PKIs. You can send encrypted e-mail messages only to people whose key you know. You should refer to data from a PKI only in transactions with people you know to be able to protect their private keys.

In this context, we have to stress once more that security mechanisms must be properly installed and operated to have their desired effect. Inevitably, users are involved during some stages of this process. At the most simple level, users will be asked to take adequate care of their smart cards. If the user's end system is a PC, we may end up asking a 'security unaware' user to become the system manager of a security relevant device. Such a constellation can easily undermine assumptions that are crucial for the security of a PKI. It is a well-rehearsed fact that security systems often break at their weakest link.

At the other end, we have to decide on the meaning of keys. Do keys represent individual persons in cyberspace or do they serve as a capability to get access to a service? A certificate that binds a name to a key makes it simpler to describe the meaning of a key in a given application. If different applications want to use the same names, they have to agree on the meaning of names. Such an arrangement will not scale well, and is by no means a necessary prerequisite for the use of public key cryptography. Just the opposite, the more applications rely on the same certificate, the greater damage is possible if a certificate is issued wrongly or a private key becomes compromised. Sharing unique identifiers (identities) between applications also raises many issues of personal privacy. Hence, a single PKI is not only unnecessary for electronic commerce, it may become an impediment when it undermines consumer confidence.

The foundations that anchor cryptography are computer security, to protect access to private keys, and security management, to assign the proper meaning to keys and to define the rules for resolving disputes relating to the binding of a key to a name. Without those foundations, strong cryptography remains a giant on clay feet.

REFERENCES

Bellare, Mihir and Phillip Rogaway. (1994). Entity Authentication and Key Distribution. In: Advances in Cryptology - CRYPTO'93, Springer LNCS 773: 232-249.

Bellovin, Steve M. and Michael Merritt. (1990). Limitations of the Kerberos Authentication System. *ACM Computer Communications Review* 20(5): 119-132.

Burrows, Michael, Martin Abadi, and Roger Needham. (1990). A Logic of Authentication. DEC Systems Research Center, Report 39 (revised February 22).

Commission of the European Communities. (1991). Information Technology Security Evaluation Criteria (ITSEC). Version 1.2.

Diffie, Whitfield, and Martin E. Hellman. (1976). New directions in cryptography. *IEEE Transactions on Information Theory* 22: 644-654.

ElGamal, Tahir. (1985). A public key cryptosystem and a signature scheme based on discrete logarithms. *IEEE Transactions on Information Theory* 31: 469-472

Ellis, J.H. (1970). The Possibility of Non-Secret Encryption. CESG. http://www.cesg.gov.uk/about/nsecret/home.htm.

Ellison, Carl M., Bill Frantz, Butler Lampson, Ron Rivest, Brian M. Thomas, and Tatu Ylonen. (1998). SPKI Certificate Theory. Internet Draft. (November).

Gollmann, Dieter. (1996). What do We Mean by Entity Authentication? In: Proceedings of the 1996 IEEE Symposium on Security and Privacy: 46-54.

Gollmann, Dieter. (1999). Insider Fraud. In: Proceedings of the Cambridge Security Protocols Workshop, B. Christiansen et al. (eds.), Springer LNCS 1550: 213-219.

International Organisation for Standardization. (1988). Basic Reference Model for Open Systems Interconnection (OSI) Part 2: Security Architecture. ISO 7498.

International Organization for Standardization. (1994). Information technology - Open Systems Interconnection - The Directory-Authentication Framework. ISO/IEC 9594-8 | ITU-T Rec X.509.

Lampson, Butler, Martin Abadi, Michael Burrows, and Edward Wobber. (1992). Authentication in Distributed Systems: Theory and Practice. *ACM Transactions on Computer Systems* 10(4): 265-310.

Longley, D. and S. Rigby. (1992). An Automatic Search for Security Flaws in Key Management Schemes. *Computers & Security* 11(1): 75-89 (March).

Lowe, Gavin. (1995). An Attack on the Needham-Schroeder Public-Key Authentication Protocol. *Information Processing Letters* 56(3): 131-133.

Lowe, Gavin. (1996). Breaking and Fixing the Needham-Schroeder Public-Key Protocol using FDR. In: Proceedings of TACAS, Springer LNCS 1055: 147—166.

Miller, S.P., B.C. Neuman, J.J. Schiller, and J.H. Saltzer. (1987). Section E.2.1: Kerberos Authentication and Authorization System. MIT Project Athena.

National Institute of Standards and Technology. (1994). Digital Signature Standard (DSS). FIPS PUB 186. (May).

Needham, Roger M. and Michael D. Schroeder. (1978). Using Encryption for Authentication in Large Networks of Computers. *Communications of the ACM* 21: 993-999.

Rivest, Ron, and Adi Shamir, and L. Adleman. (1978). A Method for Obtaining Digital Signatures and Public-Key Cryptosystems. *Communications of the ACM* 21:120-126.

UK ITSEC Scheme. (1999). UK Certified Products List. UKSP 06 (October).

US Department of Defense. (1985). DoD Trusted Computer System Evaluation Criteria. DOD 5200.28-STD.

Wobber, Edward, Martin Abadi, Michael Burrows, and Butler Lampson. (1994). Authentication in the TAOS Operating Systems. *ACM Transactions on Computer Systems* 12(1): 3-32.

ENDNOTES

1 ANSI IISP Need #106 - Security: Non-repudiation Mechanisms for Operating Mediation of Resource System Access.

2 Hashing passwords with a one-way function had been proposed much earlier but is not a 'typical' cryptographic application as no keys are involved.

3 A nonce is an unpredictable value that had not been used in any previous protocol run.

4 We are deliberately vague about the precise nature of this impersonation. Impersonation in packet-switched networks is a thorny subject in itself and a detailed discussion would detract from the argument we are pursuing here.

5 There is no generally agreed upon definition of PKI. Here, we use the term in its most general meaning.

6 The contract could include a fingerprint (hash value) of the card issuer's verification key, allowing other parties to retrieve this public key over an insecure channel and check whether they have received a clean copy.

7 These rules may not only state access rights, they may also declare which events have to be logged in an audit trail.

8 An excellent discussion of this point can be found in (Ellison et al., 1998).

9 TCB: The totality of protection mechanisms within a computer system - including hardware, firmware, and software - the combination of which is responsible for enforcing a security policy (US Department of Defense, 1985).

Chapter VIII

Developments in Security Mechanism Standards

Chris Mitchell
University of London, UK

International Standardisation

Over the last ten years, in parallel with the enormous growth in the use of cryptography, major efforts have been devoted to assembling a set of internationally agreed standards for cryptographic mechanisms. These standards have been prepared by ISO/IEC JTC1/SC27, a committee devoted entirely to security standardisation. Of course, the standards produced by SC27 are not the only cryptographic standards in existence. A number of important standards have been produced by a variety of other bodies, including the following:

- From the early 1980s onwards, the US banking community has produced a range of US (ANSI) standards covering the use of cryptography in retail and wholesale banking. The standards have had a very strong influence on subsequent international banking standards on cryptography and its use. In turn, these banking standards have motivated some of the general purpose standards developed by SC27.
- The Internet community has produced a number of RFCs covering a range of cryptographic algorithms. These RFCs have been primarily aimed at providing algorithms for use in specific secure

Internet protocols (e.g. for secure e-mail and secure IP). Nevertheless, some of the schemes adopted as RFCs have become widely used in many applications outside of the Internet sphere.

- A variety of national, regional and industry bodies have proposed standards for cryptographic techniques. Examples include the pioneering US standards for the DES block cipher, the DSA signature algorithm, and the SHA-1 hash algorithm, and the European ETSI standards for cryptographic algorithms for use in mobile telecommunications (some of which remain confidential).

Scope of This Chapter

However, despite this wide range of standardisation activity, the ISO/IEC JTC1/SC27 work is unique in being both truly international and also aimed at general applications. As such, while we mention the relevant work of other standards bodies, the main focus of this chapter is the work of ISO/IEC JTC1/SC27. The main purpose of this chapter is to bring the international standards for cryptographic techniques to the widest possible audience. Adoption of these standards, which have received detailed scrutiny from experts worldwide, can only help to improve the quality of products incorporating security features.

Note that much of the work described in this chapter is based on recent research. For brevity, references to research papers are not included here. For further information the interested reader should consult the bibliographies in the quoted standards, or the excellent encyclopaedic work (Menezes, van Oorschot and Vanstone, 1997).

Contents

The chapter will consider the full spectrum of international standardisation of cryptographic techniques. Thus, it will involve covering the following areas:

- Encryption algorithms,
- Modes of operation for block ciphers,
- Message Authentication Codes (MACs),
- Digital signatures and Hash-functions,
- Entity authentication,
- Non-repudiation, and
- Key management.

The main technical contents of the international standards covering these topics are outlined, and some motivation for their contents, as well as indications on their application, will be provided. This discussion of international standards for cryptographic techniques is prefaced by a short introduction to the main standards-making bodies, and an overview of some of the most significant parts of ISO/IEC 7498-2, the OSI Security Architecture. This latter standard is strictly outside the scope of this chapter, but it is useful in that it provides a standardised framework for the description of security services and mechanisms.

STANDARDISATION BODIES

Overview
The main international standards bodies relevant to information security are:
- International Organization for Standardization (ISO),
- International Electrotechnical Commission (IEC),
- International Telecommunications Union (ITU), the successor to CCITT and CCIR.

There is some collaboration between these bodies; for example, in the area of IT, ISO and IEC have formed a Joint Technical Committee (JTC1). At the European level, the three standards bodies roughly corresponding to ISO, IEC and ITU are respectively:
- Comité Européen de Normalisation (CEN),
- Comité Européen de Normalisation Eléctrotechnique (CENELEC),
- European Telecommunications Standards Institute (ETSI).

The National Standards bodies (members of ISO and IEC) also produce their own national standards. In Europe, ECMA (the European Computer Manufacturers Association) have produced standards for distributed system security. In North America, the IEEE (Institute of Electrical and Electronics Engineers) and NIST (the National Institute for Standards and Technology) produce IT security standards of international importance. IEEE work includes LAN security and POSIX standards. NIST (the successor to NBS) produces standards for use by Federal Government bodies. Also of global significance is the work of ANSI (the American National Standards Institute), particularly for its banking security standards.

Internet Standards

The Internet is the result of interconnecting a worldwide community of government, academic and private computer networks. It started as a project sponsored by the U.S. government and it grew organically based largely on academic and research institutions. In recent years the Internet has expanded to include many private organisations wishing to make use of the communications facilities the Internet provides. The operation of the Internet relies on interconnection standards, primarily those designed specifically for Internet operation. The Internet is managed by the Internet Activities Board (IAB), which delegates the main responsibility for the development and review of its standards to the Internet Engineering Task Force (IETF). Final decisions on Internet standards are made by the IAB.

ISO Standards
Overview

ISO, founded in 1946, is a worldwide federation of national standards bodies. A member body of ISO is the national body 'most representative of standardisation in that country' (e.g., BSI in the UK). ISO (and IEC) assigns responsibility for the development of standards in particular areas to Technical Committees (TCs). A technical committee determines its own programme of work, within the scope specified by its parent body (ISO or IEC). The main TCs responsible for security relevant standards are:

- ISO/IEC JTC1: Information technology, and
- ISO TC68: Banking and related financial services.

TCs establish Sub-Committees (SCs) to cover different aspects of their work. SCs, in turn, establish Working Groups (WGs), to deal with specific topics. While the structures of TCs, SCs and WGs evolve over time, the evolution is not rapid, and these groups typically exist for several years. An ISO standard moves through the following phases in its development:

- New Work Item (NWI) Proposal and TC Ballot,

- Appointment of editor,
- Series of Working Drafts (WDs),
- Committee Draft (CD), Final CD (FCD), and associated ballots,
- Draft International Standard (DIS), Final DIS (FDIS), and associated ballots,
- International Standard status,
- 5-year review.

Provisions are also made for standards to be revised earlier than the five-yearly review cycle if defects are found. This operates via a 'defect report' system.

ISO security standards

As previously mentioned, the main ISO TCs responsible for security are ISO/IEC JTC1 and ISO TC68. ISO TC68, responsible for banking standards, has produced a wide variety of security standards (including ISO 8730, ISO 8731-1, and ISO 8731-2 specifying integrity mechanisms, and ISO 8732, ISO 11166-1 and ISO 11166-2 specifying key management methods).

The main security-relevant SCs within JTC1 (responsible for Information Technology) are as follows:

- SC6: Telecommunications and information exchange between systems,
- SC17: Identification cards and related devices,
- SC18: Document processing and related communication,
- SC21: OSI, data management and Open Distributed Processing.
- SC27: IT Security Techniques.

The security techniques standards produced by SC27 are the main focus of this chapter. The work of SC27 is divided into three working groups:

- WG1 is responsible for security management and liaison with other standards groups.
- WG2 is responsible for security mechanism standards.
- WG3 is concerned with computer security (evaluation criteria, etc.).
- We are primarily concerned here with the work of WG2, although we do consider two standards (ISO/IEC 9979 and ISO/IEC 11770-2) developed by WG1.

THE OSI SECURITY ARCHITECTURE

We start our discussion of security standards by considering ISO 7498-2 (ISO, 1989) the OSI security architecture developed by JTC1 SC21. ISO 7498-2 is intended to serve as a security-specific addition to ISO 7498, the OSI reference model. In doing so it defines many security-related terms and ideas which are of importance to a variety of application areas, including many not covered by the OSI model. Of particular importance is the terminology it introduces for the description of security services and mechanisms.

Security model

The underlying model, implicit to the discussion in ISO 7498-2, is that there is a generic security life-cycle, containing the following steps:

- Definition of a security policy, containing a rather abstract series of security requirements for the system,
- A security requirements analysis, including a risk analysis, possibly using a tool such as CRAMM, and an analysis of governmental, legal and standards requirements,
- Definition of the security services necessary to meet the identified security requirements,
- System design and implementation, including selection of security mechanisms to provide the chosen security services, and
- Continuing security management.

In the context of this model, a security threat is something that poses a danger to a system's security. A security service is selected to meet an identified threat, and a security mechanism is the means by which a service is provided. It is important to note the distinction between a security service, i.e. what is provided for a system, and a security mechanism, i.e. the means by which a service is provided. Hence, confidentiality is a service, whereas encryption is a mechanism which can be used to provide confidentiality. In fact encryption can be used to provide other services, and data confidentiality can also be provided by means other than encryption (e.g. by physical protection of data).

When designing a secure system, the scope of the system and the set of rules governing the security behaviour of the system are of fundamental importance; these are the security domain and the security policy respectively. A security policy is defined in ISO 7498-2 as 'the set of criteria for the provision of security services'. A security domain can be regarded as the scope of a single security policy. It is possible to have nested or overlapping security domains and, thus, nested or overlapping scopes for security policies.

ISO 7498-2 gives the following statement as an example of a possible generic security policy statement regarding authorisation:

> Information may not be given to, accessed by, or permitted to be inferred by, nor may any resource be used by, those not appropriately authorised.

An initial generic policy of this type can then be refined, in conjunction with the results of a requirements analysis, into a detailed set of rules governing the operation and management of the system. Note that this generic policy only deals with preventing unauthorised access, i.e. it does not make any statement about guaranteeing access to legitimate users. Thus it does not deal with availability and, hence, does not address denial of service threats.

ISO 7498-2 distinguishes between two types of security policy: identity-based and rule-based, depending on how authorisation is granted. Identity-based policies authorise system access on the basis of the identity of the client and the identity of the resource which the client wishes to make use of. Rule-based policies rely on global rules imposed on all users, with access decisions typically made using a comparison of the sensitivity of the resources with the user attributes (e.g. the 'clearance' of the user).

Security Services

ISO 7498-2 defines five main categories of security service:
- Authentication, including entity authentication and origin authentication,
- Access control,
- Data confidentiality,
- Data integrity,
- Non-repudiation.

Parts 2-6 of the 7-part Security framework standard (ISO, 1996a) give a much more detailed discussion of the general ways in which these services can be provided.

- *Entity authentication* provides corroboration to one entity that another entity is as claimed. This service may be used at the establishment of (or during) a connection, to confirm the identities of one or more of the connected entities. This service provides confidence, at the time of usage only, that an entity is not attempting a masquerade or an unauthorised replay of a previous connection.

  Origin authentication provides corroboration to an entity that the source of received data is as claimed. However, the service does not, in itself, provide protection against duplication or modification of data units.

- The *access control* service provides protection against unauthorised use of resources. This protection may be applied to various types of access to a resource, e.g. the use of a communications resource, the reading, writing, or deletion of an information resource, the execution of a processing resource.

- ISO 7498-2 defines four types of *data confidentiality* service; all these services provide for the protection of data against unauthorised disclosure. The four types are *Connection confidentiality* — which provides for the confidentiality of all user data transferred using a connection, *Connectionless confidentiality* — which provides for the confidentiality of all user data transferred in a single connectionless data unit, i.e. a packet, *Selective field confidentiality* — which provides for the confidentiality of selected fields within user data transferred in either a connection or a single connectionless data unit, and *Traffic flow confidentiality* — which provides for the confidentiality of information which might be derived from observation of traffic flows.

- ISO 7498-2 defines five types of *data integrity* service; all these services counter active threats to the validity of transferred data. The five types are *Connection integrity with recovery* — which provides for the integrity of all user data on a connection, and detects any modification, insertion, deletion or replay of data within an entire data unit sequence, with recovery attempted, *Connection integrity without recovery* — as previously but with no recovery attempted, *Selective field connection integrity* — which provides for the integrity of selected fields within the user data of a data unit transferred over a connection, *Connectionless integrity* — which provides integrity assurance to the recipient of a data unit, and *Selective field connectionless integrity* — which provides for the integrity of selective fields within a single connectionless data unit.

- ISO 7498-2 defines two types of *non-repudiation* service: *Non-repudiation with proof of origin*, where the recipient of data is provided with protection against any subsequent attempt by the sender to falsely deny sending the data, and *Non-repudiation with proof of delivery*, where the sender of data is protected against any subsequent attempt by the recipient to falsely deny receiving the data.

Security Mechanisms

Security mechanisms exist to provide and support security services. ISO 7498-2 divides mechanisms into two types: *Specific security mechanisms*, i.e. those specific to providing certain security services, and *Pervasive security mechanisms*, i.e. those not specific to the provision of individual security services, including trusted functionality and event detection (we do not discuss these further here).

Eight types of specific security mechanism are listed, namely *Encipherment*, *Digital signature mechanisms*, *Access control mechanisms*, *Data integrity mechanisms*, which include MACs, *Authentication exchange mechanisms*, *Traffic padding mechanisms*, *Routing control mechanisms*, and *Notarisation mechanisms*. We now consider each of these eight classes in a little more detail. This lays the ground work for the detailed consideration of standards for various types of security mechanism.

- *Encipherment* mechanisms, commonly known as encryption or cipher algorithms, can help provide confidentiality of either data or traffic flow information. They also provide the basis for some authentication and key management techniques.
- A *digital signature* mechanism consists of two procedures: a signing procedure, and a verifying procedure. Such mechanisms can be used to provide non-repudiation, origin authentication and/or integrity services, as well as being an integral part of some mechanisms to provide entity authentication. Signature mechanisms can be divided into two types: Digital signatures 'with message recovery', and Digital signatures 'with appendix'. *One-*

way hash functions are an essential part of the computation of digital signatures 'with appendix'.

- *Access control* mechanisms can be thought of as a means for using information associated with a client entity and a server entity to decide whether access to the server's resource is granted to the client. Examples of types of access control mechanisms include: access control lists, capabilities and security labels. A general framework for access control mechanisms can be found in ISO/IEC 10181-3, the Access Control Framework (ISO, 1996a).
- Two types of *data integrity* mechanism exist: those concerned with the integrity of a single data unit, and those concerned with protecting the integrity of an entire sequence of data units. The first type of mechanism, e.g. a MAC, can be used to help provide both data origin authentication and data integrity (as well as being an integral part of some authentication exchange and key management mechanisms). Mechanisms of the second type, which must be used in conjunction with mechanisms of the first type, can be used to provide full connection-oriented integrity services. These mechanisms include sequence numbers and time stamps. These mechanisms are necessary since use of a MAC alone will not enable a recipient of data to detect replays of single data units, and, more generally, manipulation of a sequence of data units (including replay, selective deletion and reordering).
- *Authentication exchange mechanisms*, otherwise known as authentication protocols, can be used to provide entity authentication (as well as being the basis of some key management mechanisms).
- The term *traffic padding* describes the addition of 'bogus' data to conceal the volumes of real data traffic. It can be used to help provide traffic flow confidentiality. This mechanism can only be effective if the added padding is enciphered (or otherwise provided with confidentiality).
- *Routing control* mechanisms can be used to prevent sensitive data using insecure communications paths. For example, depending on the data's sensitivity, routes can be chosen to use only secure network components (subnetworks, relays or links). Data carrying certain security labels may be forbidden to enter certain network components.
- The integrity, origin and/or destination of transferred data can be guaranteed by the use of a *notarisation* mechanism. A third party

notary, which must be trusted by the communicating entities, will provide the guarantee (typically by applying a cryptographic transformation to the transferred data).

ENCRYPTION ALGORITHMS

In the late 1970s the DES block cipher algorithm was adopted by the NBS as a U.S. Federal Standard (FIPS, 1993); it was subsequently made into a U.S. Standard by ANSI (ANSI, 1981). Efforts to make DES an ISO standard nearly succeeded in the mid 1980s, but work was stopped for political reasons (work also stopped on efforts to standardise RSA). Instead, all efforts to standardise encryption techniques were abandoned, and work focussed instead on creating an international register of algorithms. The form of register entries is standardised in ISO/IEC 9979 (ISO, 1999e) and the register itself is actually held by NCC, Manchester. The register enables communicating entities to identify and negotiate an agreed algorithm.

The Registration Authority maintains the register and ensures that 'register entries conform to the registration procedures' in ISO/IEC 9979. It 'does not evaluate or make any judgement of quality' of registered algorithms. A registered algorithm may be an algorithm for which a complete description is contained in the register, an algorithm for which a complete description is defined in an ISO document or in a standard maintained by an ISO member body or by a liaison organisation, or an algorithm not completely described in the public domain.

Submission of entries to the register may be originated by an ISO member body, e.g. BSI, AFNOR, ANSI, DIN, etc., an ISO Technical Committee, or a liaison organisation. For each registered algorithm the corresponding register entry must contain the following details:

a. Formal algorithm name.
b. Proprietary name(s) of algorithm.
c. Intended range of applications.
d. Cryptographic interface parameters.
e. Set of test values.
f. Organisation identity that requested registration.
g. Dates of registration and modifications.
h. Whether the algorithm is the subject of a national standard.
i. Patent licence restriction information.

It may also, optionally, contain the following information.

j. List of references to associated algorithms.

k. Algorithm description.

l. Modes of operation.

m. Other information.

MODES OF OPERATION FOR BLOCK CIPHERS

Modes of operation for the DES block cipher algorithm were standardised in the U.S. in 1980 (FIPS, 1980) and 1983 (ANSI, 1983). These modes of operation are recommended ways in which to use DES to encipher strings of data bits.

Work initially started within ISO to provide corresponding international standards for DES modes of operation. When the ISO work on DES ceased, the modes of operation work continued, but now are directed towards any block cipher algorithm, resulting in two standards: ISO 8372 (ISO, 1987a) (modes of operation for a 64-bit block cipher algorithm) and ISO/IEC 10116 (ISO, 1997c) (modes of operation for an n-bit block cipher algorithm for any n).

All these standards (NBS, ANSI and ISO) contain four modes of operation:

- ECB (Electronic Code Book) Mode,
- CBC (Cipher Block Chaining) Mode,
- OFB (Output FeedBack) Mode,
- CFB (Ciphertext FeedBack) Mode.

We now describe each of these modes in a little more detail. Note that we base all our descriptions on the text in ISO/IEC 10116 (ISO, 1997c) since ISO 8372 is just a special case of ISO/IEC 10116. Throughout we suppose e is the encryption operation for an n-bit block cipher (where n is the number of bits in a plaintext and a ciphertext block), and d is the decryption operation for the same block cipher. We write

$$C = eK(P)$$

where C is an n-bit ciphertext block, K is a secret key for the block cipher, and P is an n-bit plaintext block. Similarly, we write

$$P = dK(C),$$

and hence $P = dK(eK(P))$.

Electronic Code Book (ECB) Mode

The plaintext must be in the form of a sequence of blocks $P_1, P_2, ...,$ P_q where P_i is an n-bit block. The ciphertext is then defined to be the sequence of blocks $C_1, C_2, ... , C_q$ where
$$C_i = eK(P_i)$$
for every i ($1 \leq i \leq q$). Decipherment is achieved as:
$$P_i = dK(C_i)$$
for every i ($1 \leq i \leq q$).

Cipher Block Chaining (CBC) Mode

As for ECB mode, the plaintext must be made into a series of n-bit blocks: $P_1, P_2, ... , P_q$. In addition let SV be a "starting variable." Then compute the sequence of ciphertext blocks $C_1, C_2, ... , C_q$, as follows:
$$C_1 = eK(P_1 \oplus SV), \text{ and } C_i = eK(P_i \oplus C_{i-1}) \ (i>1)$$
where $\oplus$ denotes bit-wise exclusive-or of blocks. Decipherment operates as follows:
$$P_1 = dK(C_1) \oplus SV \text{ and } P_i = dK(C_i) \oplus C_{i-1} \ (i>1).$$

Ciphertext FeedBack (CFB) Mode

We start by describing CFB mode as it appeared in the first, 1991, edition of ISO/IEC 10116. To use this mode it is first necessary to choose two parameters:

- k $(1 \leq k \leq n)$, the size of the *Feedback Variable*,
- j $(1 \leq j \leq k)$, the size of the *Plaintext Variable*.

Divide the plaintext into a series of j-bit blocks: $P_1, P_2, ... , P_q$. Let SV be an n-bit 'starting variable'. We will also use the following variables to denote 'intermediate results':

- $X_1, X_2, ..., X_q, Y_1, Y_2, ..., Y_q$, each of n bits,
- $E_1, E_2, ..., E_q$, each of j bits,
- $F_1, F_2, ..., F_{q-1}$, each of k bits.

Given an m-bit block $X = (x_1, x_2, ..., x_m)$ and a k-bit block $F = (f_1, f_2, ..., f_k)$ (where $k \leq m$), we will use the notation $S_k(X \mid F)$ to denote the m-bit block
$$(x_{k+1}, x_{k+2}, ..., x_m, f_1, f_2, ..., f_k).$$
The effect is to shift X left by k places, shifting in the k elements of F on the right.

Encipherment operates as follows. First let $X_1=SV$. Then, for $i = 1$,

2, ..., q calculate:

$$Y_i = eK(X_i)$$
$$E_i = Y_i \sim j$$
$$C_i = P_i \oplus E_i$$
$$F_i = S_j(I(k) \mid C_i)$$
$$X_{i+1} = S_k(X_i \mid F_i)$$

where $Y_i \sim j$ denotes the left-most j bits of Y_i, and $I(k)$ denotes a block of k ones. Note that the last two steps are not performed when $i = q$. Decipherment operates as follows. First let $X_1 = SV$. Then, for $i = 1, 2, ..., q$ calculate:

$$Y_i = eK(X_i)$$
$$E_i = Y_i \sim j$$
$$P_i = C_i \oplus E_i$$
$$F_i = S_j(I(k) \mid C_i)$$
$$X_{i+1} = S_k(X_i \mid F_i)$$

As for encipherment, the last two steps are not performed when $i = q$.

Output FeedBack (OFB) Mode

To use this mode it is first necessary to choose j ($1 \le j \le n$), the size of the *Plaintext Variable*.

Divide the plaintext into a series of j-bit blocks: $P_1, P_2, ..., P_q$. Let SV be an n-bit 'starting variable'. We will also use the following variables to denote 'intermediate results':

- $X_1, X_2, ..., X_q, Y_1, Y_2, ..., Y_q$, each of n bits,
- $E_1, E_2, ..., E_q$, each of j bits.

Encipherment operates as follows. First let $X_1 = SV$. Then, for $i = 1, 2, ..., q$ calculate:

$$Y_i = eK(X_i)$$
$$E_i = Y_i \sim j$$
$$C_i = P_i \oplus E_i$$
$$X_{i+1} = Y_i$$

where $Y_i \sim j$ denotes the left-most j bits of Y_i. Note that the last step is not performed when $i = q$. Decipherment operates as follows. First let $X_1 = SV$. Then, for $i = 1, 2, ..., q$ calculate:

$$Y_i = eK(X_i)$$
$$E_i = Y_i \sim j$$

$$P_i = C_i \oplus E_i$$
$$X_{i+1} = Y_i$$

As for encipherment, the last step is not performed when $i = q$.

Padding

All four modes of operation require the plaintext to be 'padded' to the right length. Annex A to (ISO, 1997c) describes the following two methods for avoiding message extension for CBC mode. First suppose that the 'unpadded' plaintext results in a final block P_q of j bits (where $j < n$).

- Method 1 modifies the encipherment of the last 'short' block. The encipherment (and decipherment) methods for this block are as follows:

  $$C_q = P_q \oplus (eK(C_{q-1}) \sim j)$$
  $$P_q = C_q \oplus (eK(C_{q-1}) \sim j).$$

- Method 2 (also known as *Ciphertext Stealing*) modifies the encipherment of the last block as follows:

  $$C_q = eK(S_j(C_{q-1} \mid P_q))$$

  and the last two ciphertext blocks are then $C_{q-1} \sim j$ and C_q. It is necessary to decipher the final block C_q before C_{q-1}. Deciphering C_q enables the recovery of the last n-j bits of C_{q-1}, and then C_{q-1} can be deciphered.

Method 1 is subject to a possible 'chosen plaintext' attack if the SV (starting variable) is not secret or has been used more than once with the same key.

Generalised CFB Mode

In the 2nd edition of ISO/IEC 10116 (ISO, 1997c) a generalised version of the CFB mode has been included. This method allows 'pipelining' to take place. In the original version of CFB mode, the result of enciphering one block of plaintext is needed as input to the enciphering of the next block, and thus it is impossible to 'pipeline' calculations, i.e. start enciphering one block before the processing of the previous block is complete. To avoid this problem, in the new version of CFB mode an r-bit *feedback buffer* (FB) is introduced, where $2n \geq r \geq n$. An r-bit SV is now needed, and after setting $FB_1 = SV$, the encipherment process becomes:

$$X_i = FB_i \sim n,$$
$$Y_i = eK(X_i),$$
$$E_i = Y_i \sim j,$$
$$C_i = P_i \oplus E_i,$$
$$F_i = S_j(I(k) \mid C_i),$$
$$FB_{i+1} = S_k(FB_i \mid F_i),$$

where FB_1, FB_2, ..., FB_q are r-bit variables representing the successive contents of the Feedback Buffer. Note also that (ISO, 1997c) recommends choosing $j = k$ for CFB mode.

MESSAGE AUTHENTICATION CODES (MACS)

The purpose of a Message Authentication Code (MAC), when applied to a message, is to enable the recipient of that message to check both where it comes from and that it has not been changed in transit. Standards for MACs date back to the early 1980s, when ANSI in the U.S. published MAC standards exclusively for banking use (ANSI, 1986a) and (ANSI, 1986b). The corresponding international banking standard, released by ISO in 1987, is (ISO, 1987b). All these standards specify use of the DES block cipher algorithm in CBC mode to produce what has become known as a CBC-MAC. Further, international (banking only) MAC standards are (ISO, 1986) which gives general requirements for such mechanisms, and (ISO, 1992), which standardises a completely different and now discredited mechanism, called the *Message Authenticator Algorithm* (*MAA*).

Following on from this banking work, ISO produced a general purpose MAC standard, ISO/IEC 9797, in 1989. This standard also uses a block cipher in CBC mode, i.e. it specifies a CBC-MAC. Unfortunately, the 1989 version was ambiguously phrased in its description of how padding operates, and a revised version (ISO, 1994a) was published in 1994.

In 1997, a major revision of the ISO/IEC MAC standard commenced. The existing 1994 standard is being replaced by ISO/IEC 9797-1 (ISO, 1999c) containing an enlarged set of CBC-MAC mechanisms. A further part ISO/IEC 9797-2 (ISO, 1998a) is also under development, which contains a series of hash-function based MAC mechanisms, including the HMAC technique.

CBC-MACs

We start by considering the CBC-MACs defined in the (1994) second edition of ISO/IEC 9797, (ISO, 1994a). We then consider what is added in ISO/IEC 9797-1, and also briefly consider the hash-function based mechanisms in ISO/IEC 9797-2.

ISO/IEC 9797 'specifies a method of using a key and an n-bit block cipher algorithm to calculate an m-bit cryptographic check value that can be used as a data integrity mechanism' to detect unauthorised changes to data. Note that m is user-selectable subject to the constraint $m \leq n$. Essentially the data is processed as follows:

- The data is padded to form a sequence of n-bit blocks.
- The data is enciphered using CBC mode with a secret key.
- The final ciphertext block becomes the MAC, after optional processing and optional truncation (which will only be necessary if $m < n$).

More specifically, if the n-bit data blocks are denoted $D_1, D_2, ..., D_q$, then the MAC is computed by first setting $I_1 = D_1$ and $O_1 = eK(I_1)$, and then performing the following calculations for $i = 2, 3, ..., q$:

$$I_i = D_i \oplus O_{i-1}$$
$$O_i = eK(I_i)$$

The output O_q from these calculations is then subjected to an 'optional process' and finally truncated to m bits to produce the MAC.

Padding Methods

ISO/IEC 9797 specifies two possible padding methods.
- **Method 1**: add as many zeros (possibly none) as are necessary to obtain a data string whose length is an integer multiple of n (old method).
- **Method 2**: add a single one and then as many zeros as are necessary (this method may involve creating an entire extra block).

It is important to note that the padding does not need to be transmitted/stored with the integrity-protected data string. If the length of the data is not reliably known by the verifier, then Method 2 should be used since it allows the detection of malicious addition/deletion of trailing zeros (unlike Method 1, which is retained for backwards compatibility with (ANSI, 1986a) and (ANSI, 1986b).

An Attack on CBC-MACs

Suppose a CBC-MAC is computed with no optional process and no truncation. Then, given two messages with valid MACs (computed using the same secret key K), we can compute a third 'composite' bogus message with a valid MAC without knowing the key.

To see how this works we illustrate the attack in the case where MACs are known for two single block messages. Suppose $MAC_1 = eK(D_1)$, and $MAC_2 = eK(D_2)$. Then MAC_2 is a valid MAC on the two block message with first block D_1 and second block: $D_2 \approx MAC_1$. To avoid such attacks, known sometimes as 'cut and paste' attacks, we either need to use one of the optional processes, or use padding method 3 from (ISO, 1999c). Note that even if two MACs are never computed with the same key, this attack still applies since we can take $D_1=D_2$.

Optional Processes

ISO/IEC 9797 specifies two optional processes which can be applied to the final block O_q obtained from the CBC encipherment of the padded data string.

The two optional processes are as follows (where O_q is the n-bit output from the CBC process and K is the key used with the CBC encipherment).

- **Optional process 1**: choose a key K_1 and compute:
  $O_q'' = eK(dK_1(O_q))$.
- **Optional process 2**: choose a key K_1 (which may be derived from K) and compute:
  $O_q' = eK_1(O_q)$.

Following the optional process, the resulting n-bit block can be truncated to m bits (if $m < n$). Note that one of the main reasons for using an optional process is to avoid 'cut and paste' attacks of the type just described.

New CBC-MAC Methods

The motivation for the new CBC-MAC methods in ISO/IEC 9797-1 is provided by some new attacks on CBC-MACs, described in detail in Annex A of (ISO, 1999c). The enhancements include the following.

- A new (3rd) padding method has been introduced.
- A new algorithm has been introduced with special processing for the first block (as well as the last block). This makes exhaustive key search more difficult.

- Two new 'parallel' variants have been introduced.

The new 'Padding Method 3' operates as follows:
- The data string D shall be right-padded with as few (possibly zero) 0 bits as are necessary to obtain a data string whose length is a multiple of n bits.
- The resulting string shall be left-padded with a single n-bit block L, consisting of the binary representation of the length in bits of the unpadded data string D (left-padded as necessary with zeros).

In summary, the six MAC algorithms in the new version of ISO/IEC 9797-1 are as follows. Note that the first three algorithms were in the 1994 version of the standard.
- MAC Algorithm 1 is simply CBC-MAC with no optional process.
- MAC Algorithm 2 is CBC-MAC with optional process equal to an additional encryption of the last block.
- MAC Algorithm 3 is CBC-MAC with optional process equal to an extra decryption and encryption. This means that, effectively, the last block is 'triple encrypted'.
- MAC Algorithm 4. In this algorithm the first and last blocks are both 'double encrypted'.
- MAC Algorithm 5 is equal to two parallel instances of MAC algorithm 1 (with different keys). The two outputs are ex-ored together to give the MAC.
- MAC Algorithm 6 is equal to two parallel instances of MAC algorithm 4 (with different keys). The two outputs are ex-ored together to give the MAC.

MACs from Hash-Functions

ISO/IEC 9797-2 (ISO, 1998a) contains a total of three different methods for deriving a MAC function from a hash-function. In each case it recommends use of one of the three hash-functions from ISO/IEC 10118-3 (1998c), described below. Thus, ISO/IEC 9797-2 defines a total of nine different MAC functions.

Superficially it is possible to derive a MAC from a hash-function by simply concatenating a secret key with the data to be MACed, and then applying the hash. That is we could put

$$MAC = h(K||D)$$

where h is a hash-function, K is a secret key, and D is the data to be MACed.

This is insecure because of the iterative nature of popular hash-functions. To see why this is the case, we first need to consider what it means for a hash-function to be iterative. Essentially it means that the hash-function is constructed from use of a special type of function called a *round-function*. To compute a hash-code, the data is first divided into blocks. The round-function is then applied repeatedly, and at each application it combines a data block with the previous output of the round-function. The first input to the round-function is a fixed IV, and the last output is the hash-code. This means that, if h is the hash-function, then knowledge of h(X) for secret X, enables h($X \mid \mid Y$) to be computed for any chosen Y. This is because the hash-code is simply the output of the last iteration of the hash-function. Thus, if the MAC is computed as suggested above, then given a MAC on data string D, a valid MAC can be computed on a data string $D \mid \mid D'$, where D' is chosen by the attacker.

The three methods described in ISO/IEC 9797-2 are as follows:

- MDx-MAC is the first scheme in ISO/IEC 9797-2. It involves modifying the hash-function in a small way. It only works with the three hash-functions from ISO/IEC 10118-3, all of which involve iterative use of a *round-function* (as described previously, the data string to be hashed is divided into blocks, and the round-function combines a block with the previous round-function output). The round-function of the underlying hash-function is first modified in a key-dependent way. An 'intermediate value' is then obtained by concatenating some key-derived information with the data string to be MACed, and then applying the (modified) hash-function. This intermediate value is then input to the round-function one more time, with the other input being further key-dependent information. The output is the MAC value.

- HMAC, as defined in Internet RFC 2104 (RFC, 1997), is the second scheme included in ISO/IEC 9797-2. The basic idea of the HMAC scheme is to compute

$$MAC = h(K \mid \mid h(K' \mid \mid m))$$

where h is a hash-function and $K \neq K'$. More specifically K and K' are two variants of a single secret key (and steps are taken to ensure that K and K' are distinct).

- The third scheme in ISO/IEC 9797-2 is a modified version of MDx-MAC applying only to short messages (at most 256 bits). It has been optimised to minimise the amount of computation required.

DIGITAL SIGNATURES

A digital signature mechanism is a function which, when applied to a message, produces a result which enables the recipient to verify the origin and integrity of a message. Moreover, it has the property that only the originator of the message can produce a valid signature (i.e. being able to verify the correctness of a signature generated by entity A, does not provide the means to compute A's signature on another message). Digital signatures can be used to provide non-repudiation of origin for a message, i.e. the recipient of a message with entity A's signature on it has evidence that A did originate the message, which even A cannot repudiate. This emulates the properties we expect of a conventional signature.

A digital signature mechanism requires every user to have a pair of keys, a *private key* for signing messages (which must be kept secret) and a *public key* for verifying signatures (which is widely distributed).

Signature mechanisms can be divided into two types:

- *Digital signatures with message recovery*, i.e. where all or part of the message can be recovered from the signature itself, and mechanisms of which type are standardised in the multipart standard ISO/IEC 9796, and
- *Digital signatures with appendix*, i.e. where the entire message needs to be sent or stored with the signature, as covered by the multipart international standard ISO/IEC 14888.

Signatures with Message Recovery

Signatures with message recovery operate in the following general way:

1. The message to be signed is lengthened by the addition of 'redundancy' according to an agreed formula, and
2. The lengthened message is then subjected to the signing process.

The verification process reveals the lengthened message, from which the original message can be recovered. Hence, with such a signature scheme, the message is contained in the signature and, thus, the message does not need to be sent or stored independently of the signature itself. Because of this property, signatures of this type can only be applied to short messages.

ISO/IEC 9796 currently has three parts:

- ISO/IEC 9796 (ISO, 1991), currently being transformed into ISO/IEC 9796-1. The signature scheme is based on a generalised version of RSA.
- ISO/IEC 9796-2 (ISO, 1997a). This scheme uses the same signature transformation as (ISO, 1991). However the method for adding redundancy is completely different, being based on use of a hash-function. It also provides for *partial message recovery*, and hence this scheme can be used to sign arbitrarily long messages.
- ISO/IEC FCD 9796-3 (ISO, 1999b). This scheme uses the same redundancy method as (ISO, 1997a), i.e. it allows for partial message recovery, will work with arbitrarily long messages, and is based on a hash-function. However the signature function is different, being based on discrete logarithms rather than being RSA-like.

ISO/IEC 9796 Scheme
Overview

The ISO/IEC 9796 standard for a 'signature with recovery' mechanism operates in the following general way.

Messages to be signed are subject to a sequence of five processes (note that use of the scheme requires choice of a parameter k_s):

1. **Padding**. This ensures the padded message contains a whole number of 8-bit bytes.
2. **Extension**. This ensures the extended message contains the 'correct' number of bytes.
3. **Redundancy adding**. This doubles the length of the extended message by interleaving it with special 'redundancy' bytes.
4. **Truncation and forcing**. This involves discarding a few of the most significant bits (if necessary) of the redundancy-added message to get a string of k_s-1 bits, then prefixing the result with a single 1 (to get a string of k_s bits), and finally changing the least significant byte according to a specified formula. The purpose of this, seemingly rather bizarre, operation on the least significant byte is to prevent certain types of cryptographic attack.
5. **Signature production**. The truncated and forced message is input to a mathematical signature algorithm which operates on strings of k_s bits (e.g. the modified RSA signature scheme described in Annex A of the standard), to obtain the signature on the message.

Although the signature production function is not specified in ISO/IEC 9796, the other four processes (which *are* specified) have been designed specifically for use with the signature production function given in Annex A of the standard, and are probably inappropriate for any other signature production function. The signature production function is in Annex A and not in the body of the standard for political and not technical reasons.

Note that Annex A of ISO/IEC 9796 is informative and not normative (i.e. the RSA-type scheme is not officially part of the standard), although this situation has been changed in ISO/IEC 9796-1, where Annex A has been made normative.

The Five Signature Generation Processes

We now examine each of the five processes in a little more detail. We assume that the signature production function operates on strings of k_s bits and produces signatures also containing k_s bits. Because of the various processes applied to the message before it is input to the signature production function, and because of the mathematical properties of the signature production function in Annex A of ISO/IEC 9796-1, this means that messages to be signed must contain a little less than $k_s/2$ bits.

1. The bit string to be signed is first padded with between 0 and 7 zeros at the 'most significant end', to get a whole number (denoted z) of bytes. The *Index r*, is defined to be the number of added zeros plus one (i.e. r will satisfy $1 \leq r \leq 8$). The output of the padding process is denoted *MP* (for *Padded Message*). The following must hold for the signature computation to be possible:

$$16z \leq k_s+3.$$

2. Define t to be the smallest integer such that $16t \geq k_s-1$ (and hence a string of $2t$ bytes will contain between k_s-1 and k_s+14 bits). The *Extended Message, ME*, is now obtained by repeating the z bytes of *MP* as many times as are necessary to get a string with exactly t bytes in it.

3. The third step involves producing a *Redundancy-added Message MR*, which will contain precisely $2t$ bytes. It is obtained by interleaving the t bytes of *ME* (in odd positions) with t bytes of redundancy (in even positions). Hence, if $m_1, m_2, ..., m_t$ are the bytes of *ME*, then Byte $2i-1$ of $MR = m_i$, and Byte $2i$ of $MR = S(m_i)$,

for every i ($1 \leq i \leq t$), where S is a function specified in ISO/IEC 9796. More precisely, ISO/IEC 9796 specifies a permutation P which acts on 4-bit 'nibbles', and if $\mu = \mu_2 \mid\mid \mu_1$ is a byte, where $\mid\mid$ denotes concatenation, then
$$S(m) = \Pi(\mu_2) \mid\mid \Pi(\mu_1).$$

Finally, byte number $2z$ of MR (denoted mr_{2z}) is modified by $mr_{2z} = r \oplus mr_{2z}$ where $\oplus$ denotes bit-wise exclusive-or and r is the index (defined in the padding step).

4. As a result of the fourth step a string IR is produced, which will contain exactly k_s bits, from MR. This is done by setting the most significant bit to a one, and then setting the other k_s-1 bits to the least significant k_s-1 bits of MR (which contains between k_s-1 and k_s+14 bits), i.e. between 0 and 14 bits are discarded. Finally the least significant byte is replaced using the following method. If $\mu_2 \mid\mid \mu_1$ is the least significant byte of MR (where μ_1 and μ_2 are 4-bit 'nibbles'), then the least significant byte of IR is set to $\mu_1 \mid\mid 6$.

5. The signature Σ is obtained as a string of k_s bits by applying the signature function to IR under the control of the secret signature key. Hence
$$\Sigma = \text{Sign}(IR)$$
where 'Sign' is the signature function. As already stated, the function 'Sign' will take as input a string of k_s bits and give as output another string of k_s bits. The details of this function are not specified in the main body of ISO/IEC 9796, but Annex A gives exact details of a function for which the whole process has been designed. This function is based on modular exponentiation.

Key Generation

To perform the signature function specified in Annex A of (ISO, 1991) it is first necessary for the signer to generate a key pair. To do this the signer must first choose:

- A *verification exponent v>1*,
- Two primes p and q, where,
  - if v is odd, then p-1 and q-1 shall be coprime to v (where two integers are *coprime* if they have highest common factor 1), and
  - if v is even then $(p$-1$)/2$ and $(q$-1$)/2$ shall be coprime to v, and p shall not be congruent to q modulo 8.

The signer's *public modulus* is then $n = pq$. The length of the modulus is denoted by k, and the choice of k also fixes k_s so that $k = k_s + 1$. Finally the signer's *secret signature exponent*, denoted s, is then set equal to the least positive integer such that:

- $sv \equiv 1 \pmod{\text{lcm}(p\text{-}1, q\text{-}1)}$ if v is odd,
- $sv \equiv 1 \pmod{\text{lcm}(p\text{-}1, q\text{-}1)/2}$ if v is even.

This is equivalent to 'standard' RSA if the exponent v is odd.

The ISO/IEC 9796 Signature Function

The signature function contains two steps. The first converts the 'Intermediate Integer' IR to a 'Representative Element' RR. The second computes the signature S from RR.

To compute RR from IR:

- If v is odd: $\qquad\qquad RR = IR$,
- If v is even and $(IR \mid n) = +1$: $\quad RR = IR$, $\qquad$ and
- If v is even and $(IR \mid n) = -1$: $\quad RR = IR/2$,

where $(a \mid n)$ denotes the *Jacobi symbol*, and in this case $(a \mid n) = (a^{(p-1)/2} \bmod p).(a^{(q-1)/2} \bmod q)$ where $n = pq$.

To compute Σ from RR, compute: $RR^s \bmod n$, $\Sigma = \min(RR^s \bmod n, n\text{-}(RR^s \bmod n))$.

Signature Verification

Signatures to be verified are subject to a sequence of three processes:

1. **Signature opening**. This is essentially the inverse to the signature function (step 5 of the signature production process).
2. **Message recovery**. This step yields the original message.
3. **Redundancy checking**. This final step is present to complete the checks that the signature is correct.

At each of these three steps it is possible that the signature may be rejected as invalid if certain checks fail (in which case there is no point in performing any further processing). The signature opening function is not specified in ISO/IEC 9796, although the other two processes are. Annex A to (ISO, 1991) does contain a precise specification of a signature opening function to go with the signature production function also specified there.

The three signature verification processes

We now examine each of the three processes in a little more detail.

1. The *Signature opening* step involves transforming the signature to be verified Σ into a string IR', the *recovered intermediate integer*. Hence

$$IR' = \text{Verif}(\Sigma).$$

   The signature Σ is rejected if IR' is not a string of k_s bits with most significant bit one and least significant nibble equal to 6. (If all is correct, then IR' should be equal to the string IR produced as a result of the fourth step of the signature generation procedure.)

2. The *Message recovery* step involves producing a $2t$-byte string MR' (the *recovered message with redundancy*) from IR'. Firstly the least significant k_s-1 bits of MR' are set to equal the corresponding bits of IR', with the most significant $16t-k_s+1$ bits of MR' being set to zeros. The least significant byte of MR' is now replaced using the following method. If $\mu_4 \mid\mid \mu_3 \mid\mid \mu_1 \mid\mid 6$ are the four least significant nibbles of IR' then the least significant byte of MR' is made equal to

$$\Pi^{-1}(\mu_4) \mid\mid \mu_1.$$

   If all is correct, then MR' should be equal to the string MR produced as a result of the fourth step of the signature generation procedure, with the possible exception of the most significant $16t-k_s+1$ bits, which in MR' are set to all zeros. A series of t checks are now performed to see which of the even bytes 'match' the odd bytes, i.e. if we label the bytes of MR': $m_{2t}, m_{2t-1}, ..., m_1$, a check is performed for successive values of i ($i = 1, 2, ..., t$) to see whether or not $m_{2i} \oplus S(m_{2i-1}) = 0$. If this equation holds for every i ($1 \le i \le t$) then the signature is rejected.

   Let z be the smallest positive integer for which $m_{2z} \oplus S(m_{2z-1}) \ne 0$. Set r equal to the least significant nibble of $m_{2z} \oplus S(m_{2z-1})$. The signature is rejected if $1 \le r \le 8$ does not hold. The *Recovered padded message MP'* is then put equal to the z least significant bytes in odd positions in MR'; MP' should now be equal to the padded message MP, produced as a result of the first step of the signature procedure. Finally the message is recovered from MP' by deleting the most significant $r-1$ bits (the signature is rejected if these deleted bits are not all zeros).

3. As a final step in verifying the signature, the recovered padded message MP' is subjected to the second and third steps of the

signature generation process (Extension and Redundancy). The least significant k_s-1 bits of the result are compared with the least significant k_s-1 bits of *MR'* (generated during the previous step). If they disagree then the signature is rejected.

Concluding Remarks

The scheme described in ISO/IEC 9796 can be adapted to produce digital signatures 'with appendix' for messages of arbitrary length. This can be achieved by using a *One-way Collision-free Hash-function, h*.

- The *one-way* property means that, given an arbitrary output string y, it is computationally infeasible to *find* a binary string x such that $h(x) = y$ (although many such strings x will typically exist).
- The *collision-free* property means that it is computationally infeasible to find two binary strings x and x' $(x \neq x')$ such that $h(x) = h(x')$, although many such pairs will exist.

A message of arbitrary length, m say, is signed by first computing $h(m)$ and then inputting $h(m)$ to the five-part ISO/IEC 9796 signature process.

ISO/IEC 9796-2

ISO/IEC 9796-2 was published in 1997 (ISO, 1997a). This mechanism has two main properties:

- The system allows for 'partial message recovery' for messages of arbitrary length, i.e., if the message is sufficiently short then all the message can be recovered from the signature, whereas if the message is too long to 'fit' then part of the message can be recovered from the signature and the rest will need to be conveyed to the verifier by some other means.
- The redundancy scheme of ISO/IEC 9796 is a little 'heavy' in that it requires half of the available space in the signature block to be used for redundancy. Thus, if the signature function is 768-bit RSA, then, with the scheme in (ISO, 1991), only 384 bits are available for conveying data bits. With the scheme specified in ISO/IEC 9796-2, around 600 bits out of the 768 could be available for data; such a gain could be critically important in certain practical applications.

The basic idea of the scheme is as follows:

1. The entire message m to be signed is input to a hash-function h to

obtain a hash-code H, i.e. $H = h(m)$.

2. If the message is too long to be totally included in the signature then some portion of the message is selected to be 'recoverable' from the signature.

3. A flag bit (called a 'more-data' bit) is added to the recoverable portion of the message to indicate whether it is all or part of the message.

4. The recoverable portion of the message, the flag and the hash-value, together with other 'formatting' bits including an optional hash-function identifier, are concatenated and input to the signature function to derive the signature Σ.

Like ISO/IEC 9796, no signature function is specified in the body of 9796-2; instead exactly the same RSA-based function is included in an informative (non-normative) annex.

ISO/IEC 9796-3

The ISO/IEC 9796-3 signature function is based on discrete logarithms (the scheme is known as Nyberg-Rueppel, after the inventors). There are two basic versions of the scheme specified in the standard: one based on the group of integers modulo a prime p, and the other based on working within an elliptic curve group. Both versions make use of the same basic idea, so we describe the first version only.

The following domain parameters must be agreed by any community of users of the scheme:

- Two large prime numbers p and q, where q is a factor of p-1,
- An element g of multiplicative order q modulo p, i.e. a number g satisfying $g^q \equiv 1$ (mod p) and $g \neq 1$.

Then a user's private signature key is a number x, where $1 < x < q$. The corresponding public verification key is: $y = g^x \bmod p$.

To use the scheme a signer needs a method for generating secret random numbers k $(1 < k < q)$, one per signature; these numbers must be different and unpredictable for each signature. To generate a signature it is necessary to first compute the integer Π, where $\Pi = g^k \bmod p$, and second compute the integer R, where $R = \Pi + D \bmod q$, and where D is the concatenation of the recoverable part of the message and a hash-code (computed on the entire message) – as in ISO/IEC 9796-2. Finally, compute the integer S as $S = k - xR \bmod q$. The signature is then the pair (R, S).

To verify a signature first compute the integer Π', where: $\Pi' = g^S y^R$ mod p, second compute the value D', where: $D' = R - \Pi'$ mod q, and third reconstruct the message from the recoverable part (embedded within D') and the non-recoverable part (which must be sent with the signature). The reconstructed message is then used to recompute the hash-code. Finally it is necessary to compare the recomputed hash-code with the value embedded in D'.

ISO/IEC 14888 – Signatures 'with Appendix'

Introduction

ISO/IEC 14888 is a multi-part standard containing a variety of 'digital signature with appendix' mechanisms. The three parts are as follows:

- **ISO/IEC 14888-1: 1998**: *General*, (ISO, 1998f),
- **ISO/IEC DIS 14888-2**: *Identity-based mechanisms*, including the Guillou-Quisquater scheme, (ISO, 1998g),
- **ISO/IEC 14888-3: 1998**: *Certificate-based mechanisms*, including NIST's *Digital Signature Algorithm (DSA)* – a version of the El Gamal signature algorithm, (ISO, 1998h).

Since this standard covers a large variety of mechanisms, we will not discuss all parts in detail. All 'signature with appendix' schemes operate roughly in the following way:

1. The message to be signed is input to a collision-free one-way hash-function,
2. The output of the hash-function (the *hash-code*) is subjected to the signing process, and
3. The signed hash-code constitutes the signature (*appendix*).

The verification process needs to take as input both the signature and the message, i.e. the message cannot be recovered from the signature.

ISO/IEC 14888-1 provides a general model for all the signature schemes specified in ISO/IEC 14888 parts 2 and 3. This general model covers both *deterministic* and *randomised* signatures. In a deterministic signature scheme, the signature of a fixed string will always be the same. In a randomised signature scheme, a random number is used as part of signing process. This means that, if the same data string is signed twice, different signatures will result. In such schemes it is always important to ensure that the randomised number is different every time, and that guessing the random number is not possible.

Identity-Based Mechanisms

ISO/IEC 14888-2 (ISO, 1998g) specifies identity-based signature techniques (with appendix). In identity-based schemes, each entity's public signature verification key is derived from that entity's identity. Thus there is no need for public key certificates. To make such a scheme work a Trusted Third Party (TTP) is needed to generate private keys (users cannot generate their own). Hence in such a scheme the TTP has access to all private keys. This means that such schemes are not suitable in all applications. However, such schemes may be suitable for certain closed domains (e.g. within a large company) where there is a 'natural' TTP.

ISO/IEC 14888-2 contains three different signature schemes, all of which are of the *randomised* type. All three schemes are, in fact, different variants of the *Guillou-Quisquater* signature scheme. We only describe the first ('basic') variant here. The scheme is essentially a variant of RSA, closely analogous to the scheme used in ISO/IEC 9796-1 and 9796-2. The TTP chooses (and makes public):

- The domain verification exponent v, and
- The domain modulus $n = pq$, where p and q are large primes (which the TTP *does not* make public), and p-1 and q-1 are both coprime to v.

The TTP calculates (and keeps secret) the key generation exponent d, where d is the multiplicative inverse of v (mod $(p$-1$)(q$-1$)$). Hence we have that u^{dv} mod $n = u$ for all non-zero u. This is just like the key generation process for RSA.

To participate in this scheme, each entity must have unique 'identification data' I (a string of bits). To generate the key pair for a user with identification data I, the TTP computes the user's public verification key y as $y = f(I)$ where f is the redundancy-adding function specified in ISO/IEC 9796-1. The private signature key for this user is then $x = y^d$ mod n.

To generate a signature, the signer first generates the *randomiser* k, and then computes $\Pi = k^v$ mod n (where v and n are the domain parameters). The signer next computes $R = h(\Pi \mid\mid M)$, where M is the message to be signed, and h is an agreed collision-resistant hash-function. Finally the signer computes $S = k.x^R$ mod n, (where R is converted from a bit string to an integer), and the signature is the pair (R, S).

To verify a signature, the verifier first computes $\Pi' = y^R.S^v$ mod n. The verifier next computes $R' = h(\Pi' \mid\mid M)$, where M is message. Finally, the verifier compares R and R'. If they agree then the signature is accepted (otherwise it is rejected).

Certificate-Based Mechanisms

ISO/IEC 14888-3 (ISO, 1998h) describes two general models for signatures with appendix, one discrete logarithm based, and the other factorisation based. A number of examples of each type of scheme are specified in the standard:

- **Discrete logarithm based schemes**: DSA, Pointcheval-Vaudenay (a DSA variant), ECDSA (Elliptic Curve DSA).
- **Factorisation based schemes**: ISO/IEC 9796 with hash, and ESIGN.

The most important of these is probably DSA, and we now describe this scheme.

The Digital Signature Algorithm

The *Digital Signature Algorithm (DSA)* is a version of the ElGamal signature algorithm, which depends for its security on the *discrete logarithm* problem (just like the Diffie-Hellman key exchange mechanism). DSA was adopted as a U.S. Federal Standard in 1993, in the *Digital Signature Standard (DSS)* (FIPS, 1994). The FIPS standard specifies which hash-function should be used with the DSA algorithm, namely the *Secure Hash Algorithm (SHA-1)*, which is itself specified in a separate U.S. Federal Standard (FIPS, 1995).

The generation of a key pair for the Digital Signature Algorithm is a two-stage process. The first stage corresponds to the selection of a triple of underlying parameters (P, Q, G) which may be common to a group of users. It involves the following steps:

- A parameter l is selected which determines the size of the modulus; l is chosen subject to the constraint that $0 \le l \le 8$. This determines the value of the 'modulus length parameter' L, where $L = 512 + 64l$.
- A prime P is selected, where $2^{L-1} < P < 2^L$, i.e. P has L bits in its binary

representation. The prime P is chosen in such a way that P-1 possesses a prime factor Q, where $2^{159} < Q < 2^{160}$, i.e. Q has 160 bits in its binary representation. An algorithm for generating P and Q is specified in FIPS 186.

- Choose a number G ($1 < G < P$-1) of multiplicative order Q (when working modulo P). To do this choose a random T ($1 < T < P$-1) and check that $T^{(P-1)/Q} \neq 1$. If this check fails then choose another T, and repeat as necessary. Finally put $G = T^{(P-1)/Q}$.

The triple (P, Q, G) is made public, and could be common for a group of users. The second stage involves selecting the private/public key pair.

- The private signature key X is randomly chosen, where $0 < X < Q$.
- The public verification key Y is calculated using $Y = G^X \bmod P$.

The signature for the message M is calculated using the following steps.

- M is subjected to the specified hash-function (SHA-1) which we denote by h, i.e. $h(M)$ is computed. For the purposes of this signature scheme $h(M)$ needs to be treated as an integer; a rule for converting the bit string $h(M)$ into an integer is given in FIPS 186.
- A random value K is selected, where $0 < K < Q$. A different and unpredictable value of K must be chosen for every signature computed (note that DSA is a *randomised* signature scheme).
- A value R is computed, where $R = (G^K \bmod P) \bmod Q$.
- A value S is computed where $S = (K^{-1}(h(M) + XR)) \bmod Q$. Note that K^{-1} is the inverse of K modulo Q. The signature on the message M is the pair (R, S), which contains only 320 bits (since R and S are both 160 bits long).

The verification process takes as input the message M, and the signature pair (R, S). The following steps are performed:

- The verifier first checks that $0 < R < Q$ and $0 < S < Q$; if not then the signature is rejected.
- The verifier next computes:
  $W = S^{-1} \bmod Q$,
  $U1 = h(M)W \bmod Q$,
  $U2 = RW \bmod Q$, and
  $V = (G^{U1}Y^{U2} \bmod P) \bmod Q$.

If $V = R$ then the signature is verified; if not, then the signature is rejected. Note that signing the message M using DSA involves calculating the two values:

$$R = (G^K \bmod P) \bmod Q, \text{ and}$$
$$S = (K^{-1}(h(M) + XR)) \bmod Q,$$

where K is a random value. Given that K is message-independent, it can be selected in advance. Moreover, R is a function only of K, i.e. it is message-independent, and thus R can also be pre-computed, as can K^{-1} and XR. Thus signing can be made very fast, at least in situations where pre-computations can be performed. All that is required to compute a signature is to hash the message (i.e., compute $h(M)$), add $h(M)$ to XR (mod Q), and multiply the result of the previous step by K^{-1} (mod Q).

However, verification includes calculating two exponentiations mod P, where both exponents will be 160 bits long. This is a non-trivial calculation. This is reverse of situation for RSA, where use of low exponent for public key can make verification very simple.

HASH-FUNCTIONS

One-way hash functions form an integral part of any digital signature with appendix. However, ISO/IEC 14888 does not specify any particular hash function – the choice is left to the user. A separate multi-part standard, ISO/IEC 10118, specifying one-way hash functions has been developed. Such cryptographic hash functions also have uses for file protection and data integrity purposes.

- **ISO/IEC 10118-1**, *General* (ISO, 1994c) provides general definitions and background for the other parts of the standard.
- **ISO/IEC 10118-2**, *Hash-functions using an n-bit block cipher algorithm* (ISO, 1994d) describes two methods for deriving a hash function from an n-bit block cipher.
- **ISO/IEC 10118-3**, *Dedicated hash-functions* (ISO, 1998c) describe three hash-functions designed specifically for the purpose (namely SHA-1, RIPEMD-128 and RIPEMD-160).
- **ISO/IEC 10118-4**, *Hash-functions using modular arithmetic* (ISO, 1998d) describes two hash-functions (MASH-1 and 2) using modular exponentiation to construct a hash-value.

All the hash-functions specified in ISO/IEC 10118 parts 2, 3 and 4 conform to the same general model (a simplified version of which is given in ISO/IEC 10118-3). The model requires a choice of two parameters m (the 'block length') and s (the length of the 'iteration value', which determines the maximum possible length for the derived hash-code), the choice of an s-bit Initialising Value (IV), the choice of the length for the hash-code L_H (where $L_H \leq s$), and the use of a *round-function* ϕ which takes as input two strings (of lengths m and s bits), and gives as output an s-bit string. Hence, if X is an m-bit string and Y is an s-bit string then $\phi(X,Y)$ is an s-bit string.

The model involves four steps in the processing of a data string D.

1. *Padding.* D is padded to ensure that its length is a multiple of m bits.
2. *Splitting.* The padded version of D is split into m-bit blocks $D_1, D_2, ..., D_q$.
3. *Iteration.* The s-bit blocks $H_1, H_2, ..., H_q$ are calculated iteratively in the following way:
$$H_i = \phi(D_i, H_{i-1})$$
where $H_0 = IV$.
4. *Truncation.* The hash-code H is derived by taking L_H of the s bits from H_q.

Block Cipher Based Hash-Functions

ISO/IEC 10118-2 contains two methods for deriving a hash-function from an n-bit block cipher. Method 1 produces hash-codes of length L_H bits, where $L_H \leq n$. Method 2 produces hash-codes of length L_H bits, where $L_H \leq 2n$. The padding techniques for these two methods are not specified in ISO/IEC 10118-2, although examples are given in an annex to the standard.

Method 1 (single length hash-codes)

For Method 1, the block length (m) is equal to n, the plaintext/ciphertext length for the block cipher. Hence, the data string to be hashed is padded and split into a sequence of n-bit blocks
$$D_1, D_2, ..., D_q.$$
The parameter s is also set to n, the block cipher plaintext/ciphertext length. If encipherment of block M using key K is denoted $e_K(M)$, then the round-function ϕ is defined so that

$$\phi(X,Y) = e_{u(Y)}(X) \oplus X$$

where u is a function which maps n-bit blocks into blocks suitable for use as keys in the chosen block cipher. Hence, $H_i = \phi(D_i, H_{i-1}) = e_U(D_i) \oplus D_i$ where $U = u(H_{i-1})$. The truncation function involves taking the left-most L_H bits of H_q.

Method 2 (double length hash-codes)

To define the round-function for ISO/IEC 10118-2 Method 2, we first need to define three special functions.

- I, which takes as input a $2n$-bit block and gives as output a $2n$-bit block. Suppose n is even and $X = X_1 \mid\mid X_2 \mid\mid X_3 \mid\mid X_4$ is a $2n$-bit block, where X_i $(i = 1, 2, 3, 4)$ are $n/2$ bit sub-blocks. Then $I(X) = X_1 \mid\mid X_4 \mid\mid X_3 \mid\mid X_2$, i.e. sub-blocks X_2 and X_4 are interchanged.
- L, which takes as input a $2n$-bit block and gives as output an n-bit block containing the n left-most bits of the input.
- R, which takes as input a $2n$-bit block and gives as output an n-bit block containing the n right-most bits of the input.

For Method 2 we have $m = n$ (as for Method 1), and hence the data string to be hashed is padded and split into a sequence of n-bit blocks $D_1, D_2, ..., D_q$. We set s to $2n$, i.e. twice the block cipher plaintext/ciphertext length. The round-function f is now defined so that

$$\phi(X,Y) = I(e_{u(L(Y))}(X) \oplus X \mid\mid e_{u'(R(Y))}(X) \oplus X)$$

where u and u' are functions which map n-bit blocks into blocks suitable for use as keys in the chosen block cipher. Hence

$$H_i = \phi(D_i, H_{i-1}) = I(e_{u(L(i))}(D_i) \oplus D_i \mid\mid e_{u'(R(i))}(D_i) \oplus D_i).$$

where $L(i) = L(H_{i-1})$ and $R(i) = R(H_{i-1})$.

In Annex A to ISO/IEC 10118-2, choices for the Initialising Value (*IV*) and transformation u are suggested which are appropriate for method 1 when the block cipher in use is DES. In the same annex, choices for the Initialising Value (*IV*) and transformations u, u' are suggested which are appropriate for method 2 when the block cipher in use is DES. Worked examples of these choices are given in a further annex.

Dedicated Hash-Functions

ISO/IEC 10118-3 (*Dedicated hash functions*) contains three functions specifically designed for use as hash-functions. In all cases the Initialising Values are specified in the standard, as are the padding methods. Two of the hash-functions, *Dedicated Hash-functions 1* and *2*, are identical to RIPEMD-128 and RIPEMD-160 respectively, European algorithms developed as part of the EC-funded RIPE project. In the first case the round-function has $m = 512$ and $s = 128$, i.e. it can generate hash-codes of up to 128 bits in length, and in the second case the round-function has $m = 512$ and $s = 160$, i.e. it can generate hash-codes of length up to 160 bits. The third function, *Dedicated Hash-function 3*, is NIST's *Secure Hash Algorithm (SHA-1)*, already a U.S. Federal Standard (FIPS, 1995). In this case, like RIPEMD-160, the round-function has $m = 512$ and $s = 160$, i.e. it can generate hash-codes of up to 160 bits in length.

Modular Arithmetic-Based Hash-Functions

ISO/IEC 10118-4 (*Modular arithmetic based hash-functions*) contains a pair of hash-functions, *MASH*-1 and *MASH*-2, based on modular exponentiation. They are improved variants of the function given in the original 1988 version of X.509 (CCITT, 1988) which was found to be prone to attack and, hence, it has been removed from later versions of the standard.

The initialising values and padding methods for these functions are specified in the standard. The values of m and s will depend on the modulus for the arithmetic operations. The round-functions for both versions of MASH are based on exponentiation using a fixed exponent; this fixed exponent is 2 for MASH-1 and 257 for MASH-2.

ENTITY AUTHENTICATION

Authentication forms the basis of the provision of other security services in the majority of network security systems. The OSI Security Architecture (ISO 7498-2) distinguishes between *data origin authentication* (i.e., verifying the origin of received data—a connectionless operation), and *(peer) entity authentication* (i.e. verifying the identity of one entity by another —a connection-oriented operation).

We are primarily concerned here with the second of these two services, namely entity authentication. Entity authentication is typically achieved using an *authentication exchange mechanism*. Such a mechanism consists of an exchange of messages between a pair of entities and is usually called an *authentication protocol*. In OSI-speak, the term 'protocol' should strictly be reserved for the specification of the data structures and rules governing communication between a pair of peer entities, and this is why ISO 7498-2 speaks of authentication exchange mechanisms. However, here we abuse the OSI notation slightly and follow generally accepted practice and call them authentication protocols.

ISO/IEC JTC1/SC27 has produced a multi-part standard, ISO/IEC 9798, specifying a general-purpose set of authentication protocols. The five parts published so far are as follows:

- ISO/IEC 9798-1 – General model, (ISO, 1997b).
- ISO/IEC 9798-2 – Protocols based on symmetric encipherment, (ISO, 1994b).
- ISO/IEC 9798-3 – Protocols based on digital signatures, (ISO, 1998b).
- ISO/IEC 9798-4 – Protocols based on data integrity mechanisms, (ISO, 1995).
- ISO/IEC 9798-5 – Zero knowledge protocols, (ISO, 1999d).

The protocols specified in these standards have been specified for use in a variety of application domains. As such they have been designed to be as 'robust' as possible, i.e. they have been designed to resist all known attacks (as long as they are used in the way specified).

ISO 7498-2 defines entity authentication as 'the corroboration that an entity is the one claimed'. We also need to distinguish between protocols providing *unilateral authentication* and *mutual authentication*. Unilateral authentication is 'entity authentication which provides one entity with assurance of the other's identity, but not vice versa. Mutual authentication is 'entity authentication which provides both entities with assurance of each other's identity'. Entity authentication can only be achieved for a single instant in time.

Typically, a mutual authentication protocol is used at the start of a connection between communicating entities. If security (e.g. confidentiality, integrity) is required for information subsequently exchanged during the life of the connection, then other cryptographic mechanisms will need to be used, e.g. encipherment or the use of *Message Authentication Codes (MACs)*, to protect that data. The keys needed for these cryptographic operations can be agreed and/or exchanged as part of the authentication protocol, and so one application of entity authentication is 'authenticated session key establishment'. Other applications exist which are not directly related to session key exchange, including secure clock synchronisation, secure RPC (remote procedure call) and secure transactions.

Mechanisms Underlying Authentication Protocols

Authentication protocols require the use of a combination of either shared secrets (keys or passwords) or signature/verification key pairs, and accompanying cryptographic mechanisms. These are used to ensure that the recipient of a protocol message knows where it has come from (origin checking), that it has not been interfered with (integrity checking). Note that cryptographic mechanisms (by themselves) cannot provide *freshness checking*, i.e., the verification that a protocol message is not simply a replay of a previously transmitted (valid) protocol message, protected using a currently valid key. We consider the provision of freshness verification later.

A variety of different types of cryptographic mechanism can be used to provide integrity and origin checking for individual protocol messages. We consider three main possibilities: encipherment, integrity mechanism (MAC), and digital signature. The use of MACs and digital signatures and MACs for integrity protection of messages is standard practice; however the use of encipherment for this purpose is much less straightforward, and hence we discuss this a little more before proceeding.

To protect a message in a protocol, the sender enciphers it with a secret key shared with the recipient. The recipient can then verify the origin of the message using the following process. The recipient first deciphers the message and checks that it 'makes sense'; if this is the case then the recipient reasons that it must therefore have been enciphered using the correct secret key, and since only the genuine sender knows this key, it must therefore have been sent by the claimed originator. This reasoning makes a number of assumptions about the nature of the encipherment algorithm and the capabilities of the recipient. First and foremost, if this process is to be performed automatically by a computer (as we would expect), then we need to define what 'makes sense' means for a computer, especially as the contents of the message might include random session keys and random 'challenges'.

We are also assuming that an interceptor cannot manipulate an enciphered message (without knowledge of the key used to encipher it) in such a way that it still 'makes sense' after decipherment. This constrains the type of encipherment algorithm that is suitable for use in this application; for example, stream ciphers are usually unsuitable for use as part of an authentication protocol. The usual solution to this problem is the addition of deliberate 'redundancy' (according to some agreed formula) to the message prior to encipherment. The presence of this redundancy can then be automatically checked by the recipient of the message (after decipherment). One common method of adding redundancy to a message is to calculate a *Manipulation Detection Code (MDC)*, a sort of checksum dependent on the entire message, and append it to the message prior to encipherment. The MDC calculation function will typically be a public function.

Classifying Authentication Protocols

One way of classifying authentication protocols is by the type of cryptographic mechanism they use. This is the approach followed by ISO/IEC 9798. However, it is also possible to classify authentication protocols by the 'freshness checking' mechanism they use. As we have already briefly noted, providing origin and integrity checking for protocol messages is not all that is required. We also need a means of checking the 'freshness' of protocol messages to protect against replays of messages from previous valid exchanges. There are two main methods of providing freshness checking:

- The use of *time-stamps* (either clock-based or 'logical' time-stamps),
- The use of *nonces* or challenges.

Timestamp-Based Protocols

Clearly the inclusion of a date/time stamp in a message enables the recipient of a message to check it for freshness, as long as the time-stamp is protected by cryptographic means. However, in order for this to operate successfully all entities must be equipped with **securely** synchronised clocks. It is non-trivial to provide such clocks, since the clock drift of a typical work-station can be 1-2 seconds/day.

Every entity receiving protocol messages will need to define a time acceptance 'window' either side of their current clock value. A received message will then be accepted as 'fresh' if and only if it falls within this window. This acceptance window is needed for two main reasons:

- Clocks vary continuously, and hence no two clocks will be precisely synchronised, except perhaps at some instant in time, and
- Messages take time to propagate from one machine to another, and this time will vary unpredictably.

The use of an acceptance window is itself a possible security weakness since it allows for undetectable replays of messages for a period of time up to the length of the window. To avert this threat requires each entity to store a 'log' of all recently received messages, specifically all messages received within the last t seconds, where t is the length of the acceptance window. Any newly received message is then compared with all the entries in the log, and if it is the same as any of them then it is rejected as a replay.

Another problem associated with the use of time-stamps is the question of how synchronised clocks should be provided. One solution is to use an authentication protocol **not** based on time-stamps (e.g. nonce-based) at regular intervals to distribute a master clock value which is then used to update each entity's individual clock. Another solution is for all entities to have reliable access to an accurate time source (e.g. a national radio broadcast time such as the Rugby time signal).

One alternative to the use of clocks is for every pair of communicating entities to store a pair of *sequence numbers*, which are used only in communications between that pair. For example, for communications between A and B, A must maintain two counters: N_{AB} and N_{BA} (B will also need to maintain two counters for A). Every time A sends B a message, the value of N_{AB} is included in the message, and at the same time N_{AB} is incremented by A. Every time A receives a message from B, then the sequence number put into the message by B (N say) is compared with N_{BA} (as stored by A), and:

- If $N > N_{BA}$ then the message is accepted as fresh, and N_{BA} is reset to equal N,
- If $N \leq N_{BA}$ then the message is rejected as an 'old' message.

These sequence numbers take the role of what are known as *logical time-stamps*, a well-known concept in the theory of Distributed Systems, following (Lamport, 1978).

Nonce-Based Protocols

Nonce-based (or *challenge-response*) protocols use a quite different mechanism to provide freshness checking. One party, A say, sends the other party, B say, a *nonce* (*Number used ONCE*) as a *challenge*. B then includes this nonce in the *response* to A. Because the nonce has never been used before, at least within the lifetime of the current key, A can verify the 'freshness' of B's response (given that message integrity is provided by some cryptographic mechanism). Note that it is always up to A, the nonce provider, to ensure that the choice of nonce is appropriate, i.e. that it has not been used before.

The main property required of a nonce is the 'one-time' property. Thus, if that is all that is ever required, A could ensure it by keeping a single counter and whenever a nonce is required, for use with any other party, the current counter value is used (and the counter is incremented). However, in order to prevent a special type of attack, many protocols also need nonces to be *unpredictable* to any third party. Hence nonces are typically chosen at random from a set sufficiently large to mean that the probability of the same nonce being used twice is effectively zero.

Example Protocols

We now consider a variety of examples of authentication protocols taken from parts 2, 3 and 4 of ISO/IEC 9798. We give examples based on both types of freshness mechanism.

A Unilateral Authentication Protocol Using Timestamps
and Encipherment

The first example can be found in clause 5.1.1 of ISO/IEC 9798-2. It is based on the use of time-stamps (for freshness) and encipherment (for origin and integrity checking). It provides *unilateral authentication* (B can check A's identity, but not vice versa). In the message description (here and subsequently) we use the following notation:

- $x \mid \mid y$ denotes the concatenation of data items x and y,
- Text1 and Text2 are data strings, whose use will depend on the application of the protocol,
- K_{AB} denotes a secret key shared by A and B,
- eK_{AB} denotes encryption using the shared secret key K_{AB}, and
- T_A denotes a time-stamp (or sequence number) generated by A.

The mechanism has one message pass, as follows:

$A \rightarrow B$: Text2 $| | e_{KAB}(T_A | | B | |$ Text1)

When B receives the message from A, B deciphers the enciphered string, and checks that the deciphered message 'makes sense' (has the appropriate redundancy), that the time-stamp is within its current window (and, using its 'log', that a similar message has not recently been received), and that B's name is correctly included. If all three checks are correct, then B accepts A as valid. Use of the data strings 'Text1' and 'Text2' will depend on the application domain ('Text1' might, for example, be used for session key transfer). Either or both of these strings may be omitted.

A Unilateral Authentication Protocol Using Nonces and MACs

This example can be found in clause 5.1.2 of ISO/IEC 9798-4. It is based on the use of nonces (for freshness) and a data integrity mechanism (for origin and integrity checking). It provides *unilateral authentication* (B can check A's identity, but not vice versa). In the message descriptions we use the following notation (in addition to that defined for the first example):

- Text1, Text2 and Text3 are data strings, whose use will depend on the application of the protocol,
- fK_{AB} denotes a cryptographic check value (the output of a data integrity mechanism) computed using the shared secret key K_{AB},
- R_B denotes a random nonce generated by B.

The mechanism has two message passes, as follows:

$B \rightarrow A$: $R_B | |$ Text1

$A \rightarrow B$: Text3 $| | f_{KAB}(R_B | | B | |$ Text2)

When B sends the first message, B stores the nonce R_B. When B receives the second message, B first assembles the string $R_B | | B | |$ Text2, then computes $fK_{AB}(R_B | | B | |$ Text2) using the shared secret K_{AB}, and finally checks that the newly computed value agrees with the one in the message. If the check is correct, then B accepts A as valid. Note that, in order for B to perform the desired check, B must have the means to obtain the data string 'Text2'. One possibility is that Text3 contains a copy of Text2, perhaps in an enciphered form.

A mutual authentication protocol using nonces and encipherment

This example can be found in clause 5.2.2 of ISO/IEC 9798-2. It is based on the use of nonces (for freshness) and encipherment (for origin and integrity checking). It provides *mutual authentication* (*B* can check *A*'s identity and vice versa). In the message descriptions we use the following notation (in addition to that defined for previous examples):

- Text1-Text5 are data strings, whose use will depend on the application of the protocol,
- R_A and R_B denote random nonces generated by *A* and *B* respectively.

The mechanism has three message passes, as follows:

$B \rightarrow A$: R_B | | Text1

$A \rightarrow B$: Text3 | | $e_{KAB}(R_A$ | | R_B | | B | | Text2)

$B \rightarrow A$: Text5 | | $e_{KAB}(R_B$ | | R_A | | Text4)

When *B* sends the first message, *B* stores the nonce R_B. When *A* sends the second message, *A* stores the nonces R_A and R_B. When *B* receives the third message, *B* deciphers the enciphered string and checks that the deciphered message 'makes sense' (has the appropriate redundancy), that the nonce it includes is the one *B* sent in the first message, and that *B*'s name is correctly included. If all checks are correct, then *B* accepts *A* as valid, and sends the third message. When *A* receives the third message, *A* deciphers the enciphered string and checks that the deciphered message 'makes sense' (has the appropriate redundancy), and that the nonces it includes are the expected ones. If both checks are correct, then *A* accepts *B* as valid.

A Mutual Authentication Protocol Using Timestamps and MACs

This example can be found in clause 5.2.1 of ISO/IEC 9798-4. It is based on the use of time-stamps (for freshness) and an integrity mechanism (for origin and integrity checking). It provides *mutual authentication* (*B* can check *A*'s identity and vice versa). In the message descriptions we use the following notation (in addition to that defined for previous examples):

- Text1-Text4 are data strings, whose use will depend on the application,
- T_A and T_B denote time-stamps (or sequence numbers) generated by *A* and *B* respectively.

The mechanism has two message passes, as follows:

$A \rightarrow B$: T_A || Text2 || $f_{KAB}(T_A$ || B || Text1)
$B \rightarrow A$: T_B || Text4 || $f_{KAB}(T_B$ || A || Text3)

When B receives the first message, B first assembles the string T_A||B||Text1 and then computes $fK_{AB}(T_A$||B||Text1), using the shared secret K_{AB}. B checks that the time-stamp T_A is within its current window (and, using its 'log', that a similar message has not recently been received), and that the newly computed check value agrees with the one in the message. If the checks are correct, then B accepts A as valid and sends the second message. When A receives it, A first assembles the string T_B||A||Text3 and then computes $fK_{AB}(T_B$||A||Text3), using the shared secret K_{AB}. A checks that the time-stamp T_B is within its current window (and, using its 'log', that a similar message has not recently been received), and that the newly computed check value agrees with the one in the message. If the checks are correct, then A accepts B as valid.

Note that, in order for A and B to perform their checks, A and B must have the means to obtain the data strings Text3 and Text1 respectively. One possibility is that Text4 (Text2) contains a copy of Text3 (Text1), perhaps in enciphered form.

A Mutual Authentication Protocol Using Timestamps and Signatures

This example can be found in clause 5.2.1 of ISO/IEC 9798-3. It is based on the use of time-stamps (for freshness) and digital signature (for origin and integrity checking). It provides *mutual authentication* (B can check A's identity and vice versa). In the message descriptions we use the following notation (in addition to that defined for previous examples):

- S_A and S_B are the private signature keys of A and B respectively.
- sS_A denotes the signature function computed using private key S_A.

The mechanism has two message passes, as follows:

$A \rightarrow B$: T_A || B || Text2 || $sS_A(T_A$ || B || Text1)
$B \rightarrow A$: T_B || A || Text4 || $sS_B(T_B$ || A || Text3)

When B receives the first message, B first checks that the time-stamp T_A is within its current window (and, using its 'log', that a similar message has not recently been received). *B* then assembles the string $T_A \mid \mid B \mid \mid$ Text1 and checks that the signature is a valid signature on this string, using a copy of *A*'s public verification key. If the checks are correct, then *B* accepts *A* as valid and sends the second message. When *A* receives it, *A* first checks that T_B is within its current window (and, using its 'log', that a similar message has not recently been received), and then assembles the string $T_B \mid \mid A \mid \mid$ Text3 and checks that the signature is a valid signature on this string. If the checks are correct, then *A* accepts *B* as valid.

Note that, in order for *A* and *B* to perform their checks, *A* and *B* must have the means to obtain the data strings Text3 and Text1 respectively. One possibility is that Text4 (Text2) contains a copy of Text3 (Text1), perhaps in enciphered form.

A Mutual Authentication Protocol Using Nonces and Signatures

This example can be found in clause 5.2.2 of ISO/IEC 9798-3. It is based on the use of nonces (for freshness) and digital signature (for origin and integrity checking). It provides *mutual authentication* (*B* can check *A*'s identity and vice versa). We use identical notation to the previous examples. The mechanism has three message passes, as follows:

$B \rightarrow A: R_B \mid \mid$ Text1
$A \rightarrow B: R_A \mid \mid R_B \mid \mid B \mid \mid$ Text3 $\mid \mid sS_A(R_A \mid \mid R_B \mid \mid B \mid \mid$ Text2)
$B \rightarrow A: R_B \mid \mid R_A \mid \mid A \mid \mid$ Text5 $\mid \mid sS_B(R_B \mid \mid R_A \mid \mid A \mid \mid$ Text4)

When *B* sends the first message, *B* stores the nonce R_B. When *A* sends the second message, *A* stores the nonces R_A and R_B. When *B* receives the second message, *B* first assembles the string $R_A \mid \mid R_B \mid \mid B \mid \mid$ Text2, and then checks that the signature is a valid signature on this string (using a copy of *A*'s public verification key). If the check is correct, then *B* accepts *A* as valid and sends the third message. When *A* receives it, *A* assembles the string $R_B \mid \mid R_A \mid \mid A \mid \mid$ Text4 and checks that the signature is a valid signature on this string. If the check is correct, then *A* accepts *B* as valid.

Note that, in order for *A* and *B* to perform their checks, *A* and *B* must have the means to obtain the data strings Text4 and Text2 respectively. One possibility is that Text5 (Text3) contains a copy of Text4 (Text2), perhaps in enciphered form.

Comparing Different Approaches

We now briefly consider the relative merits of time-stamps and nonces for freshness checking. Time-stamps have the following advantages with respect to nonces:

- time-stamp based protocols typically contain less messages then nonce-based protocols (typically one less),
- time-stamp based protocols fit well to the client-server model of computing (e.g. RPC).

The main disadvantages of time-stamp based protocols are as follows:

- there is a need to maintain either synchronised clocks (and a log of recently received messages) or sequence number pairs (if logical time-stamps are used),
- problems arise in securely linking the messages of the protocol together.

The need for this latter property depends on the application of the authentication protocol. If the protocol is used for time synchronisation, or database query protection, then linking of a 'request' message to a 'response' message is needed (to prevent a malicious interceptor 'shuffling' responses to requests issued within a short time of one another). To address this problem, time-stamp protocols can use a 'transaction ID' to securely link a request to a reply.

Note that, because of the many problems that have been encountered with authentication protocols in the past, a variety of various 'logics of authentication' have been proposed. The purposes of these logics are to provide a framework to reason formally about the 'soundness' (or otherwise) of candidate protocols. The most celebrated example is the *BAN Logic* (names after its inventors: Burrows, Abadi and Needham). The BAN logic actually makes it possible to reason about one particular application of authentication, namely key distribution.

Keying Requirements for Authentication Protocols

As we have already noted, almost all authentication protocols use either shared secret keys, or public/private key pairs (for digital signatures). More specifically, protocols based on symmetric cryptography (either 'symmetric' encipherment or data integrity mechanism) make use of a shared secret between A and B. Digital signature based protocols need A and B to have a trusted copy of each other's verification key.

We start by considering the keying requirements for symmetric (secret key) cryptography based protocols, i.e. where A and B need to share a secret key. Of course, if A and B already share a secret key, then there is no problem. We therefore suppose that A and B want to engage in an authentication protocol but they do not yet share a secret key. To provide the required shared secret key we assume that there is a trusted third party (TTP) with whom both A and B share a secret. The (on-line) TTP co-operates to enable A and B to authenticate one another. This process requires more elaborate protocols. Two examples of such protocols can be found in ISO/IEC 9798-2 (ISO, 1994b) although we do not explore them further here. Further examples are provided in ISO/IEC 11770-2 (ISO, 1996c).

When using public key cryptographic techniques such as digital signatures, there is a need for a means to distribute *trusted* copies of user public keys instead of shared secrets. Public verification keys can be *certified* by applying the digital signature of a Trusted Third Party (TTP). The result (i.e. a public key, an entity name, an expiry date, and the signature of a TTP on these three items) is called a public key *certificate*. In order to obtain a verified copy of a user's public key, one first obtains a copy of their public key certificate. To verify a certificate signed by a TTP requires a trusted copy of TTP's public verification key (this could typically be obtained by a user at the time the user's own certificate is generated).

If two entities have certificates signed by different TTPs, then a *cross-certificate* is needed (i.e. one a copy of one TTP's public verification key signed by the other TTP). This leads to the notion of *certification paths*, i.e. sequences of cross-certificates with the subject of one certificate being the signer of the next certificate in the sequence.

Applications

One very important application of authentication protocols is during connection establishment. An authentication protocol can be used to set up session key(s) to protect data which is transferred during the lifetime of the connection. Keys can be transferred by inclusion in the data string elements of protocol messages. Parts 2 and 3 of the key management standard, ISO/IEC 11770 (ISO, 1996c) and

(ISO, 1999f) contain examples of how this can be achieved.

NON-REPUDIATION

A multi-part standard (ISO/IEC 13888) on mechanisms for the provision of non-repudiation services has recently been completed. This overlaps to some extent with the work on digital signatures since digital signatures can be used to provide non-repudiation services.

The non-repudiation standards seek a rather wider scope, with ISO/IEC 13888-1 (ISO, 1997d) giving a general model for the provision of non-repudiation, including a discussion of the role of the trusted third party. ISO/IEC 13888-2 (ISO, 1998e) discusses the provision of non-repudiation services using symmetric cryptographic techniques. Such schemes require the on-line involvement of a trusted third party or *Notary*. ISO/IEC 13888-3 (ISO, 1997e) covering asymmetric cryptography, is concerned with how digital signature techniques can be used to provide these types of service.

ISO/IEC 13888-1

ISO/IEC 13888-1 (ISO, 1997d) provides a high-level discussion of the ways in which non-repudiation services can be provided. Among other topics, the roles of TTPs and the use of tokens are discussed. A total of eight non-repudiation services are defined; amongst them are the following four services which are likely to be the most important:

- *Non-repudiation of origin*, protects against the message originator falsely denying having sent the message.
- *Non-repudiation of submission*, protects against a message delivery authority falsely denying acceptance of the message from the originator.
- *Non-repudiation of transport*, protects against a message delivery authority falsely denying delivery of the message to the recipient.
- *Non-repudiation of delivery*, protects against the message recipient falsely denying receipt of the message.

Each of these services is provided by giving evidence to the party being given protection. For the above four services, evidence is provided to the message recipient for service 1, and to the message originator for services 2, 3 and 4.

ISO/IEC 13888-2

ISO/IEC 13888-2 (ISO, 1998e) describes a set of mechanisms for providing a variety of non-repudiation services using a combination of symmetric cryptography and a Trusted Third Party. Possible non-repudiation services covered by these mechanisms include:

- *Non-repudiation of origin* - a service which protects against an originator's false denial of being the originator of the message, and
- *Non-repudiation of delivery* - a service which protects against a recipient's false denial of having received the message.

We describe one TTP-based mechanism for providing non-repudiation of origin.

Suppose entity A is to send a message m to entity B, and suppose also that A and B both trust a Trusted Third Party TTP. Suppose also that A has identity ID_A, and B has identity ID_B. We also suppose that $f_k(D)$ is a MAC computed on data D using the key k, A and TTP share a secret key a, B and TTP share a secret key b, the TTP possesses a secret key x, h is a hash-function, and z denotes a string of data items including ID_A, ID_B, ID_{TTP}, a timestamp, and $h(m)$.

The mechanism has five message passes, as follows:

1. $A \rightarrow TTP$: $z \mid \mid f_a(z)$
2. $TTP \rightarrow A$: $z \mid \mid f_x(z) \mid \mid f_a(z \mid \mid f_x(z))$
3. $A \rightarrow B$: $m \mid \mid z \mid \mid f_x(z)$
4. $B \rightarrow TTP$: $z \mid \mid f_x(z) \mid \mid f_b(z \mid \mid f_x(z))$
5. $TTP \rightarrow B$: $PON \mid \mid z \mid \mid f_x(z) \mid \mid f_b(PON \mid \mid z \mid \mid f_x(z))$

where *PON* is one bit (*Positive or Negative*) indicating whether or not the non-repudiation information is valid.

After receiving the final message, B retains the string $z \mid \mid f_x(z)$ as evidence that A really did send message m to B. This evidence can be verified by the TTP at any later stage, using the TTPs' secret key x (and the TTP does not need to retain a record of the transaction).

ISO/IEC 13888-3

ISO/IEC 13888-3 (ISO, 1997e) describes how to construct and use digitally signed tokens to provide various non-repudiation services. For example, a non-repudiation of delivery token is defined as the recipient's signature on a data string containing the following data items:

$ID_{originator}$, $ID_{recipient}$, a timestamp, and a hash of the message.

To provide the non-repudiation of delivery service, the message recipient will be required to provide a non-repudiation of delivery token upon request by the message originator.

An informative annex to ISO/IEC 13888-3 describes the use of a TTP to provide a time-stamping service. Such a service involves a TTP adding a timestamp and its signature to data provided by a requester. This data could be a previously signed non-repudiation token. The use of such a time-stamping service is vital if signatures, and hence non-repudiation tokens, are to have long term validity. The addition of a Trusted Third Party timestamp protects against subsequent revocation and/or expiry of the private key used to sign the non-repudiation token.

KEY MANAGEMENT

We now consider the multi-part ISO/IEC standard concerned with key management, namely ISO/IEC 11770. We divide our discussion into three parts, corresponding to the three parts of ISO/IEC 11770:

- *Part 1* - Key management framework (ISO, 1996b) under which heading we consider basic definitions and concepts,
- *Part 2* - Mechanisms using symmetric techniques (ISO, 1996c) i.e. mechanisms for distributing keys using symmetric cryptographic techniques,
- *Part 3* - Mechanisms using symmetric techniques (ISO, 1999f) i.e. mechanisms for distributing keys (for both symmetric and asymmetric algorithms) using asymmetric cryptography.

The earliest key management standards work was started in the early 1980s by the ANSI banking standards community. It has resulted in a series of important banking key management standards (e.g. X9.17-1985, X9.24, X9.28, X9.30 and X9.31). This work was then taken up by ISO TC68, the banking standards committee for ISO, and has resulted in a series of parallel ISO standards, e.g. ISO 8732 for wholesale key management (based on X9.17), ISO 11568 for retail key management, ISO 11649 (based on X9.28), and ISO 11166 (a multi-part standard covering key management using asymmetric algorithms completed in 1994, and related to X9.30 and X9.31). More recently SC27 has developed a generic key management multi-part standard: ISO/IEC 11770.

The ISO/IEC JTC1/SC27 work has primarily focussed on key establishment mechanisms, although 11770-1 is the *Key Management Framework*, containing general advice and good practice on key management, and which is distantly related to ISO/IEC 10181, the multi-part security frameworks standard (ISO, 1996a). ISO/IEC 11770-2 contains key distribution mechanisms based on the use of symmetric (conventional) cryptography, and ISO/IEC 11770-3 contains key distribution/agreement mechanisms based on asymmetric cryptography.

Key Management Framework

ISO/IEC 11770-1 (ISO, 1996b) covers the following main topics:
- A list of definitions relevant to key management.
- Methods for key protection and a definition of the key 'lifecycle'.
- Key management 'concepts', covering: key generation, registration, certification, distribution, installation, storage, derivation, archiving, revocation, de-registration, and destruction.
- Models for key distribution.
- A series of appendices covering: Threats to key management, Key Management Information Objects (an ASN.1 definition for a data structure containing key(s) and associated information), Types of keys, and Certificate lifecycle management.

Some of the most important ISO/IEC 11770 definitions (mostly but not exclusively contained in Part 1) are as follows.
- *Certification authority (CA)* – a centre trusted to create and assign public key certificates. Optionally, the CA may create and assign keys to the entities.
- *Implicit key authentication to A* – the assurance for one entity A that only another identified entity can possibly be in possession of the correct key.
- *Key* – a sequence of symbols that controls the operation of a cryptographic transformation.

- *Key agreement* – the process of establishing a shared secret key between entities in such a way that neither of them can predetermine the value of that key. [This means that neither entity has key control.]
- *Key confirmation* – the assurance for one entity that another identified entity is in possession of the correct key.
- *Key control* – the ability to choose the key, or the parameters used in the key computation.
- *Key distribution centre (KDC)* – an entity trusted to generate or acquire, and distribute keys to entities that share a key with the KDC.
- *Key establishment* – the process of making available a shared secret key to one or more entities. Key establishment includes key agreement and key transport.
- *Key translation centre (KTC)* – an entity trusted to translate keys between entities that each share a key with the KTC.
- *Key transport* – the process of transferring a key from one entity to another entity, suitably protected.
- *Private key* – that key of an entity's asymmetric key pair which should only be used by that entity. [A private key should not normally be disclosed.]
- *Public key* – that key of an entity's asymmetric key pair which can be made public.
- *Secret key* – a key used with symmetric cryptographic techniques and usable only by a set of specified entities.

Keys are typically organised in *key hierarchies*. Keys in one level of the hierarchy may only be used to protect keys in the next level down in the hierarchy. Only keys in the lowest level of the hierarchy are used directly to provide data security services. This hierarchical approach allows the use of each key to be limited, thus limiting exposure and making attacks more difficult. For example, the compromise of a single session key (i.e. a key at the lowest level of the hierarchy) only compromises the information protected by that key. The key at the top level of the hierarchy is referred to as the *master key*. Disclosure of a master key will potentially enable the possessor to discover or manipulate all other keys protected by it (i.e. all keys in that particular hierarchy). It is therefore desirable to minimise access to this key, perhaps by arranging that no single user has access to its value.

Certificate Management

Annex D of ISO/IEC 11770-2 (ISO, 1996c) contains a detailed discussion of certificate lifecycle management. This discussion covers the role of the Certification Authority (CA), the 'certification process' (covering the relationships between the main entities involved in the generation and management of certificates), distribution and use of certificates, certification paths, and certificate revocation.

A *public key certificate* is a list of data items associated with a particular user, including the public key(s) of that user, all signed by a Certification Authority. Every user will subscribe to a particular CA, and possess a (trusted) copy of the verification key for that CA; they are thus able to verify certificates generated by that CA. Information in a certificate will typically include:

- The name of the user,
- An expiry date (or, more generally, a period of validity),
- A serial number,
- One or more public key(s) belonging to the user,
- The algorithm identifier(s) for the public key(s),
- Information regarding the security policy under which this certificate has been created.

Various standards exist for the structure of a certificate. Most important is ITU-T recommendation X.509 (ITU, 1997) and the corresponding ISO/IEC standard: ISO/IEC 9594-8 (ISO, 1999a). Recent revisions to these standards (which enable policy information to be included in these 'standard' certificates) have resulted in the 'Version 3' X.509 certificate format.

The CA is trusted by its subscribers for the purposes of certificate generation. The CA is responsible for identifying the entities whose public key information is to be incorporated into a certificate, ensuring the quality of the CA's own key pair used for generating certificates, and securing the certificate generation process and the private key used in the certificate generation process.

One issue of major importance not addressed in ISO/IEC 11770-1 concerns the situation where a user generates his/her own asymmetric key pair, and then requests the CA to generate a certificate for his/her public key. It is generally considered good practice for the CA to ask the user to provide assurance that the user possesses the private key corresponding to the public key offered for signature (e.g. in the case of a signature key by signing a date-stamped statement to this effect, which the CA can then verify using the offered public key). Such a procedure can avoid one user claiming to possess another user's key pair, with undesirable consequences in certain situations.

Certificates may be revoked before their scheduled date of expiry by the issuing CA. Possible reasons include: key compromise, request for cancellation by an entity, termination of the entity, etc. Thus, there needs to be a means to inform all relevant users that an apparently valid certificate is no longer valid. This is typically done by means of a *Certificate Revocation List (CRL)*. A CRL is a time-stamped list of serial numbers or other certificate identifiers for those certificates which have been revoked by a particular CA. The CRL is signed by the relevant CA. Updates should be issued at regular intervals, even if the list has not changed (thus enabling users possessing a CRL to check that it is the current one). Means need to be provided for the effective and timely distribution of CRLs.

Key Establishment Using Symmetric Techniques

ISO/IEC 11770-2 (ISO, 1996c) defines key establishment mechanisms using symmetric cryptographic techniques (mainly using symmetric encipherment but also using cryptographic check functions). The text is primarily, but not exclusively, based on using authentication protocols from ISO/IEC 9798-2 (ISO, 1994b) for key distribution.

ISO/IEC 11770-2 includes 13 'key establishment mechanisms' for:
- Session key distribution between a pair of entities with a pre-established shared 'master key',
- Key distribution between a pair of parties employing a trusted third party acting as a Key Distribution Centre, and
- Key distribution between a pair of parties employing a trusted third party acting as a Key Translation Centre.

We consider four representative examples. In these examples we use the following notation.
- A and B are the two entities wishing to establish a new secret key.
- $e_K(X)$ denotes encipherment of data block X using secret key K (note that the encipherment technique is not specified). Note that the encipherment technique is assumed to provide data integrity and origin authentication. Hence it is implicit that an MDC or

MAC will be computed on the data and appended to the data prior to encryption.

- $X \mid \mid Y$ denotes the concatenation of data items X and Y, *in the order specified*.

Authenticated key establishment using timestamps and encipherment
For this mechanism to be usable, entities A and B must already share a secret key KAB. A and B must also maintain synchronised clocks or sequence numbers. This mechanism is based on the one-pass (unilateral) authentication mechanism given in ISO/IEC 9798-2, Clause 5.1.1. It provides *unilateral authentication* of A to B, and *implicit key authentication* to A. A chooses the key and therefore has *key control*.

The mechanism has one message pass:
$$A \to B: \; e_{KAB}(T/N \mid \mid B \mid \mid F \mid \mid \text{Text1})$$
T/N denotes either a timestamp T or a sequence number N, B denotes the distinguishing name of B, and F contains keying material. On receipt of the message, B deciphers the enciphered part, and then checks for the presence of its identifier and the correctness of the timestamp/sequence number. The key established between A and B is contained in F.

Authenticated Key Establishment Using Nonces and Encipherment
Mechanism 6 (a nonce-based key distribution mechanism) is derived from the 3-pass authentication protocol in Clause 5.2.2 of ISO/IEC 9798-2. To use this mechanism, A and B must share a secret key KAB. It provides *mutual authentication* between A and B. In the most general version of its use, no individual entity has *key control*.

The mechanism has three message passes:
$$B \to A: \; R_B$$
$$A \to B: \; e_{KAB} (R_A \mid \mid R_B \mid \mid B \mid \mid F_A \mid \mid \text{Text1})$$
$$B \to A: \; e_{KAB} (R_B \mid \mid R_A \mid \mid F_B \mid \mid \text{Text2})$$

R_A and R_B are (unpredictable) nonces. F_A and F_B contain keying material. A and B calculate their new shared key as a function of the keying material F_A and F_B. The standard permits either F_A or F_B to be null; however if both F_A and F_B are used, then the properties required for the function used to combine them mean that neither entity has key control.

TTP-aided authenticated key establishment using nonces

Mechanism 9 (a nonce-based key distribution mechanism) is based on the 5-pass authentication protocol in clause 6.2 of ISO/IEC 9798-2. Note that, in this protocol, T is a third party (a KDC) trusted by both A and B. Moreover T shares the secret keys KAT and KBT with A and B respectively. The mechanism provides *mutual authentication* between A and B. The KDC has *key control*.

The mechanism has five message passes:

$B \rightarrow A$: R_B

$A \rightarrow T$: $R_A \mid\mid R_B \mid\mid B$

$T \rightarrow A$: $e_{KAT}(R_A \mid\mid F \mid\mid B \mid\mid \text{Text1}) \mid\mid e_{KBT}(R_B \mid\mid F \mid\mid A \mid\mid \text{Text2})$

$A \rightarrow B$: $e_{KBT}(R_B \mid\mid F \mid\mid A \mid\mid \text{Text2}) \mid\mid e_K(R'_A \mid\mid R_B \mid\mid \text{Text3})$

$B \rightarrow A$: $e_K(R_B \mid\mid R'_A \mid\mid \text{Text4})$

K is the new shared key generated by T, and it is contained in the keying material field F. R_A, R_B and R'_A are nonces.

TTP-aided Authenticated Key Establishment Using Timestamps

Mechanism 12 (a timestamp-based key distribution mechanism) is based on, but is not fully compatible with, the 4-pass authentication protocol in clause 6.1 of ISO/IEC 9798-2. Note that, in this protocol, T is a third party (a KTC) trusted by both A and B. Moreover T shares the secret keys KAT and KBT with A and B respectively. T, A and B must also maintain synchronised clocks or sequence numbers. The mechanism provides *mutual authentication* between A and B. Entity A has *key control*.

The mechanism has four message passes:

$A \rightarrow T$: $e_{KAT}(TVP_A \mid\mid B \mid\mid F \mid\mid \text{Text1})$

$T \rightarrow A$: $e_{KAT}(TVP_A \mid\mid B \mid\mid \text{Text2}) \mid\mid e_{KBT}(T_T/N_T \mid\mid F \mid\mid A \mid\mid \text{Text3})$

$A \rightarrow B$: $e_{KBT}(T_T/N_T \mid\mid F \mid\mid A \mid\mid \text{Text3}) \mid\mid e_K(T_A/N_A \mid\mid B \mid\mid \text{Text4})$

$B \rightarrow A$: $e_K(T_B/N_B \mid\mid A \mid\mid \text{Text5})$

TVP_A is a time variant parameter (random number, timestamp or sequence number) chosen by A and used by A to match the response from T with the request to T (it is not checked by T). T_X/N_X denotes either a timestamp T_X or a sequence number N_X generated by entity X.

K is the new shared key generated by A, and it is contained in the keying material field F.

Key Establishment Using Asymmetric Techniques

ISO/IEC 11770-3 (ISO, 1999f) defines key establishment mechanisms based on asymmetric cryptographic techniques. It provides mechanisms using asymmetric techniques to agree to a shared secret key between two entities (seven key agreement mechanisms), transport a secret key from one entity to another (six key transport mechanisms), and make an entity's public key available to other entities in a verifiable way (three public key transport mechanisms). The first two types of mechanism include uses of some of the protocols defined in ISO/IEC 9798-3 (ISO, 1998b), but also include a variety of other asymmetric techniques (e.g., Diffie-Hellman key exchange). The third type of mechanism includes the use of certificates.

The seven key agreement mechanisms specified in ISO/IEC 11770-3 all make use of a 'mathematical context', which essentially means the pre-agreement by the relevant parties (A and B) of a readily computed function F with certain very special properties. More specifically:

$F: H \times G \rightarrow G$,

where G and H are sets. F satisfies:

- $F(h, F(h', g)) = F(h', F(h, g))$ for every $h, h' \in H$ and every $g \in G$, and
- Given $F(h, g)$, $F(h', g)$ and g it is computationally infeasible to find $F(h, F(h', g))$. Among other things this implies that $F(\cdot, g)$ is one-way, for every g.

A and B must share a common element $g \in G$ (which may be public).

One example of a candidate for F provided in ISO/IEC 11770-3 is the discrete logarithm mechanism which underlies Diffie-Hellman key exchange, namely: $G = Z_p$ (the integers modulo p for some prime p), $H = \{ 1, 2, \dots , p\text{-}2 \}$, g is a primitive element from Z_p, and $F(h, g) = g^h$ mod p. Note that, on this case, the prime number p needs to be chosen with care.

Key Agreement with Mutual Implicit Key Authentication

This example is specified in ISO/IEC 11770-3 as 'Key agreement mechanism 5'. If entities A and B wish to use this mechanism to

establish a new shared secret key, then:
- Entity A must have a private key $h_A \in H$ known only to A and a public key $p_A = F(h_A, g)$ known to B,
- Entity B must have a private key $h_B \in H$ known only to B and a public key $p_B = F(h_B, g)$ known to A.

This mechanism provides mutual implicit key authentication, but does not, however, allow A and B to choose the value or form of K_{AB} in advance, i.e. neither A nor B has key control. Hence, this mechanism is inappropriate for systems where the key needs to have a special form - in such a case a *key transport* mechanism needs to be used. Prior to starting the mechanism, A chooses a random (secret) $r_A \in H$, and B chooses a random (secret) $r_B \in H$. The protocol is simply:

$A \rightarrow B$: $F(r_A, g)$ || Text1
$B \rightarrow A$: $F(r_B, g)$ || Text2

After receipt of the first message, B computes the shared secret key as

$$K_{AB} = w(\, F(h_B, F(r_A, g)), F(r_B, p_A)\,),$$

and after receipt of the second message A computes the shared secret key as

$$K_{AB} = w(\, F(r_A, p_B), F(h_A, F(r_B, g))\,),$$

where w denotes an (unspecified) commonly agreed one-way function.

Key Transport with Mutual Authentication

Transport Mechanism 5 (a nonce-based key transport mechanism) is based on the 3-pass authentication protocol in clause 5.2.2 of ISO/IEC 9798-3. Note that, in this protocol:
- A, B have signing/verification transform pairs (S_A, V_A) and (S_B, V_B) respectively. Both parties must have access to each other's public verification transformation.
- A, B have encrypt/decrypt transform pairs (E_A, D_A) and (E_B, D_B) respectively. Both parties must have access to each other's public encipherment transformation.

The mechanism provides *mutual authentication* and optional *key confirmation* to B. Two keys are established (one transported in each direction).

The mechanism has three message passes:

$$A \rightarrow B: r_A \mid\mid \text{Text1}$$
$$B \rightarrow A: S_B(r_B \mid\mid r_A \mid\mid A \mid\mid E_A(B \mid\mid K_B \mid\mid \text{Text2}) \mid\mid \text{Text3})$$
$$\mid\mid \text{Text4}$$
$$A \rightarrow B: S_A(r_A \mid\mid r_B \mid\mid B \mid\mid E_B(A \mid\mid K_A \mid\mid \text{Text5}) \mid\mid \text{Text6})$$
$$\mid\mid \text{Text7}$$

r_A, r_B denote nonces. The keys K_A and K_B are established between A and B. For key confirmation to B, user A can include a check-value computed on K_B in Text6. Mutual key control can be achieved by combining the two keys K_A and K_B using a one-way function, yielding a key agreement mechanism.

OTHER STANDARDS

A multi-part standard specifying security mechanisms based on elliptic curves, ISO/IEC 15946, is at an early stage of development.
- *Part 1* contains mathematical background on elliptic curves.
- *Part 2* covers elliptic curve signatures.
- *Part 3* covers elliptic curve key establishment techniques.

A further new area for standardisation currently being investigated within SC27/WG2 concerns methods for key generation. Whilst this is potentially an extremely important area, no substantive document exists as yet.

REFERENCES

ANSI. (1981). ANSI X3.92. American National Standard – Data Encryption Algorithm. American National Standards Institute.

ANSI. (1983). ANSI X3.106, American National Standard for Information Systems – Data Encryption Algorithm – Modes of Operation. American National Standards Institute.

ANSI. (1986a). ANSI X9.9 (revised), American National Standard – Financial institution message authentication (wholesale). American Bankers Association.

ANSI. (1986b). ANSI X9.19, American National Standard – Financial institution retail message authentication. American Bankers Association.

CCITT. (1988). X.509, The Directory – Authentication Framework. CCITT.

FIPS. (1980). FIPS 81, DES Modes of Operation. National Bureau of Standards.

FIPS. (1993). FIPS 46, Data Encryption Standard. National Bureau of Standards, (FIPS 46-2: 2nd revision).

FIPS. (1994). FIPS 186, Digital signature standard. National Institute of Standards and Technology.

FIPS. (1995). FIPS 180-1, Secure hash standard. National Institute of Standards and Technology, 1st revision.

ISO. (1986). ISO 8730, Banking – Requirements for message authentication (wholesale). International Organization for Standardization.

ISO. (1987a). ISO 8372, Information processing – Modes of operation for a 64-bit block cipher algorithm. International Organization for Standardization.

ISO. (1987b). ISO 8731-1, Banking – Approved algorithms for message authentication – Part 1: DEA. International Organization for Standardization.

ISO. (1989). ISO 7498-2, Information processing systems – Open Systems Interconnection – Basic reference model – Part 2: Security architecture. International Organization for Standardization.

ISO. (1991). ISO/IEC 9796, Information technology – Security techniques – Digital signature scheme giving message recovery. International Organization for Standardization.

ISO. (1992). ISO 8731-2, Banking – Approved algorithms for message authentication – Part 2: Message authenticator algorithm. International Organization for Standardization, 2nd edition.

ISO. (1994a). ISO/IEC 9797, Information technology – Security techniques – Data integrity mechanism using a cryptographic check function employing a block cipher algorithm. International Organization for Standardization, 2nd edition.

ISO. (1994b). ISO/IEC 9798-2, Information technology - Security techniques - Entity authentication - Part 2: Mechanisms using symmetric encipherment algorithms. International Organization for Standardization.

ISO. (1994c). ISO/IEC 10118-1, Information technology – Security techniques – Hash-functions – Part 1: General. International Organization for Standardization.

ISO. (1994d). ISO/IEC 10118-2, Information technology – Security techniques – Hash-functions – Part 2: Hash-functions using an n-bit block cipher algorithm. International Organization for Standardization.

ISO. (1995). ISO/IEC 9798-4, Information technology - Security techniques - Entity authentication - Part 4: Mechanisms using a cryptographic check function. International Organization for Standardization.

ISO. (1996a). ISO/IEC 10181 Parts 2 to 6, Information technology – Open Systems Interconnection – Security frameworks for open systems. International Organization for Standardization.

ISO. (1996b). ISO/IEC 11770-1, Information technology - Security techniques - Key management - Part 1: Framework. International Organization for Standardization.

ISO. (1996c). ISO/IEC 11770-2, Information technology - Security techniques - Key management - Part 2: Mechanisms using symmetric techniques. International Organization for Standardization.

ISO. (1997a). ISO/IEC 9796-2, Information technology – Security techniques – Digital signature schemes giving message recovery – Part 2: mechanisms using a hash-function. International Organization for Standardization.

ISO. (1997b). ISO/IEC 9798-1, Information technology - Security techniques - Entity authentication - Part 1: General. International Organization for Standardization, 2nd edition.

ISO. (1997c). ISO/IEC 10116, Information technology – Security techniques – Modes of operation for an n-bit block cipher. International Organization for Standardization, 2nd edition.

ISO. (1997d). ISO/IEC 13888-1, Information technology – Security techniques – Non-repudiation – Part 1: General. International Organization for Standardization.

ISO. (1997e). ISO/IEC 13888-3, Information technology – Security techniques – Non-repudiation – Part 3: Mechanisms using asymmetric techniques. International Organization for Standardization.

ISO. (1998a). ISO/IEC CD 9797-2, Information technology – Security techniques – Message Authentication Codes (MACs) – Part 2: Mechanisms using a hash-function. International Organization for Standardization.

ISO. (1998b). ISO/IEC 9798-3, Information technology - Security techniques - Entity authentication mechanisms - Part 3: Mechanisms using digital signature techniques. International Organization for Standardization, 2nd edition.

ISO. (1998c). ISO/IEC 10118-3, Information technology – Security techniques – Hash-functions – Part 3: Dedicated hash-functions. International Organization for Standardization.

ISO. (1998d). ISO/IEC 10118-4, Information technology – Security techniques – Hash-functions – Part 4: Hash-functions using modular arithmetic. International Organization for Standardization.

ISO. (1998e). ISO/IEC 13888-2, Information technology – Security techniques – Non-repudiation – Part 2: Mechanisms using symmetric techniques. International Organization for Standardization.

ISO. (1998f). ISO/IEC 14888-1, Information technology – Security techniques – Digital signatures with appendix – Part 1: General. International Organization for Standardization.

ISO. (1998g). ISO/IEC FDIS 14888-2, Information technology – Security techniques – Digital signatures with appendix – Part 2: Identity-based mechanisms. International Organization for Standardization.

ISO. (1998h). ISO/IEC 14888-3, Information technology – Security techniques – Digital signatures with appendix – Part 3: Certificate-based mechanisms. International Organization for Standardization.

ISO. (1999a). ISO/IEC DIS 9594-8, Information technology – Open Systems Interconnection – The Directory – Part 8: Authentication framework. International Organization for Standardization.

ISO. (1999b). ISO/IEC FCD 9796-3, Information technology – Security techniques – Digital signature schemes giving message recovery – Part 3: Discrete logarithm based mechanisms. International Organization for Standardization.

ISO. (1999c). ISO/IEC FDIS 9797-1, Information technology – Security techniques – Message Authentication Codes (MACs) – Part 1: Mechanisms using a block cipher. International Organization for Standardization.

ISO. (1999d). ISO/IEC 9798-5, Information technology - Security techniques - Entity authentication - Part 5: mechanisms using zero knowledge techniques. International Organization for Standardization.

ISO. (1999e). ISO/IEC 9979, Information technology – Security techniques – Procedures for the registration of cryptographic algorithms. International Organization for Standardization, 2nd edition.

ISO. (1999f). ISO/IEC 11770-3, Information technology - Security techniques - Key management - Part 3: Mechanisms using asymmetric techniques. International Organization for Standardization.

ITU. (1997). X.509, Information technology – Open Systems Interconnection – The Directory – Authentication Framework. ITU-T, 3rd edition.

Lamport, L. (1978). Time, clocks, and the ordering of events in a distributed system. Communications of the ACM **21**:558–565.

Menezes, A.J., van Oorschot, P.C., and Vanstone, S.A. (1997). *Handbook of Applied Cryptography*. CRC Press.

RFC. (1997). RFC 2104, HMAC: Keyed hashing for message authentication. Internet Request for Comments 2104, H. Krawczyk, M. Bellare and R. Canetti.

Part IV

Security and the Law

Chapter IX

Electronic Mail, Employee Privacy and the Workplace

Charles Prysby
University of North Carolina, USA

Nicole Prysby
Attorney at Law, Virginia, USA

Electronic mail (e-mail) has become increasingly important in the workplace. The growth of this new medium of communication has generated important legal questions about the privacy and monitoring of e-mail messages, so much so that most experts strongly recommend that organizations adopt explicit policies about e-mail for their own legal protection. The legal questions concerning e-mail in the workplace include both: (a) employee rights to privacy regarding e-mail messages; and (b) employee obligations to monitor e-mail to ensure a suitable workplace or to prevent illegal behavior. We discuss both of these topics in this chapter, attempting not only to outline current legal thinking in the area, but also to raise questions that managers and policy makers should consider.

It is worth noting at the start that many of the legal issues surrounding the use of e-mail are direct extensions of principles that apply to other forms of communications. Indeed, much of the law that governs e-mail is not legislation that was written explicitly to cover this particular form of communication. Issues of the privacy of employee e-mail messages, for example, are directly analogous to issues of the privacy of employee phone calls or written correspondence. To be sure, there are questions about exactly how legal principles that were established for older communication technologies should be applied to a new one, and perhaps not all of these questions are fully settled at this point in time, but our understanding of this topic is broadened if we appreciate the application of legal principles across communication media.

PRIVACY ISSUES AND BELIEFS

Many employees probably believe that their e-mail messages should be private. Most employees probably also have thought for a long time that it would be highly inappropriate for supervisors to listen to their phone conversations at work—except perhaps for the monitoring of employees who primarily handle public phone calls, such as tax department workers responding to taxpayer questions. Similarly, most employees undoubtedly would be upset if their employer opened and read their personal correspondence. By extension, employees may also feel that e-mail falls into the same category and that supervisors should not be reading their e-mail without permission, except in certain narrowly defined cases. Many employees undoubtedly use their work e-mail system to send personal messages, both internally and externally, or they may mix personal and professional items in the same message, in much the same way that both may be mixed together in a phone conversation with a colleague. Employees may believe that they are entitled to privacy in these matters, and the fact that passwords are required to access their computer accounts, and thus their e-mail, may be considered confirmation of this belief (Dixon, 1997; Greengard, 1996).

Regardless of what many employees might believe should be the case, their legal right to privacy is quite limited when it comes to e-mail messages. The possible basis for a right to privacy of e-mail messages from the scrutiny of the employer might come from several sources. First of all, the Fourth Amendment prohibits the government from unreasonable searches and seizures, and this restricts public (but not private) sector employers. Second, federal legislation, most notably the Federal Electronic Communications Privacy Act of 1986, provides some protection for communications. Third, many states may have their own constitutional and statutory provisions, which may even go beyond what the U.S. Constitution or federal laws stipulate. Finally, under common law an individual may assert a tort claim for invasion of privacy. However, the application of the above legal and constitutional principles to workplace e-mail is extremely limited, as we shall see.

The various legal protections of an individual's privacy stem from general societal beliefs that individuals are entitled to privacy. Unwanted intrusion into an individual's personal affairs violates the respect and dignity to which an individual is entitled (Adelman and Kennedy, 1995: xiii). The concept of privacy is a complex one that is not easily captured with a simple definition. Doss and Loui (1995) argue that the philosophical concept of privacy has at least three aspects: confidentiality, anonymity, and solitude, the first two of which are relevant for this discussion. Confidentiality refers to the right to keep personal information private. Anonymity refers to the absence of unwanted attention. Solitude refers to a lack of intrusion upon a person's physical seclusion, which does not appear to apply to workplace e-mail. Confidentiality and anonymity do apply when individuals send communications (via e-mail, telephone calls, or surface mail) that are for the intended recipient only. When a third party intercepts such a communication without permission, one or both individuals suffer a loss of confidentiality, because personal or private information is divulged to others, and a loss of anonymity, as they now are the subject of undesired attention (Doss and Loui, 1995). Of course, putting these general philosophical principles into a workable legal framework can be difficult.

FOURTH AMENDMENT PROTECTIONS

The Fourth Amendment protects citizens against unreasonable searches by government officials, a protection that extends to unreasonable searches of public employees by their employers. Since federal, state, and local government employees constitute about one-sixth of the labor force, this protection is relevant for a large number of employees. However, the Fourth Amendment provides only limited protection in this situation. One limitation on the application of the Fourth Amendment stems from the legal principle that an employee has no valid objection to a search by the employer unless the employee has a reasonable expectation of privacy in the situation (White, 1997). This legal principle applies not just to e-mail, but to other aspects of the workplace. For example, the employee may or may not have a reasonable expectation of privacy regarding his or her desk drawers or file cabinets. In one case, the U.S. Supreme Court ruled that a public hospital employee did have a reasonable expectation of privacy regarding the desk and file cabinets in his office (*O'Conner v. Ortega*). The Court also said, however, that such expectations would have to be determined on a case-by-case basis, depending on the particular facts of each case (Cole, 1997).

The determination of whether a reasonable expectation of privacy exists would depend on a variety of factors, including the context of the search, the uses to which the searched area is put, and the societal expectation of the extent to which the area deserves protection from governmental intrusion. For example, an expectation of privacy in an office might be reduced by actual office practices, including broad access to co-workers (Jenero and Mapes-Riordan, 1992). In one case, *Simmons v. Southwestern Bell Telephone Company*, a deskman at a phone company's test center was subject to monitoring of all calls he made from the testboard telephones. The employee was aware that the telephones were monitored and that other telephones were available for personal calls and were not monitored. Although the court dismissed the Fourth Amendment claim because the telephone company was a private employer, the court did note in dicta that under the circumstances, the employee would have no reasonable expectation of privacy in the calls made from the testboard telephone. The court did state, however, that it would have found a violation of the Fourth Amendment if the company had been a public employer and had monitored the employee's calls from the telephones designated for personal calls (Jenero and Mapes-Riordan, 1992).

Some commentators suggest that an employee would have no reasonable expectation of privacy in e-mail messages because most people would realize that the system administrator has access to individual employees' e-mail messages (Lee, 1994). In addition, if the employer has publicized a policy providing that e-mail may be subject to monitoring, the employee will have assumed the risk that his e-mails are subject to searching. Furthermore, even if a password is required to log on to a computer, if the employee's supervisor or the network administrator knows the password, the employee would not have a reasonable expectation of privacy, even for files that were stored in a location requiring the password (Dawes and Dallas, 1997). Therefore, it is likely that in many situations, there would be no reasonable expectation of privacy.

Even if the employee is able to assert a reasonable expectation of privacy, the employer may still have a right to read the employee's e-mail messages, as the Fourth Amendment only prohibits unreasonable searches. The Supreme Court ruled in *O'Conner* that even though the employee had a reasonable expectation of privacy regarding his file cabinets and desk drawers, the employer nevertheless had a right to search these locations because the search was not unreasonable (Cole, 1997; Cozzetto and Pedeliski, 1997). The general rule is that a search must be reasonable both at its inception and in its scope. A search is reasonable at its inception if there are reasonable grounds to suspect that it would turn up evidence of work-related misconduct or if it is necessary for a noninvestigatory work related purpose. A search is reasonable in its scope if the extent of the search is reasonably related to the accomplishment of the objectives of the search (Jenero and Mapes-Riordan 1992).

While the *O'Conner* case did not involve e-mail, the principles are clearly extendable. An employer's search of an employee's files is reasonable if the employer has a necessity or valid business reason to conduct the search (Cole, 1997; White, 1997). This necessity would be indicated in a variety of circumstances. One situation would be where the employer needs to retrieve information to conduct business, such as if an important message must be obtained from an absent employee's electronic mailbox. Another possibility would be a situation where an employee was suspected of violating organizational policies or otherwise engaging in inappropriate or even illegal conduct, and where searching the individual's e-mail might reasonably provide the employer with evidence pertaining to the suspected activity. In order for the search to be reasonable, the employer must also conduct the search in a fashion that is designed to obtain the information without unnecessarily intruding into the individual's privacy (Cole, 1997).

STATE PROTECTIONS

State and local public employees also can claim privacy rights under applicable state constitutional provisions or state statutes, which also might apply to private sector employees. Some states have privacy clauses in their constitutions, and most states have statutes that protect privacy in personal communications (Fitzpatrick, 1997; White, 1997). Between 1968 and 1980, eight states amended their constitutions to add an explicit right to privacy. In five of the states (Arkansas, California, Florida, Hawaii, and Montana), the privacy guarantee was broadly drawn (Tarr, 1998: 207-208). For example the Florida constitution states that every person "has the right to be let alone and free from governmental intrusion into the person's private life except as otherwise provided herein," and the Hawaiian constitution states that the "right of the people to privacy is recognized and shall not be infringed without the showing of a compelling state interest" (Rodriquez, 1998). These provisions provide public employees with some protection against employee monitoring of their e-mail. Moreover, the California constitutional provision has been interpreted by the courts to apply to private employers as well (Rodriquez, 1998). In *Hill v. NCAA*, the California Supreme Court stated that a balancing test should be applied, in which the privacy interest of the employee should be weighed against legitimate interests of the employer, which is similar to the Fourth Amendment "reasonableness" test discussed above.

In recent years, some states have added legislation to deal specifically with electronic communications and/or unauthorized access to computer systems (see Perritt, 1996, and Rodriquez, 1998, for a state-by-state summary of such legislation). Several states have legislation prohibiting unauthorized access to computer systems or data, which presumably would cover e-mail. (for example, see Cal. Penal Code § 502, Conn. Gen. Stat. Ann. § 53a-251, Iowa Code Ann. § 716A.2, S.C. Code Ann. § 16-16-20). However, these statutes are not specifically written for the protection of employees, and it is unclear if they could even be enforced against an employer. The statutes generally refer to the owner of the system as the enforcer of the law; because the employer is almost certain to be the system owner, employees would probably not be able to use these statutes.

Nebraska, however, does have a specific employer-employee monitoring statute. Under the Nebraska statute, an employer, on the business premises, may intercept, disclose, or use electronic monitoring in the normal course of employment. The employer may not randomly monitor employees unless notice of the policy is given to the employees (Neb. Rev. Stat. § 86-702). Similarly, Colorado employers who maintain an e-mail system are required to adopt a policy on the monitoring of e-mail, including the circumstances under which monitoring may take place (Dawes and Dallas, 1997; Col. Rev. Stat. Ann. § 24-72-204.5). Connecticut law also requires public and private employers to give prior written notice to employees, informing them of the type of monitoring of their e-mail that make take place (Walker, 1999a).

Adding statutory protections for employee e-mail privacy may be controversial in many states. For example, in California, the legislature passed a bill in 1999 that would have prohibited employers from inspecting or reviewing any personal electronic mail without the consent of the employee, but the governor vetoed the bill, stating that it would be an undue regulatory burden on businesses (Davis, 1999). Among other things, the governor argued that there was likely to be undesirable controversy over whether proper notification was provided to the employee. Furthermore, the governor stated that employees should understand that computers provided by the employer are for business purposes and may be monitored by the employer, particularly because employers have a legitimate need to monitor e-mail to prevent improper, inappropriate, or even illegal behavior.

TORT LAW PROTECTIONS

Finally, employees, public or private, may be able to assert a violation of privacy under common law if their e-mail is monitored by their employer. Tort law varies from state to state, but in most states it is now recognized that violation of privacy torts do apply to employment situations (Fitpatrick, 1997). Invasion of privacy is a tort with four possible causes of action, two of which might apply to e-mail. The first would be an intrusion into affairs that an individual has a right to keep private, by a method objectionable to the reasonable person; the second would be a public disclosure of private matters, where the disclosure is highly offensive and not of public concern (Perritt, 1996: 93).

The reasonable expectation of privacy is an essential element in common law tort claims, just as it is in cases asserting constitutional (federal or state) protections. An employee cannot claim that his or her privacy has been invaded if there was no reasonable expectation of privacy in the employment situation. With regard to e-mail at work, privacy expectations have been very narrowly defined by the courts. First of all, if the employer has a written statement that e-mail messages may be monitored, which many employers do have, the employee probably will find it very difficult to claim an expectation of privacy. Even in the absence of a written statement, it may still be difficult for an employee to assert a reasonable expectation. In fact, in one case involving a private company, *Smyth v. Pillsbury Co.*, the court ruled against an employee who sued his employer for wrongful discharge following his firing, which was based on information gathered by the employer through reading his e-mail. The court's decision was that the employee had no reasonable expectation of privacy despite the fact that the employer had assured employees that their e-mail messages were considered confidential items (Farber, 1997; White, 1997).

Several important cases have reaffirmed the employer's right to inspect employee e-mail. In a well-known case, *Shoars v. Epson*, an employee claimed that her employer wrongfully terminated her after she complained that her supervisor was reading employee e-mail (Adelman and Kennedy, 1995: 310-315). Her attorney also filed a companion class action invasion of privacy lawsuit, *Flanigan v. Epson*. The California Superior Court rejected the invasion of privacy claim, stating that the California statute protecting privacy of communications did not extend to e-mail at work (Adelman and Kennedy, 1995: 315). In *Bourke v. Nissan Motor Co.*, two employees sued their employer because they were terminated after their supervisor read their e-mail message and found that they had been making fun of him, but the court rejected their argument that the company had violated their privacy (Cozzetto and Pedeliski, 1997). In *Bohach v. City of Reno*, the court rejected any claim of a reasonable expectation of privacy on the part of police personnel using the departmental computer system (Bramsco, 1997).

However, at least one court has recognized a cause of action for invasion of privacy based on the employer's reading of employee e-mail (*Restuccia v. Burk Technologies, Inc.*). The *Restuccia* case involved a supervisor who read subordinates' e-mail and discovered that they had a variety of nicknames for him and that they were aware of his extramarital affair. The employees were terminated, and they then filed a lawsuit claiming, among other things, invasion of privacy and wrongful discharge in violation of the public policy against invasion of privacy. The court found that there were issues of fact as to whether the employees had a reasonable expectation of privacy in their e-mail messages and whether the reading of the messages constituted an unreasonable, substantial, or serious interference with the employees' privacy. The ruling was based on a Massachusetts statute that guarantees a right to privacy and contains language analogous to that found in a common law cause of action. To date, other courts have not followed the *Restuccia* decision.

From the limited number of cases that have been decided, it appears that employees may have fewer privacy rights for e-mail than for other forms of communications. This difference may be explained in part by the fact that the employee is using the employer's computer system, and therefore the employer may be regarded as having a right to monitor what is transmitted on the system. The argument is that if the employer owns the computer, then the employer should be able to read what is stored on the computer. In most cases the employer can do so very easily and surreptitiously, making the action perhaps seem less intrusive than opening personal mail, for example. Moreover, since the e-mail messages generally are stored in a common location, such as on a network server, the employee cannot regard them in the same light as personal items stored in a desk drawer in one's office. In addition, actual knowledge that the system is not private may be inferred. For example, the *Bourke* court cited the fact that the plaintiffs knew that their e-mail was occasionally read by individuals other than the sender and recipient as evidence that the plaintiffs had no reasonable expectation of privacy.

It also may be that the relatively newness of e-mail means that social conventions have not firmly developed in this area. While most people would regard listening in on another person's phone conversation as very impolite, perhaps the same social stigma is not attached to the reading of someone else's e-mail (Doss and Loui, 1995). Societal perceptions are important because for recovery under most privacy common law an intrusion, even if regarded as outside usual social norms, must usually be shown to be "highly offensive" to a reasonable person.

THE ELECTRONIC COMMUNICATIONS PRIVACY ACT

The Federal Electronic Communications Privacy Act (ECPA), enacted by Congress in 1986, is the most recent attempt by Congress to legislate in this area. The ECPA attempted to extend the legal restrictions on wiretapping of phone conversations to electronic communications, providing both criminal and civil penalties for illegal interception and disclosure of protected communications (Perritt, 1996). However, the legislative history of the ECPA suggests that Congress did not intend to restrict employers from reading the e-mail of employees (Cole, 1997; Cozzetto and Pedeliski, 1997).

First of all, ECPA does not prohibit the monitoring of communications in situations where one of the parties consents (Cole, 1997; White, 1997). Thus, if an employer has a policy stating that e-mail will be monitored, which employees were aware of and at least implicitly agreed to, that alone would appear to provide legal justification for reading of employee e-mail. However, there are employment situations where the implied consent might be questioned. For example, in a case involving telephone monitoring (*Watkins v. L. M. Berry & Co.*), the court ruled that the employee had not given consent for the monitoring of personal calls; the employer could intercept the calls to determine if they were personal or business calls, but once it was determined that they were personal, monitoring was no longer permitted (Cole, 1997; Cozzetto and Pedeliski, 1997; White, 1997).

Similarly, another court found that an employer violated the ECPA by listening to all of the personal telephone calls of an employee that were tape recorded by the employer, even though the employee was suspected of theft and the employer therefore had a legitimate reason for monitoring (Greenberg, 1994, citing *Deal v. Spears*). Still, even the absence of clear consent on the part of the employee does not guarantee e-mail privacy, as other provisions of the ECPA may provide employers with broad rights in this area.

The ECPA includes a business exemption, which essentially states that the provider of the communications system being used by employees in the ordinary course of business, which almost always will be the employer in the case of e-mail systems, has a right to intercept messages, at least if there is a legitimate business purpose for doing so (Cole, 1997; White, 1997).   Moreover, the ECPA also distinguishes between intercepting a communication and accessing a stored communication, providing more latitude for the latter. This is particularly applicable to e-mail, which almost always would be accessed by the employer from stored files, rather than during transmission. Specifically, the ECPA states that restrictions on the reading of stored files do not apply to the provider of the electronic communications service (Bramesco, 1997; Cole, 1997; Perritt, 1996: 109-110). Thus, any employer who owns the computer network in which the employee e-mail messages reside could cite both the general employer-owned system exemption and the stored communications provision. The combination of these would appear to confer a very broad right to read stored e-mail, at least as far as federal law is concerned.

While internal e-mail messages usually travel and are stored on the organization's own computer system, external messages might be in a different category. An external e-mail message traveling over the Internet would appear to fall under the jurisdiction of the ECPA, which prohibits third party interception of electronic communications traveling over public networks. Whether the employer could intercept the message after it arrived on the local system, presumably owned by the employer, without violating the ECPA is unclear. However, if the employer accesses the message after it has been stored on the local system, the "stored communications" principle, discussed above, probably would apply, thus permitting employer reading of employee e-mail, even that which came from external sources over public lines. At this point, the law appears unclear on this matter (Perritt, 1996: 110). In one case (*U.S. v. Simons*), the court found that e-mail obtained from an employee's hard drive was copied while in storage and was not an interception. Using that logic, because e-mail is often stored on a server or hard drive almost instantaneously from the time of sending, it would appear that for e-mail cases, the interception clause would almost never apply, and from a practical standpoint, all e-mail could be accessed by the employer (Wigod, 1998). However, in another case (*U.S. v. Smith*), a person's act of retrieving a voice mail message from someone else's voice mailbox and recording was found by a court to be covered by the interception, not storage clause, under the ECPA.

While the employer may be able to read the employee's e-mail, the ECPA clearly prohibits outside third parties from doing so. The same rule generally applies to state wiretap statutes. A private third party who surreptitiously accessed an e-mail conversation between two individuals would be guilty of criminal conduct, just as if that person tapped the phone conversation between two individuals. However, many experts feel that even in these cases the ECPA provides little real protection against such actions. Computer hackers are capable of breaking into the computer network of an organization and accessing stored files, including stored e-mail, perhaps far more so than people suspect (Behar, 1997). Many individuals undoubtedly feel that such a threat is extremely remote, in large part because they have nothing in their stored e-mail files that would be of interest to an outside individual. But as one expert puts it, a hacker "has to learn how to hack, and will start off by breaking into a computer system that is relatively easy to break into" (Garcia, 1996). Organizations often feel that e-mail messages do not contain the kind of sensitive information that requires elaborate security measures, so e-mail files may be left more vulnerable to external hackers than other computer files (Garcia, 1996). Hackers may often operate without great fear, either because they believe there is little chance that they will be caught, or because they do not believe that they will be severely penalized if apprehended.

While many observers have noted the limitations of the ECPA in this area, there has been little subsequent effort at the federal level to provide privacy protection for employee e-mail. One attempt, legislation entitled the Privacy for Consumers and Workers Act (PCWA), was introduced into Congress in the early 1990s (Schnaitman, 1999; Wilborn, 1998). The PCWA attempted to protect employees from secret electronic monitoring in the workplace. The law would have allowed employers to monitor employee e-mail, but only after informing employees of the scope and form of the monitoring and the intended use of the information collected in the course of monitoring (Schnaitman, 1999). The legislation failed to pass either house of Congress, however. Some experts believe that federal legislation even stronger than the proposed PCWA is needed. Gantt (1995) argues that federal law should provide public and private sector employees with privacy rights that would be limited only when the employer has a compelling business interest in monitoring workplace e-mail.

CONCLUDING POINTS ON EMPLOYEE PRIVACY

While recent court cases involving the monitoring of workplace e-mail have almost always upheld the right of the employer to engage in such monitoring, it would be a mistake to conclude that there are no restrictions on the extent and nature of this monitoring. The cases that have been decided have usually involved monitoring that was in some way job-related. The employer was capable of making an argument that the monitoring was necessary for business purposes. Furthermore, it should be noted that in many of these cases, the employee had engaged in some sort of inappropriate or illegal behavior toward which most people would be unsympathetic. For example, the *Smyth* employee had communicated unprofessional comments over the company e-mail system, and the court noted that the comments were voluntarily communicated (as opposed to a forced disclosure, such as a property search) and that the employer's interest in preventing inappropriate or illegal activity over its e-mail system outweighed any privacy rights the employee may have had in the messages. It is not at all clear that the courts would rule that an employer had the right to routinely read the personal e-mail messages of an individual when there was no good reason to believe that the contents of the messages were in any way job-related (Cozzetto and Pedeliski, 1997).

While employers have broad power to read the e-mail of their employees, there may be political restrictions on such behavior when it comes to the public sector. What might be tolerated if carried out in a private company could be seen as objectionable if it occurred in a public organization. There may be more concern on the part of the public, or the media, or elected officials, to the monitoring of e-mail in public agencies. Public universities in particular tend to stress the privacy of individual e-mail (Doss and Loui, 1995). Even though the courts might rule otherwise, there may be widespread perceptions that the Fourth Amendment prohibits e-mail monitoring of public employees, except in carefully defined situations, and these beliefs may impose practical limits on such monitoring.

It should, of course, be understood that nothing prevents the recipient of an e-mail communication from divulging its contents. An individual has no reasonable expectation of privacy regarding information communicated to another person, except in some narrowly defined situations of "privileged" communications, such as between an individual and his or her attorney (Garcia, 1996). The recipient of the message is free to tell anyone, including law enforcement officials, about its contents (Sundstrom, 1998). In the case of e-mail, this could include forwarding the message to others, a common practice. All of our discussion of possible privacy rights concerns the situation where the employer or supervisor accesses an employee's e-mail message to someone else without the permission of one of the two parties directly involved in the communication.

Moreover, if the recipient of an e-mail message chooses to divulge its contents to third parties, those parties are equally free to disseminate the message to others. Even if the third parties received the message from the original recipient with the understanding that they would keep it confidential, they are not bound by statutory or tort law to maintain secrecy. Again, with the power to easily forward e-mail to many individuals, the divulgence of messages is a very real possibility.

Finally, the public has some right to see the e-mail messages in a public agency, and this may impinge on employee privacy. At the federal level, the 1982 Freedom of Information Act (FOIA) outlines the public's right to access written materials and documents, and e-mail communications are included in this category (Garson, 1995: 77-79). At the state level, public access will depend on the specifics of state legislation. Many states have freedom of information acts that provide for even more public access to e-mail than does the federal FOIA (Prysby and Prysby, 1999).

The FOIA stipulates that federal agencies must make public records available when requested. Government reports, notices, bulletins, newsletters, publications, and policy statements would be considered public documents. Exemptions are made for information defined as private or confidential, which would include certain aspects of personnel records, proprietary data contained in government contracts or proposals, certain criminal records, and so on. Most of the exemptions are the usual and familiar ones. Also included in the exemptions are internal communications prior to a policy decision (Garson, 1995: 78). Thus, while a policy is being discussed within an agency, the employees are free to send messages to each other, either written or via e-mail, expressing thoughts about various aspects or implications of some possible policy, and those messages are not considered part of the public record. The exemption is designed to protect only those materials bearing on the formulation or exercise of policy-oriented judgment; peripheral documents are not protected (*Ethyl Corporation v. U.S. E.P.A.*). To meet the exemption, the agency would need to show that the document in question is (1) predecisional and (2) deliberative (*City of Virginia Beach v. U.S. Department of Commerce*).

Depending on how this exemption is interpreted, it potentially could exclude a considerable amount of e-mail communication. However, in one case, *Armstrong v. Executive Office of the President*, the court ruled that the National Archive could not refuse to provide a computer tape of certain e-mail created during the Reagan administration, as these e-mail messages could qualify as public records (Hunter, 1995). Furthermore, the court ruled that the e-mail messages had to be retained in electronic form; printing and saving the hard copies was not equivalent to saving the electronic versions. The court explained that the printed version might not contain all of the information found in an electronic file, such as the headers stating who sent the message, the recipients, and any attachments.

EMPLOYER OBLIGATIONS TO MONITOR

Under some circumstances, the employer may have not only the right but also the responsibility to monitor e-mail communications. When one employee is suspected or accused of harassment by sending offensive e-mail messages to another employee, the employer's obligation to ensure that employees do not have to work in a hostile environment may require the monitoring of the employee's e-mail. If, for example, an employee is known to have sent harassing e-mail to a co-worker previously, some monitoring might be considered necessary to shield the employer from further liability.

Also, employers may be concerned about potential illegal behavior, on the part of some employees, and monitoring e-mail messages may be necessary to investigate this possibility. Since employers can in some circumstances be held liable for the illegal behavior of their employees, the employer has a responsibility to monitor possible illegal actions. For example, if an employee with apparent authority were to use the employer's e-mail to libel a competitor or inflict trade disparagement against a competitor's product, the employer could be liable for the action of the employee (McChrystal, Gleisner, and Kuborn, 1999).

SEXUAL HARASSMENT AND OTHER CIVIL RIGHTS CLAIMS

In some cases, employers may have an obligation to monitor employee e-mail in order to protect against legal liability for civil rights violations. In recent years, e-mail has been introduced as evidence in sexual harassment and other civil rights lawsuits. Under federal and state civil rights laws, employers may be liable for harassment occurring in the workplace, unless they exercise reasonable care to prevent and correct promptly any harassing behavior. E-mail evidence might arise in a couple of ways. First, the e-mail might be used as direct evidence of intentional discrimination, such as if an e-mail between managers explicitly stated that an employee was terminated because of his race. Second, e-mail might be used as circumstantial evidence of discrimination. For example, e-mails containing sexist or racist humor might be used as evidence of a hostile environment based on sex or race.

E-mail has been used to support claims of discrimination in several reported cases to date. In one case (*Peterson v. Minneapolis Community Development Agency*), a court overturned summary judgment for the employer by the court below, and cited as one of the facts in support of the decision the e-mail from a supervisor to a subordinate, pressing for a relationship. (Towns and Girard, 1998). It is unclear at this point exactly what e-mail will need to contain to support a claim of a hostile environment. Several courts have found that a few offensive e-mail messages do not create a hostile environment. (*Owens v. Morgan-Stanley, Harley v. McCoach, Curtis v. DiMaio*).

However, some courts have been willing to allow the introduction of e-mail evidence to demonstrate general behavior at an office. In *Strauss v. Microsoft Corp.*, the plaintiff alleged that she had not been promoted because she was female. Microsoft tried to exclude evidence of e-mail messages, sent by her supervisor, that contained comments of a sexual nature. The court found that while the e-mail did not prove sexual discrimination, it was relevant evidence for the jury to consider.

An employer may escape liability if an appropriate response is taken following a complaint of harassment. In a case decided under Texas law, an employer received a complaint that racially-harassing e-mail was being sent over the company's e-mail system. The employer reprimanded the employees responsible for the e-mail and had two company-wide meetings to discuss appropriate use of company e-mail. The court found that the employer's prompt action relieved it of liability. (Towns and Girard, 1998, citing *Daniels v. Worldcom Corp.*).

The potential duty to monitor employee e-mail raises the question of an appropriate response. Employers may be caught in a "Catch-22" situation. If they do not monitor e-mail, they may open themselves up for liability on civil rights or other claims, and if they do monitor e-mail, they may face invasion of privacy claims (Ciapciak and Matuszak, 1998). Some employers are following a simple policy with respect to senders of inappropriate e-mail by firing those who are found to have violated company policy. In December, 1999, the New York Times fired more than 20 staff employees for the sending of e-mail that contained offensive material (Kurtz, 1999). In addition, a St. Louis brokerage firm, Edward Jones & Company, fired 19 employees over e-mail containing off-color jokes and pornography (Seglin, 1999). In both of these cases, the offensive e-mail was discovered following a complaint to the employer. This tact of monitoring following knowledge of inappropriate behavior may be a good balance for the rights of employer and employees.

TOWARD A MODEL E-MAIL POLICY

We conclude this discussion with an examination of possible components of an e-mail policy for an organization. All authorities in this field recommend that organizations, pubic or private, develop clear policies regarding e-mail and communicate those policies to their employees. Differences of opinion exist on what features an e-mail policy should have, however, and we attempt to outline some of the thinking in this area.

A number of attorneys recommend that employers tell their employees that the workplace e-mail system is for business use only, that e-mail can and will be monitored, and that employees should not expect any privacy regarding their e-mail (Fitzpatrick, 1997; White, 1997). Such recommendations frequently appear in state employment law newsletters (for example, see Coie, 1999; Walker, 1999b). Some attorneys even recommend that the policy appear on the computer monitor screen every time the user logs on and that the user be required to acknowledge consent in order to proceed. Others suggest that employees be required to sign a statement acknowledging the employer's e-mail policy. As earlier discussions make clear, such a policy provides the employer with almost complete protection in the event employee e-mail is monitored. Of course, many of those who recommend a policy of this nature would not recommend that employee e-mail be regularly monitored; they simply are recommending a course of action that is likely to minimize potential legal problems for an employer.

Another opinion is that employees should be allowed to use their e-mail for personal purposes (Doss and Loui, 1995). First of all, limiting the workplace e-mail system to business use only is a substantial restriction. Many employees find it extremely convenient to use their e-mail for personal use, just as they use their workplace telephone for personal calls. While a stronger argument can be made for permitting personal telephone calls at work—urgent or even emergency calls might be necessary, for example—prohibiting personal e-mail would be a significant inconvenience that would raise several questions. What happens if an employee receives an external e-mail message of a personal nature? What if a communication between two colleagues contains both business and personal items, just as the two can easily be contained in one phone call? Should an employee be prohibited from using the workplace e-mail system for personal messages during a lunch hour or after work? Rather than completely prohibiting personal e-mail, public employers might consider appropriate guidelines for allowable personal messages. For example, personal e-mail might be permitted if it: (1) is not excessive in amount and/or does not overburden the e-mail system; (2) is not used for private business (i.e., profit-making) purposes; and (3) is not in violation of organizational policies or federal or state laws.

It also may be desirable to provide employees with some privacy rights regarding their e-mail, especially if personal communications are allowed (Etzioni, 1999). Rather than stating that all e-mail is subject to monitoring, possible conditions for monitoring could be spelled out. Monitoring naturally would be conducted when there was some legitimate business reason for doing so, such as a situation in which there was reason to believe that the employee was violating organizational policies. In such cases, however, monitoring of e-mail should be limited in duration and scope (Fitzpatrick, 1997). Moreover, the results of the monitoring should be kept confidential. Thus, employees should expect that their e-mail communications would not be randomly monitored without cause, but that they could be monitored under appropriate situations.

There are possible benefits from a policy that provides employees with privacy expectations, as opposed to a policy that provides maximum legal protection for the employer. First of all, employee morale is likely to be higher. Employees do not like being distrusted. They are likely to resent monitoring of their e-mail, even if perfectly legal, just as they would object to their employer routinely searching their office. Recognizing and respecting these privacy desires undoubtedly contributes to a healthier atmosphere in the organization (Doss and Loui, 1995). Second, employees may feel freer to use e-mail for honest and open discussions when they have some privacy expectation. Encouraging such interchange is desirable, especially for public organizations. A free flow of ideas should contribute to better decisions and policies (Gantt, 1995). Thus, establishing an e-mail policy that provides employees with some privacy rights can be defended on pragmatic as well as ethical grounds, and these considerations might outweigh the desire to have maximum legal protection.

There is universal agreement that an e-mail policy should contain a prohibition of obscene, hostile, threatening, or harassing communications (Cozzetto and Pedeliski, 1997; Fitzpatrick, 1997). An employee should not have any expectation of privacy for communications that contain offensive language. As we discussed earlier, the employer has certain responsibilities to maintain a workplace that is free of harassing or hostile behavior, which mandates that certain language be restricted. Suspicion of violating this policy naturally would be a valid reason for monitoring an employee's e-mail. Some authorities go as far as recommending a "zero tolerance" policy regarding this behavior (Cozzetto and Pedeliski, 1997). The employer's ability to monitor e-mail for prohibited content has been enhanced by the development of software designed just for such a purpose. Several programs will scan all e-mail messages and single out those that appear to contain a significant number of questionable items (Etzioni, 1999). These messages can then be scrutinized by supervisors to determine if they truly are inappropriate communications.

Another important part of the e-mail policy for a public organization is a clear statement of what types of e-mail messages qualify as public records and what requirements exist to save qualifying e-mail communications. As we have noted above, there are two competing public interests here—the desire to encourage open discussion of alternatives and the desire to inform the public. Of course, government organizations must operate within established legal parameters, which may not allow much flexibility on the part of the organization. To the extent that flexibility in interpreting and implementing the laws exists, the agency or organization has to decide what the proper balance is between keeping e-mail private, especially communications that are advisory or preliminary to an action or decision, and providing the public with the information that legitimately should be available for scrutiny. However this is decided, an important part of the policy is to communicate to employees what the legal requirements are and what constitutes acceptable implementation of the legislation. What employees need are clear guidelines that allow them to make appropriate decisions regarding the retention of their e-mail. Given the lack of long-standing conventions in this area, there is considerable potential for confusion over how to treat e-mail communications.

To conclude, there are important legal questions surrounding e-mail in the workplace. These questions involve issues that are not unique to e-mail, such as questions of employee privacy rights, employer obligations to provide a non-hostile workplace, and public access to information from government organizations. The application of these more general issues to e-mail can be ambiguous. It is useful for managers to understand current legal thinking and to consider the issues involved in order to develop an appropriate and useful organizational e-mail policy.

REFERENCES

Adelman, Ellen, and Caroline Kennedy. (1995). *The Right to Privacy*. New York: Knopf.

Behar, Richard. (1997). Who's Reading Your E-mail? *Fortune* 135:56-61 (Feb. 3).

Bramsco, Julienne W. (1997). Employee Privacy: Avoiding Liability in the Electronic Age. *Litigation and Administrative Practice Course Handbook Series*. Number H-562. New York: Practicing Law Institute.

Ciapciak, James J. and Lynne Matuszak. (1998). Employer Rights in Monitoring Employee E-Mail. *For the Defense* 40:17-20.

Coie, Perkins. (1999). Does Your Employee Handbook Have an E-mail Policy? *Washington Employment Law Letter* 6 (August).

Cole, W. Scott. (1997). E-Mail: Public Records and Privacy Issues. Paper presented at the Annual Meeting of the National Association of College and University Attorneys.

Cozzetto, Don A., and Theodore B. Pedeliski. (1997). Privacy and the Workplace: Technology and Public Employment. *Public Personnel Management* 26:515-527.

Davis, Gray. (1999). Message to the Califrnia State Senate Vetoing SB1016. Available at <http://www.lginfo/ca.gov/pub/bill.../SB_1016_vt.19991010.html>

Dawes, Steven J., and Susan E. Dallas. (1997). Privacy Issues in the Workplace for Public Employees, Parts I and II. *Colorado Lawyer* 26:61-85.

Dixon, Rod. (1997). Windows Nine-to-Five: Smyth v. Pillsbury and the Scope of an Employee's Right to Privacy in Employer Communications. *Virginia Journal of Law and Technology* 2:4. Available at <http://www.vjolt.student.virginia.edu/graphics/vol2/vol2_art4.html>.

Doss, Erini, and Michael C. Loui. (1995). Ethics and the Privacy of Electronic Mail. *The Information Society* 11:223-235.

Etzioni, Amitai. (1999). Some Privacy, Please, for E-mail. *Chicago Daily Law Bulletin* (Nov. 24).

Farber, Mark. (1997). Employee Privacy and E-Mail. Available at <http://wings.buffalo.edu/academic/.../Complaw/CompLawPapers/farber.html>.

Fitzpatrick, Robert B. (1997). Technology Advances in the Information Age: Effects on Workplace Privacy Issues. Current Developments in Employment Law. ALI-ABA Course of Study, Sante Fe, NM (June 17-19). Washington, DC: Fitzpatrick and Associates.

Gantt, Larry O. Natt. (1995). An Affront to Human Dignity: Electronic Mail Monitoring in the Private Sector Workplace. *Harvard Journal of Law and Technology* 8:345-411.

Garcia, Erik C. (1996). E-Mail and Privacy Rights. Available at <http://wings.buffalo.edu/academic/.../Complaw/CompLawPapers/garcia.html>.

Garson, G. David. (1995). *Computer Technology and Social Issues*. Harrisburg, PA: Idea Group Publishing.

Greenberg, Thomas R. (1994). E-mail and Voice Mail: Employee Privacy and the Federal Wiretap Statute. *American University Law Review* 44:219-253.

Greengard, Samuel. (1996). Privacy: Entitlement or Illusion? *Personnel Journal*

75:74-88.

Hunter, Daniel F. (1995). Electronic Mail and Michigan's Public Disclosure Laws: The Argument for Public Access to Governmental Electronic Mail. *University of Michigan Journal of Law Reform* 29:977-1013.

Jenero, Kenneth A. and Lynne D. Mapes-Riordan. (1992). Electronic Monitoring of Employees and the Elusive "Right to Privacy." *Employee Relations Law Journal* 18:71-102.

Kurtz, Howard. (1999). Not Fit to Print—or Transmit: New York Times Fires 20 Workers for Sending Offensive E-Mail. *The Washington Post* (December 1).

Lee, Laurie Thomas. (1994). Watch Your E-mail! Employee E-mail Monitoring and Privacy Law in the Age of the "Electronic Sweatshop." *John Marshall Law Review* 28:139-177.

McChrystal, Michael K., William C. Gleisner III, and Michael J. Kuborn. (1999). Employee E-Mail: Coping With the Legal Perils. *Wisconsin Lawyer* (March).

Perritt, Henry H., Jr. (1996). *Law and the Information Superhighway.* New York: John Wiley.

Prysby, Charles, and Nicole Prysby. (1999). Legal Aspects of Electronic Mail in Public Organizations. *Information Technology and Computer Applications in Public Administration*, ed. by G. David Garson. Idea Group Publishers.

Rodriquez, Alexander I. (1998). All Bark, No Byte: Employee E-Mail Privacy Rights in the Private Sector Workplace. *Emory Law Journal* 47:1439-1473.

Schnaitman, Peter. (1999). Building a Community Through Workplace E-Mail: The New Privacy Frontier. *Michigan Telecommunications and Technology Law Review* 5:177-197.

Seglin, Jeffrey L. (1999). You've Got Mail. You're Being Watched. *The New York Times* (July 18).

Sundstrom, Scott A. (1998). You've Got Mail! (and the Government Knows it): Applying the Fourth Amendment to Workplace E-mail Monitoring. *New York University Law Review* 73:2064-2102.

Tarr, G. Alan. (1998). *Understanding State Constitutions.* Princeton University Press, 207-208.

Towns, Douglas M. and Jeana Girard. (1998). Superhighway or Superheadache? E-Mail and the Internet in the Workplace. *Employee Relation Law Journal* 24:5-29.

Walker, Anne N. (1999a). Adopting an Internet-Use Policy. *Connecticut Employment Law Letter* 7 (June).

Walker, Anne N. (1999b). Monitoring of Electronic Communications. *Connecticut Employment Law Letter* 7 (March).

White, Jarrod J. (1997). E-Mail@Work.Com: Employer Monitoring of Employee E-Mail. *Alabama Law Review* 48:1079-1104.

Wigod, Myrna L. (1998). Privacy in Public and Private E-Mail and On-Line Systems. *Pace Law Review* 19:95-146.

Wilborn, S. Elizabeth. (1998). Revisiting the Public/Private Distinction: Employee Monitoring in the Workplace. *Georgia Law Review* 32:825-887.

COURT CASES

Armstrong v. Executive Office of the President, 877 F.Supp. 690 (D.D.C. 1993).

Bohach v. City of Reno, 932 F.Supp. 1232 (D.Nev. 1996).

Bourke v. Nissan Motor Co., No. YC 00379 (Cal. Sup. Ct., Los Angeles 1991).

City of Virginia Beach v. U.S. Department of Commerce, 995 F.2d 1247 (4th Cir. 1993).

Curtis v. DiMaio, 46 F.Supp. 2d 206 (E.D.N.Y., 1999).

Daniels v. Worldcom Corp., 1998 WL 91261 (N.D.Tex., February 23, 1998).

Deal. v. Spears, 980 F.Supp. 2d 1153 (8th cir. 1992).

Ethyl Corporation v. U.S. E.P.A., 25 F.3d 1241 (4th Cir. 1994).

Flanigan v. Epson, No. BC 007036 (Cal. Sup. Ct., Los Angeles 1992).

Harley v. McCoach, 928 F.Supp. 533 (E.D. Pa. 1996).

O'Conner v. Ortega, 480 U.S. 709 (1987).

Owens v. Morgan Stanley & Co., 1997 WL 403454 (S.D.N.Y. July 17, 1997).

Peterson v. Minneapolis Community Development Agency, 1994 WL 455699 (Minn. App. August 23, 1994).

Restuccia v. Burk Technologies, Inc., No. 95-2125 (Mass. App. Ct. August 12, 1996).

Shoars v. Epson, No. SWC 112749 (Cal. Sup. Ct., Los Angeles 1992).

Simmons v. Southwestern Bell Telephone Co., 452 F.Supp. 392 (W.D.Okla. 1998).

Smyth v. Pillsbury Co., 914 F.Supp. 97 (E.D.Pa. 1996).

Strauss v. Microsoft Corp., No. 91 civ. 5928 (SWK), 1995 WL 324692 (S.D.N.Y., June 1, 1995).

United States v. Simons, 29 F.Supp.2d 24 (E.D.Va. 1998).

United States v. Smith, 155 F.3d 1051 (9th Cir. 1998).

Watkins v. L.M. Berry & Co., 704 F.2d 577 (11th Cir. 1983).

Chapter X

Protecting Personal Privacy in Cyberspace: The Limitations of Third Generation Data Protection Laws Such as the New Zealand Privacy Act 1993

Gehan Gunasekara
University of Auckland, New Zealand

The Orwellian conception of the ultimate surveillance society has, fortunately, failed to materialise although it may be that its arrival has merely been postponed until the application of the appropriate technology. In several metropolitan areas in New Zealand there is an extensive network of video surveillance cameras used by the police to deter crime. On a different technological playing field Government Agencies in New Zealand now regularly engage in data matching programmes[1] with the view to detecting and deterring a variety of frauds and benefit abuse. A new driver's licence has just been introduced featuring a digitised photograph, the uses for which have not been clearly articulated. Software already exists whereby photographs can be matched with those on police databases of known criminals. Private firms, ranging from supermarkets and pizza delivery companies to credit agencies, maintain electronic databases on clients and other individuals. In short, more information about citizens can be compiled and used (or misused) than ever before. This has made all the more dangerous with the arrival of the "Information Superhighway" or what has more accurately been described as the "combined power of the computer linked with telecommunications" (Slane, 1995, appendix 3).

It is widely anticipated that in the next century, an increasing volume of business and personal transactions will be conducted through this medium - the term "internet" is used here in its wide sense to encompass all on-line services. As ever increasing numbers of people are connected to on-line services, the amount of information about them is likely to proliferate. Branscomb (1995) has commented that we now live in the "information age" where information is arguably the most important form of property, although the law has been slow to recognise it. Information about individuals, known as personal information, has the potential to cause the greatest harm if misused. It is now trite to describe privacy as the first road-kill on the information superhighway.

This enormous "privacy deficit" has to some extent been re-dressed, in New Zealand, by legislation to protect personal privacy in both the private and public sectors. The Privacy Act 1993 (hereafter referred to as "the Act") covers all the examples above, from the police video to the pizza delivery company. The Act sets up a regime for the protection of individual's privacy and anyone in New Zealand[2] can complain about interference with his or her privacy. The New Zealand legislation is a so called "third generation" data protection statute because, as will be explained it is technologically neutral. The Act was not designed specifically with cyberspace in mind. Nevertheless, it is a forward looking piece of legislation which has the flexibility to survive into the next century.

This chapter canvasses the impact of the Privacy Act 1993 on those who transact their business in cyberspace who fall within the Act's definition of "agency"[3] . The writer argues that, for the most part, the Act can be effective in protecting individuals' privacy in cyberspace. Privacy protection does not place restrictions on freedom of expression and communication on the internet. The internet has proved to be extremely difficult to regulate, perhaps not surprisingly given its origins and function. It has exhibited a high degree of resistance to regulation of any kind, thus confirming a type of "frontier" image.

Privacy legislation, such as the New Zealand Act, is however, conceptually different to other types of legislation which impacts on the internet — for example legislation to restrict pornographic or culturally undesirable material. There are two reasons for this. First, the Act is transaction or process based — for the most part it does not regulate substance. The Act controls the use to which personal information is put and the manner of its collection; it does not attempt to control content[4]. Secondly, privacy protection originates from the needs of the individual, not for the propagation of a particular political, social or religious ideology. It is to give the individual control over fundamental aspects of his or her life, and is, therefore, a basic human right. Indeed, the protection of privacy has been recognised by most countries as reflected by international documents to which New Zealand is committed.[5] Furthermore the Act provides that in most instances the individual can give informed consent to non-compliance of the rules. Attempts to introduce internet censorship in Australia were opposed, significantly, on the grounds that censorship (particularly of personal e-mail) would encroach on the privacy of individuals. The application of privacy laws to cyberspace can therefore be distinguished from the application of other laws such as censorship provisions.

The writer argues that, if the New Zealand experience is reflected elsewhere, third generation privacy laws such as the Privacy Act might actually diminish, rather than enhance, privacy in the technological arena, especially where electronic data flows, intranets and the internet is concerned. This is because, while the Act protects privacy of personal information in all spheres, the natural human response has been to invoke the legislation in everyday human disputes not involving technology where violations are easily observed and detected. The litigation typically involves scenarios such as doctors wrongly disclosing patient information to a third party, bank employees allowing client details to be overheard and so on. More sinister and pervasive technological privacy intrusions are not as easily detected. Few if any reported cases involve internet misuse. In the latter context the only effective enforcement mechanism in the Act is the pivotal role played by the Privacy Commissioner as an advocate for privacy concerns. The Commissioner has been alert to technological concerns, especially where intranets and the internet itself is concerned. Unfortunately, though both the law and the office of Privacy Commissioner have been subjected to considerable media and business criticism with the result that many see the legislation as an unnecessary impediment to business. Hence the effectiveness of the Commissioner as a privacy watch-dog is somewhat questionable.

The discussion concludes by challenging the information technology industry to come up with appropriate products which first, inform individuals of their rights and second, have built in privacy safeguards. Such a task should not be difficult if the analogy of telephone companies is considered. Finally, an important caveat is added: the writer's perspective is legal and nontechnical, and it is possible that technological developments may ultimately overtake many of the concerns raised. The law has always struggled to keep abreast of technology.

Information Privacy

It may be helpful, at the outset, to define the nature of the interest it is sought to protect. Privacy has been notoriously difficult to define although clearly, it is tied to personal autonomy and personal freedom. "Information Privacy" is somewhat easier to define: it is the ability to *control* information about oneself. In the modern world it may not be possible to prevent the collection and storage of information about individuals. However those individuals should be able to access the information, check its accuracy and have some control over its use in order to ensure that it is not misused. Obviously, the right to privacy needs to be balanced against competing social and individual rights, for instance the need to prevent criminal activities and the rights of individuals to receive and impart information.[6] The twin pillars on which any information privacy law is based must, therefore, be firstly the right of individuals to access information about them and secondly to have some control on its use and/or disclosure.

The New Zealand Act is to be commended because it covers both private and public sectors. The New Zealand Privacy Commissioner has observed that "With development of seamless technology seamless laws are essential"(Slane, 1995, appendix 3). This is no more demonstrable than in New Zealand where in recent years wholesale agencies which were in the public domain were privatised and in many cases sold to overseas interests with consequent loss of control. Many other government responsibilities were contracted out to the private sector. The information highway, which facilitates the transfer between sectors is the other main reason why public sector controls alone are inadequate.

The Challenge of the Information Superhighway

What are the dangers to privacy which are peculiar to the new technology? Not only may individuals' physical movements be recorded as they move about within a metropolis, but their "digital footprints" may be tracked and recorded as they "surf the net" or move around within cyberspace. Indeed, unlike the quite limited coverage of the cameras, there is no transaction which can take place within cyberspace without creating a record which may be traced. Edwards (1996 A) gives a vivid illustration as follows:

> If you go to the library and look at the *New York Times*, you have completely anonymously gained access to information. There will be no record of your visit. You may appear as a statistic on the number of people who have entered the library, but no one will know that you looked at a particular article, in a particular issue of the paper. If you access the eight-page internet edition of the same publication, your local server will know you have been there, as will any servers you pass through en route, and the *New York Times* will know that you have looked at their newspaper (p.10).

This ability of the Web to collect information may not concern most people apart from those who, perhaps, frequent pornographic sites and the like. Branscomb (1995, p.6) recalls an instance where journalists in the United States attempted to secure from video outlets, a list of videos rented for personal entertainment by a candidate for high judicial office. This type of attention is only likely to focus on select groups of individuals although it is a debatable point whether public figures should sacrifice their right to privacy.[7]

Consider, however, a more common use of information we generate. It was reported in 1996 (*Herald*, 1996 A, p.2) that thousands of people in New Zealand and possibly elsewhere received an unsolicited electronic junk mail message (in the jargon this is referred to as "spam") offering them interactive child pornographic material. Obviously the recipients' e-mail addresses were obtained from data contained somewhere within the web. The New Zealand Privacy Act 1993 does not prohibit the sending of unsolicited junk mail of the electronic or paper variety. What it does allow people to do, however, is to monitor to what use information about them on databases is put.

In theory an individual who objects to information being made available to direct marketers could refuse to supply the information when made aware of its potential use. However if disclosure of information to direct marketers is a purpose for collection at the outset and the individual is made aware of this, he or she cannot then complain if they receive junk mail. The individual does not have to consent under the Act to all subsequent disclosures. However, if the individual was not made aware of the possibility at the outset or if information collected for a quite unrelated purpose was accidentally or otherwise to fall into the hands of direct marketers, the Act does give individuals a remedy against the person who allowed this to happen.

Electronic mail poses the most immediate (in terms of its wide-spread use) danger to privacy. It is actually much easier for e-mail messages to be intercepted and read by unintended readers than it is for traditional paper mail to be intercepted. In a New Zealand case a worker was dismissed for harassing a colleague and in the resulting unjustifiable dismissal suit the employer's defence relied, in part, on intercepted e-mail communications of the employee in question (Slane, 1995, appendix 3). It has been observed that many employers make e-mail systems available to their employees without first establishing any clear policy as to how the system can be used — whether personal communications are allowed and who has the right to see the messages (Edwards, 1996 A, p.18). In this area many North American companies are more advanced than their New Zealand counterparts at present. These companies not only have consistent e-mail policies in place but have also adopted systems that automatically inform users when they log on that the company reserves the right to monitor messages and that the system is intended for business and not personal use (Edwards, 1996 A, p.18).

One of the most insidious developments in most western societies has been the activities of direct marketing and direct mail companies who compile data bases on consumers which they then exploit for direct marketing purposes. There is effectively no means of escaping the inevitable deluge of direct mail solicitations and the like. Even changing one's address will not provide a sure escape as the companies which engage in the practice can obtain these details from public registers (see below). Following approaches adopted elsewhere, most notably the 1995 European Union directive on Data Protection, New

Zealand's Privacy Commissioner has recommended in his recent Review of the Privacy Act that individuals should be given the right to have their names taken off direct marketing lists (Slane, 1998 p78).

Other issues canvassed by the Privacy Commissioner include the bulk transfer of personal information from public registers and the electronic transmission of personal information from public registers, including the difficulties posed by making personal information available on-line. Theses issues are discussed below.

There is no doubt that the internet challenges common assumptions about the control and storage of information. For instance it is not always possible to identify a single record-keeper who is responsible for controlling data or indeed an organisation that has the capacity to correct data on which it relies - the trend is for information on networks neither to originate from nor reside in a single focal point (Slane 1995, appendix 3).

Along with this Edwards (1996 A) indicates that a more practical difficulty, that faced by any single jurisdictional approach is:

> what good are strict domestic laws when a myriad of other jurisdictions are only a keystroke or mouse click away (p.16)

These difficulties are real and cannot be ignored. They should not, however, be used as a reason to avoid protecting privacy rights. Until the advent of a global treaty or system of "cyberlaw" or perhaps even "cybercourts", the focus of any legal controls will be in individual jurisdictions and the New Zealand model is as good a starting point as any other.

PRIVACY LEGISLATION IN NEW ZEALAND: A BRIEF HISTORY

In New Zealand it was the Government's own use of new information technologies (to store and process information about citizens) which led, almost as a by-product, to measures to protect privacy. The Wanganui Computer Centre Act of 1976 provided for a Privacy Commissioner to facilitate the investigation of complaints relating to use of the Centre. In more recent times the Privacy Commissioner Act 1991 (which arguably was inappropriately named as one of its principal objects was to permit data matching between government agencies) provided for the appointment of a Privacy Commissioner to monitor government data matching programmes and safeguard the rights of individuals affected by the matching.

An important contributing factor in New Zealand's privacy consciousness has been the ground breaking open government legislation of the early 1980s.[8] This legislation reversed a tradition of secrecy by establishing that, in principle, all information held by the Government should be available to citizens as a right. Part of this legislation provided for automatic access by individuals to information held about them by government. It was only a short step from this position to argue for access to information about individuals held by the private sector. It was probably inevitable that the culture of openness fostered by the open government legislation would eventually permeate the private sector.

THE PRIVACY ACT 1993

The Privacy Act 1993 came into force on July 1 1993.[9] It repealed the Privacy Commissioner Act 1991, while taking over that Act's functions governing data   matching. The purposes of the Act are stated to be:

a) To establish certain principles with respect to-
   (i)   The collection, use, and disclosure by public and private sector agencies, of information relating to individuals; and
   (ii) Access by each individual to information relating to that individual and held by public and private sector agencies; and

b) To provide for the appointment of a Privacy Commissioner to investigate complaints about interferences with individual privacy.

Scope of the Act

The Act governs the collection (including the manner of collection), use and disclosure of "personal information" which is defined to mean information about an identifiable natural person (as opposed to artificial entities such as corporations). The Act also governs information matching[10] between government agencies. There are various safeguards to protect the rights of the individuals affected by such programmes and to ensure they are not misused. However, consideration of these is beyond the confines of this chapter.

The obligations imposed by the Act apply to all "agencies" which are widely defined to cover both private and public sector organisations.[11] The wide definition of "agency" should cover local internet service providers or gateways as well as web sites and the like. The obligations extend to individuals although not where the information is collected or held by the individual solely or principally for the purposes of or in connection with that individual's personal, family or household affairs.

Another exception in the definition of "agency"[12] is its non application to the "news activity" of the "news media". Thus, internet news services such as the *New York Times ,CNN* and the like will not have to comply with the Act. Commentaries and current affairs are within the definition of "news activity". While bulletin boards and news groups may well be covered also, the definition of "news medium" is restricted to agencies whose business or part of whose business consists of a news activity — therefore those who are unable to demonstrate a revenue generating news activity cannot invoke this exception.

Both New Zealand's privacy and open government legislation are *information*-based, as opposed to being document or data based (Edwards, 1996 B). Thus, as pointed out at the outset, information stored on magnetic tape as well as on paper and digitally stored information are covered and it has been suggested that even telepathic communication would in principle be subject to the regime (Edwards 1996 B). Indeed in one reported case a successful request was made for information which was "held" in an official's memory - it was found that the Official Information Act is not limited to written or otherwise recorded information, but also applies to any information which is "held" in a person's memory and which can be recalled.[13] The open ended concept of "information" is significant from the technological viewpoint as well as for the reason that both transactional information about individuals and substantive information are covered by the New Zealand approach.

On the other hand, as already indicated, this approach has had the inevitable consequence that individuals have tended to focus almost exclusively on privacy violations arising through the misuse of personal information through human rather than technological instruments.

Extra-Territorial Application?

One intriguing issue, one which could be of overriding importance posed by the new technology, is the potential application of the Act beyond New Zealand's jurisdiction. As observed already, a myriad of other jurisdictions are only a keystroke or mouse click away, hence the Act must be able to exert some control beyond New Zealand or at least within the new cyberspace frontier.

The Act provides that "any person" may complain about interferences with privacy to the Privacy Commissioner.[14] This does not have to be the person who suffered an infringement of his or her privacy — it could be on behalf of another person. Likewise, the person who suffered the infringement could reside outside New Zealand, provided a New Zealand agency committed the breach.

But what if the breach occurred outside the jurisdiction? What if, say, a New Zealand agency maintained personal information on a server in Australia and that information was, for instance incorrect or subsequently used or downloaded in breach of the Act's requirements? Unlike some other jurisdictions, New Zealand does not generally apply its laws with extra-territorial effect. Nevertheless, in the scenario raised it is conceivable that under existing jurisdictional rules, the Act may be applicable, provided there is some connection with this jurisdiction. Otherwise, local agencies would be able to evade the Act's requirements by maintaining information outside the jurisdiction. Indeed section 10 of the Act expressly contemplates extra-territorial application of the principles, but presumably only in relation to New Zealand agencies. It should be emphasised, however, that this is a complex issue whose discussion perhaps merits separate treatment. This is more so because the Act's rules are not, for the most part, enforceable through the courts but through an alternative enforcement procedure.[15] What it does point to is the need for international solutions to the problem, perhaps even an "Internet Privacy Commissioner".

The Information Privacy Principles

At the core of the Act are twelve information privacy principles which govern the collection, use and disclosure of personal information.

While the principles should be read in full in order to appreciate them, a brief summary follows here together with some observations as to their likely impact as far as cyberspace is concerned. It should be noted that the principles themselves are subject to several qualifications and exceptions. These are, for the most part, summarised below:

Principle 1 requires that only information necessary for a lawful purpose of the agency is collected. The stricture that the collection must be for a lawful purpose probably does not add anything new. However, it is a requirement that the purpose must be connected with the functions or activities of the agency and that the collection of the information is necessary for that purpose. In terms of agencies freedom, this does restrict the quality of the information which is allowed to be collected and stored. However, such restrictions are justifiable for at least two reasons.

Firstly, in terms of economic efficiency, an agency which collected information which is not connected with its functions, or where it is connected is nevertheless unnecessary for its purposes, would not be operating efficient information management practices. Thus, the Act, despite its compliance costs, which raised some initial concern in New Zealand, is pro-business in terms of encouraging sound management.

An agency connected to the internet which wished to, for example, collect information about individuals visiting its site could do this provided it can point to a valid reason connected with its activities. However, this is subject to the other principles outlined below.

Principle 2 requires that information is only collected from the individual concerned. This needs to be read alongside Principle 3 below — it would be undermined if agencies could collect information indirectly. The principle also encourages accuracy of personal information.

Principle 3 requires that the individual is made aware why the information is sought and who is seeking it. The requirement also extends to informing subjects of the consequences if information is not supplied as well as informing subjects of their access and correction rights.[16] These are important rights. Anyone who collects information from or about individuals as they go about the internet, without informing them of the collection and the purposes of the collection, will be in breach of this principle. If an agency having collected the information in compliance with this principle, subsequently decides to use the information for a new or different purpose, it must seek the consent of the individual concerned. This may be difficult to accomplish in practice, hence the importance of articulating and planning the use of information at the outset.

The principle provides real protection against the surreptitious collection of information about visitors to an internet site: firstly, they must be made aware personal information is being collected and secondly the purposes of the collection must be accurately described (is it to merely identify the pages of the Web site of interest to the visitor or less innocently, in order to build up a profile of data about the individual which might subsequently, for example, be used for direct marketing purposes).

Principle 4 requires that information is not collected by unlawful, unfair or unreasonable means. This principle covers such conduct as electronic bugging, phone tapping and so on, and potentially, the interception of electronic mail. This is discussed briefly below.

Principle 5 covers the storage and security of personal information and requires that information be securely held. Under this principle, system administrators must take steps to ensure that substantive data is kept secure. What is a "reasonable" standard of security is left undefined and justifiably so, in order to allow for developing technologies and standards. The need for national, regional and international security standards is paramount and work is already in progress in this direction.[17] The issue of data encryption is clearly relevant in this context. An issue of recent concern addressed by the Privacy Commissioner is where people are allowed to inspect or "browse" personal information; this is clearly a violation of personal privacy even where no permanent alteration or loss of the information occurs (Slane, 1998. P74). Amendments to the Act have been recommended.

Principles 6 & 7 are related in that they deal with access to and correction of personal information. They require that a person whose information has been collected be given a right of access to the information and to have inaccurate information corrected. Where correction is refused the individual is entitled to have an attachment of notation to that effect on the information. This is of obvious significance for credit reporting.

It has been pointed out that the right of access to information underpins all the other aspects of information privacy in that it is impossible to know whether inaccurate information is being disseminated about an individual or whether information has been collected from an improper source, unless the individual can find out what information is held in the first place (Slane, 1995, appendix 3).

Principle 8 requires that agencies holding personal information take reasonable steps to ensure that the information is accurate prior to using it. Again the efficiency gains of ensuring information is up to date, complete and not misleading, must outweigh the compliance costs. It should be noted that only reasonable steps need be taken.

Principle 9 requires that agencies keep information for no longer than necessary. Again this highlights the fact that information, especially of the personal kind, becomes rapidly out of date.

Principle 10 requires that information is used only for the purposes for which it was collected. There are several exceptions to this, the most important being that the information may be used for purposes directly related to the purpose in connection with which information was obtained. This principle ties in with Principles 1 and 3: if the purposes were clearly articulated at the outset, it is unlikely that an agency will need to infringe Principle 10. It should be again emphasised that the purposes for the collection must be those which existed at the time the information was first collected.

If information is to be used for direct marketing purposes (or to be sold to direct marketers—caught by Principle 11) or to build up customer profiles, this needs to have been explained at the outset.

Principle 11 requires that personal information not be disclosed by an agency to anyone else unless disclosure is one of the purposes in connection with which the information was obtained or is a directly related purpose. As with Principle 10, this is a key principle, giving individuals control over the way information about them is used.

Principle 12 deals with unique identifiers and requires that unique identifiers not be assigned to individuals except to enable the agency to carry out its functions efficiently and that the same identifier that another agency has already assigned not be assigned.

Qualifications & Exceptions

The principles outlined above are subject to several qualifications and exceptions.

First, the Privacy Commissioner has a quasi legislative power and can modify the principles (prescribing greater or lesser standards) by issuing codes of practice which have the same force as the principles. This allows the Act to be flexible in relation to industries and sectors which have peculiar requirements. However the flexibility of the principles themselves has been reflected in the fact that there have, to date been only four codes of practice issued. Of these the most important has been undoubtedly the code governing the health sector. Interestingly, the first code to be promulgated was the GCS[18] Information Privacy Code 1994. This was to clarify issues relating to a government owned company (which supplied computer processing services to a number of important departments of state) prior to its transfer into the private sector.

Secondly, the Commissioner is also empowered to grant specific exemptions from Principles 2, 10 and 11 provided certain criteria are met.

Thirdly, non compliance may be authorised by the individual concerned. Unfortunately, the early tendency in New Zealand was to regard individual consent as a panacea to ensure compliance with the Act. Lengthy and impressive looking forms were designed by companies which customers were required to sign. However, as indicated earlier, consent is not needed in many cases (where, for instance disclosure of the information is one of the purposes in connection with which it was obtained) especially where the individual is made aware, at the outset, of the reasons why the information is sought. Likewise, consent does not, under the Act, have to be in writing—it could be inferred from conduct in appropriate cases. Finally, it is suggested that when the issue is tested, the Commissioner and Tribunal are unlikely to regard the consent as genuine when the individual had, in essence no choice but to consent and consent must in any case be fully informed.

Fourthly, non compliance is allowed in the case of information collected for research and statistical purposes to be published in non-identifiable form.

Other exceptions include law enforcement and public health and safety. This reflects the fact that privacy is not an absolute right but is one which needs to be balanced against other public interests.

Finally, there are numerous grounds for denying access to personal information under Principle 6. These are based largely on the parallel provisions of the Official Information Act and include for example references supplied in confidence by an individual's previous employer to prospective employers of that person.

Complaints Procedure and Remedies

Only the right of access to information held by public sector agencies is enforceable in court.

The Act provides an alternative dispute resolution which is similar to that provided in New Zealand's Human Rights protection legislation. This is to be commended, for the reason that it is not only cheaper and quicker than traditional court litigation but is also likely to foster specialisation, especially important when new technologies such as the internet are concerned.

There is a three step procedure: First, "any person" can complain to the Privacy Commissioner[19] . Secondly, the Commissioner investigates (again the inquisitorial approach is more suitable for dealing with new technology) and attempts to conciliate an agreed outcome between the parties. The Commissioner has the power to summon parties to a compulsory conference (could an on-line conference be a possibility?). Lastly, failing a settlement, the Proceedings Commissioner can bring proceedings before the Complaints Review Tribunal, although the individual can bring proceedings himself or herself if the Commissioners do not. A variety of remedies may be granted, including declarations, prohibitory and mandatory orders and damages, (currently up to $200,000).

Finally, it should be noted that an interference must cause some actual loss or injury to the individual (which may be of a nonmaterial nature such as humiliation or injury to feelings) and that in the case of requests for access, the reasonableness of any charges levied or conditions imposed may be challenged.

It has recently been pointed out that while all this is good in theory the reality of the New Zealand complains model (perhaps because it is free) is that there are lengthy delays — it often takes over a year perhaps two for the Commissioner to conclude an investigation — which is possibly undermining the legislation (Slane, 1998, p267).

PROBLEM AREAS

While the applicability of the principles outlined above to the new technology appears to pose no conceptual barrier, certain difficulties remain. Some of the most pressing of these will now be addressed.

Automated Processes as Opposed to Collection by Agencies

It has been argued that the internet can create records automatically without being a process or activity attached to or done by any particular "agency"; records may be created not through deliberate action but as an automatic process set up by the software attached to or part of internet use (Liddell, 1996). Accordingly, the argument is made that the agency concept of the New Zealand Act fails to address this type of collection on the internet. With respect, it is suggested that this problem is exaggerated. There is no reason why local internet service providers should not be made responsible for whatever processes or software are part of internet use.

More problematic is the fact that the Act defines "collection" to exclude the unsolicited receipt of information. However, it is suggested that emphasis should shift from the automated process itself to those who instigate the process or allow it to occur. Likewise, once information is "held", regardless of how it was obtained, the principles of the Act apply. Significantly, unlike the summary of the principles attempted above, Principles 10 and 11 refer to information "obtained", not "collected" and this suggests a wide interpretation of the range of information within the Act's coverage.

E - mail

The dangers of inadequate e-mail policies in the employment sector have already been canvassed. However the problems associated with private communications between individual users of e-mail are no less intractable. This is especially so where unsolicited intrusions and junk mail is concerned. There have been several instances of the receipt of "spam", both of the pornographic as well as of the more innocent nature. There is difficulty policing the boundary between the wider cyberspace environment and the e-mail system. It has been observed that while access to internet sites whose content falls outside the law can be controlled by internet service providers or by the use of software which effectively bans the use of certain keywords in searching cyberspace, there are no such constraints on e-mail - the internet can be used to send e-mail to randomly chosen electronic addresses (*Herald*, 1996 B, p.A12).

In the case of truly "individual" as opposed to workplace e-mail, there is, however, an emerging culture protective of privacy. This was reflected in one editorial from New Zealand's largest circulation newspaper:

"...electronic mail presents a dilemma. The public of New Zealand regards correspondence between individuals as confidential while it is being carried through the mail system. With the exception of ...illegal...material, the authorities are expected to respect the confidentiality of communication.... How, then, can society reconcile the right to privacy with the need to protect itself against the exploitation of children and other victims of pornography? It would be wrong for the deviant behaviour of a small group to proscribe the public's use of a service which will one day replace conventional letter delivery." (*Herald*, 1996 B, p.A12).

Public Registers

An area of recent concern in new Zealand has been the potential for the misuse of personal information contained on public registers. These are publicly available government databases such as those pertaining to motor vehicles or property valuation records. Some agencies already make records available on the internet. It has been suggested that once the information is made available electronically it is no longer feasible for the agency maintaining the register to attempt to protect privacy interests or to control the purposes for which people using the register are searching it. The privacy Commissioner has hinted at some of the privacy risks of electronic transmission (Slane, 1998, pp243-244):

- Thousands of records can be matched against others within fractions of a second;
- Data can be added to other records with ease creating new databanks and enabling the profiling of individuals;
- Sophisticated and unexpected searches can be made with ease (for example, a search of 'red BMW cars owned by women living in Seatoun' is feasible electronically but not with manual records);
- Errors in records can be rapidly transmitted to other databases and the effects on individuals multiplied;
- Registers may be vulnerable to hacking;
- Electronic transmission of data may enable persons to construct a full copy or substantial extract from a public register which could then be reworked so as to be put to different private uses.

The Privacy Commissioner has recommended that the existing Public Register Privacy Principle 3 be amended so that such information not be made available by electronic transmission unless the purpose of the transmission is to make the information available to a member of the public in New Zealand (Slane, 1998, p243). If adopted, this would have the effect that personal information contained in public registers could not be made available for search on the internet unless there was a mechanism established for limiting searches to people in New Zealand – this would appear somewhat fanciful at present as by definition the internet does not respect national boundaries.

Another recommendation targets the activities of direct marketers. There is good cause for the concern. In June 1998 thousands of Auckland (the largest city in New Zealand) valuation records were sold to a marketing company in Queensland, a jurisdiction having no privacy laws. In the first wave of marketing, Auckland property owners were the recipients of letters inviting them to "pay off your home loan four times faster without paying any more!!!" Press reports suggested "hard sell" tactics applied to those responding to the invitation.

The Privacy Commissioner has accordingly proposed the insertion of a new principle that personal information containing an individual's name, together with the individual's address or telephone number, not be made available from a public register on a volume or bulk basis unless this is consistent with the purpose for which the register is maintained (Slane, 1998, p.249).

Unique Identifiers and Intranets:
Applications in the Health Information Sphere

Recent developments in the management of health information have seen the adoption of measures with significant privacy implications. These measures have been implemented despite the existence of the Privacy Act and with little, if any public debate. Where health data is concerned both speediness of retrieval and the accuracy of the data are key attributes. The extent to which advanced information systems facilitate these goals has not yet been debated. For example, when making diagnosis and treatment decisions good medical practice might suggest not trusting information recorded by others, especially where the accuracy of the information is vital – there is seemingly little or no empirical research linking better patient health outcomes with centralised medical records.

Both private and public sector health providers in New Zealand have already begun using information systems which break new ground. These include, for instance, the use of electronic data interchange for sending and receiving laboratory test orders and results or exchanging patient details for admission and discharge. While these programmes may, with time, coalesce into larger groupings, the process was considerably speeded up in the public health sector by the adoption, in 1991, of a national health information strategy which resulted in the establishment of a new agency, the New Zealand Health Information Service (NZHIS). In turn, the NZHIS has recently established a national health register with three components: the National Health Index, the Medical Warnings System and the National Minimum Data Set. A stated goal of the NZHIS is the establishment of a Health Intranet which will provide access to all health information systems for all healthcare providers registered to use the intranet (NZHIS, 1998). The NZHIS has been active in this regard: for instance, in coordination with the agency responsible for managing pharmaceutical expenditure, the NZHIS was contracted to establish and store a data warehouse for all pharmaceutical information from across New Zealand.

It is difficult to quarrel with many of the uses of these databases. For example the Medical Warnings System enables a provider anywhere in the country to obtain potentially lifesaving information about a specific patient in their care (for instance allergies, past significant history and the like). On the other hand, it should be obvious that such information systems can be put to less benign use. For example the National Health Index (NHI) enables an individual to be positively and uniquely identified for the purposes of healthcare services and records. It is a population based register of all healthcare users in New Zealand. Each patient is assigned a unique identifier which enables linkage between different information systems. Access to the NHI is restricted to authorised users and is permitted by the Health Information Privacy Code.

While the requirements of the Act have, therefore, been satisfied, this is a superficial approach. A focus of the New Zealand law is not only in stopping leaks but also in determining where the pipes lead.

In brochures encouraging the use of the NHI number, for instance, no explanation was offered as to the information which would be collected through its use or as to the ultimate uses and recipients of it. This is contrary to both the letter and spirit of the Act. Numerous motives possibly exist for centralising health information management. They include goals such as reducing cost, eliminating fraud (in regard to government subsidies) and planning and research. However patients have not been sufficiently informed of these objectives which in itself constitutes a breach of the Act. More sinister applications of the databases include the identification of "high risk" users and possibly steps to increase the cost to them of healthcare if an "insurance" model of healthcare is adopted

There appears to be a distinct lack of public awareness of the implications of these developments. The possible ramifications of the setting up of a health intranet are evidently of little interest to members of the public. On the other hand, ordinary citizens are particularly sensitive to the potential misuse by health agencies of information about them only when such uses are physically brought to their attention.

In one case, for example, a customer complained when a pharmacy (where she was due to collect medicines which had earlier been out of stock) delivered medicines to her home without prior warning — it was a case of the extra customer service not being appreciated. While a simple phone call would have avoided the problem an interesting question arises as to whether delivering medicines are directly connected with the pharmacist's purpose for holding the customer's name and address. Another complaint arose over the wording of a form asking parents to consent to immunisation. The form did not state how the information would be used. It also contained a number without explanation. The complainant assumed that children had been allocated identification numbers and that the information would be entered into a database. In fact the number was simply a batch coding for the vaccines, so that if something went wrong with one of the batches, the affected children could be contacted. Apart from statistical data, the main use of the information was in fact to inform the children's doctors so they would know whether to offer immunisation. These cases demonstrate that members of the public exercise their privacy rights only when they are aware of the uses of information. While the Privacy Act mandates the fostering of such awareness, many agencies especially in the health sector have not lived up to the Act's expectations.

There is indeed a danger that the very existence of the Privacy Act will serve as a smokescreen for privacy violations and encourage complacency. For example it emerged, during an investigation by the Privacy Commissioner's office, that the Health Ministry's statement in its web site that the Privacy Commissioner had been involved in ensuring the highest standards of privacy had been without foundation – the office had not even been consulted (Stevens, 1998).

SUGGESTED SOLUTIONS

It is suggested that legislation such as the New Zealand Privacy Act, can protect an individual's privacy in cyberspace as in any other medium. However, this presupposes a degree of awareness of privacy rights both on the part of individuals and service providers. Some further legislative reform is needed in peripheral areas (such as interception authority for law enforcement) but, in most instances, the Act is flexible enough to adapt to the new technology. The remaining difficulties posed by the new technology may be resolved in numerous ways and some suggestions are briefly outlined below.

A Cyberspace Code?

As explained above, the Act allows the Privacy Commissioner to issue binding codes of practice governing particular activities or sectors. One could argue that the internet, because of its unique features, is one of the most pressing areas where a code is required. Such a code could protect and clarify the responsibilities of internet service providers in New Zealand although at the time of writing no such code has yet been sought by service providers. There is indeed some precedent for this in New Zealand with the GCS Code mentioned earlier. That code (now renamed the EDS Code) recognises that the agency concerned does not collect and use information for its own purposes, but rather for the client agencies it services. Nevertheless, obligations are imposed such as the duty to transfer access requests to the relevant agency.

The writer's view is that such a code is unnecessary, provided local agencies take practical steps (see below) to minimise the danger of non-compliance. This belief is reinforced by the fact that at present, very few sectors in New Zealand have considered a code to be necessary for their unique needs.

Despite this, a code may be useful to clarify certain issues, such as those which relate to automated processes mentioned above.

Encryption

One solution which has several applications is the use of encryption programs. Both the integrity of messages and the privacy of sender and receiver can be protected. However the development of more sophisticated encryption programs has led to concern on the part of law enforcement agencies whose abilities might be hindered by the same technology, hence the search for common international standards for a system of "key escrow" whereby keys to access encrypted data will be deposited with trusted third parties (Edwards, 1996 A, p.16). At the time of this writing, work on this is ongoing.

Market Regulation

It has been suggested that the market is the best arbiter of acceptable conduct by business and according to Reidenberg (1995) "when citizens learn how their information is used, they are likely to react negatively against the offending company" (p.122). This is especially relevant because under the New Zealand law, individuals *must* be told how their information is to be used.

Coercion need not be used to secure compliance with the principles of the Act. If one company offering on-line services adopts the practice of informing customers about what information it plans to hold about them and for what purposes, competitors would risk a consumer backlash if they failed to follow suit.

Information technology firms should be challenged to develop programs and software with a privacy focus. This can be of the simple informative type — informing users as they log on of the purposes of collection and uses of the information - or of the more technologically challenging type hinted at below. The utilisation of privacy templates is already widespread in New Zealand. Software developers and internet service providers have a lucrative market to develop here.

Technological Solutions

Ultimately, technological innovations might solve the very problems created by technology in the first place.

The developments in encryption techniques have already been discussed. In the related telecommunications field, caller line identification has recently been made available in New Zealand. The telephone companies have offered along with this the option, free of charge, of complete or selective blocking options to customers who do not wish their telephone numbers to be displayed at the other end of the line.

This idea could be applied to cyberspace. The technology should be developed, if it does not already exist, for those who desire it to mask their digital footprints — a sort of blocking option. The technology should also be made available to trace those who collect unauthorised data — a "counter intelligence" measure. These could be marketed as cutting edge tools on the net and would be largely self policing.

Finally the existing obligations require New Zealand internet service providers not to use or disclose individuals' traffic details except in accordance with the principles of the Act. These requirements cannot be enforced once the information has left this jurisdiction, but the enforcement will be directed at the immediate gateway from where it left. The local agency will be required to act as a type of "screen". However, once information has validly been transferred overseas, there is no guarantee that it will not be misused later. In this respect the New Zealand Act falls short of the OECD and EC standards, whereas Hong Kong and Taiwan, for instance, have much stricter transborder data flow controls.

CONCLUSION

The threat to individual privacy of cyberspace is real and growing. The response must realistically take the form of a multi-track approach, utilising regulation (at both national and international levels), greater consumer awareness as well as technological innovation. As far as the regulatory response is concerned, New Zealand has made a bold attempt with its Privacy legislation, which adopts a set of principles which apply across the board to private and public sectors. The focus is on enhancing individuals' rights to access and control the use of information about them, rather than constricting the free flow of information. The legislation applies to all forms of information, whether in cyberspace or outside it, and is flexible. Unfortunately, however, while the Act applies *in theory* to cyberspace, the over-whelming focus of the public to date has been with less unobstrusive interferences with privacy with the result that many technological based privacy concerns have yet to be addressed.

ENDNOTES

1   Comparing information about individuals collected and held by one government department for a specific purpose with information about those individuals collected by another government department for a different purpose(this is not the statutory definition).

2   And possibly even persons outside New Zealand: as to the potential extraterritorial application of the Act see infra.

3   As to which see infra.

4   The most obvious exception to this is Principle 1, see infra.

5   Article 17 of the 1966 United Nations Covenant on Civil &Political Rights reproduces Article 12 of the 1948 Universal Declaration of Human Rights which provides: "no one shall be subjected to arbitrary or unlawful interference with his privacy" and that "everyone has the right to the protection of the law against such interference"; the 1980 recommendation by the Organisation for Economic Cooperation & Development (OECD) of Guidelines Concerning the Protection of Privacy and Transborder Flows of Personal Data; the 1981 adoption by the Council of Europe of the Convention for the Protection of Individuals with Regard to Automatic Processing of personal Data; the 1980 adoption by the United Nations General Assembly of Guidelines for the Regulation of Computerised Personal Data Files are amongst the most important.

6   The freedom of expression is now enshrined in the New Zealand Bill of Rights Act 1990 s14.

7   See infra for a brief discussion of this issue.

8   Starting with the Official information Act 1982.

9   Several of its provisions were not fully enforceable in respect of conduct occuring before 1 July 1996.

10   Section 97 defines information matching to mean "the comparison (whether manually or by means of any electronic or other device) of any document that contains personal information about 10 or more individuals with 1 or more other documents that contain personal information about 10 or more individuals, for the purpose of producing or verifying information that may be used for the purpose of taking adverse action against an identifiable individual."

11   With a few exceptions, for instance the legislature and the judiciary.

12   In section 2.

13   *Ombudsman Quarterly Review* (1995) 1 (4) December 1995
14   Section 67; the complaints procedure under the Act is briefly explained infra.
15   See infra.
16   See infra.
17   Several International and Regional Security Standards already exist.
18   Government Computing Service
19   See supra.

REFERENCES

Bedingfield, D. (1992). Privacy or Publicity? The enduring confusion surrounding the American tort of invasion of privacy. *Modern Law Review*, 55, 114.

Branscomb, A.W. (1995). *Who Owns Information? From Privacy to Public Access.* New York. Basic Books.

Edwards, J. (1996 A). The Potential Impact of the Internet on Privacy Rights. *Human Rights Law and Practice*, 2(June), 10,16,18.

Edwards, J. (1996 B). Current privacy Issues In Telecommunications. Paper presented at Privacy Forum, Christchurch Convention Centre, June 13.

Liddell, G. (1996). The Internet and the Privacy Act. Paper presented at Privacy Forum, Christchurch Convention Centre, June 13.

New Zealand Herald. (1996 A). 25 October, 2.

New Zealand Herald. (1996 B). 28 October, A12.

NHIS (1998) *Health intranet project.* Http://www.nzhis.govt.nz/projects/intranet.html.

Reidenberg, J. (1995). The Fundamental Role of privacy and Confidence in the Network. *Wake Forest law Review*, 30(1), 122.

Slane, B. (1995). Privacy and Technology - Keynote address to the *LAWASIA Conference on Intellectual Property Law in the Asia Pacific Region*, Hyatt Regency, Adelaide, March 29. Appendix 3.

Slane, B. (1998). *Necessary and Desirable privacy Act 1993 Review* Office of the Privacy Commissioner, Wellington.

Stevens, R. (1998) *Medical record databases; Just what you need?* A Report for the privacy Commissioner, April

About the Authors

Chapter 1

Jonathan Palmer is an Assistant Professor at the University of Maryland, College Park. His research interests include the strategic use of IT, electronic commerce, and virtual organizations. His work has appeared or been accepted for publication in Information Systems Research, Communications of the ACM, Journal of World Business, Journal of Computer-Mediated Communication, European Management Journal, The Information Society, International Journal of Electronic Commerce, International Journal of Human-Computer Studies, JASIS. Palmer serves on the editorial board of International Journal of Electronic Markets and Electronic Journal of Organizational Virtualness. He served on the faculty at the University of Oklahoma and taught at the University of Southern California. Palmer was director of corporate relations at The Peter F. Drucker School the Claremont Graduate University in California. His previous academic experience includes administrative positions at The Fletcher School of Law and Diplomacy and The Harvard Business School. Ph.D. Claremont Graduate University.

Jamie Kliewer is currently teaching computer science in Phnom Penh, Cambodia. He is a graduate of the University of Oklahoma in Management Information Systems where he was a J.C. Penney Leadership Fellow.

Mark Sweat is a consultant and analyst in MIS and electronic commerce at Koch Industries in Wichita, Kansas. He is a graduate of the University of Oklahoma in Management Information Systems where he was a J.C. Penney Leadership Fellow and worked for the Center for MIS Studies.

Chapter 2

Jairo Gutierrez is a Senior Lecturer in Information Systems at The University of Auckland. Previously he worked as an R&D Manager, Systems Integration Consultant, and Information Systems Manager. He also conducted seminars on LAN/WAN technologies. He teaches data communications and computer networking. His current research topics are in network management systems, programmable networks, and high-speed computer networking. He received a Systems and Computer Engineering degree from The University of The Andes (Colombia, 1983), a Masters degree in Computer Science from Texas A&M University (1985), and a Ph.D. (1997) in Information Systems from the University of Auckland (New Zealand).

Chapter 3

Dieter Fink is Associate Professor in the School of Management Information Systems at Edith Cowan University in Perth, Western Australia. Prior to joining academe he worked as a Systems Engineer for IBM and as Manager Consultant for Arthur Young & Co (now Ernst & Young). His teaching and research interests are in IS management where he specialises in IT security, investment justification and benefits management. Dr Fink is the author of "Information Technology Security - Managing Challenges and Creating Opportunities", published by CCH Australia. Other publications have appeared in journals such as Long Range Planning, Australian Journal of Information Systems and Internal Journal of Information Management . A current research project is the delivery of knowledge services by professional service firms using Internet technologies.

Chapter 4

Lech Janczewski, (MEng - Warsaw, MASc - Toronto, DEng - Warsaw) has over thirty years experience in information technology. He was the managing director of the largest IBM installation in Poland and project manager of the first computing center in the Niger State of Nigeria. He is currently with the Department of Management Science and Information Systems of the University of Auckland, New Zealand. His area of research includes management of IS resources with the special emphasis on data security and information systems investments in under-developed countries. Dr Janczewski wrote over 60 publications presented in scientific journals, conference proceedings and chapters in books. He is the chairperson of the New Zealand Information Security Forum.

Chapter 5

Fredj Dridi is a Ph.D. student at the Dept. of Information Systems and Software Techniques at the University of Essen, Germany. He received his diploma degree in Computer Science 1995 from the University of Kaiserslautern. Between 1992 and 1996 he was working at DFKI on intelligent engineering systems. Currently, his working areas are Information Systems, Security Management, Internet/Intranet Technologies and Software Engineering.

Gustaf Neumann was appointed Chair for Information Systems / New Media at the Vienna University of Economics and Business Administration in November 1999. A native of Vienna, Austria, he graduated from the Vienna University of Economics and Business Administration (WU), Austria, in 1983 and holds a Ph.D. from the same university. He joined the faculty of WU in 1983 as Assistant Professor at the MIS department and served as head of the research group for Logic Programming and Intelligent Information Systems. Before joining the Vienna University, Gustaf Neumann was Prof. of Information Systems and Software Techniques at the University of Essen, Germany. Earlier he was working as a visiting scientist at IBM's T.J. Watson Research Center in Yorktown Heights, NY, from 1985-1986 and 1993-1995. In 1987, he was awarded the Heinz-Zemanek award of the Austrian Association of Computer Science (OCG) for best dissertation

(Metainterpreter Directed Compilation of Logic Programs into Prolog). Professor Neumann has published books and papers in the areas of program transformation, data modeling, information systems technology and security management. He is the author of several widely used programs that are freely available, such as the TeX-dvi converter dvi2xx and the graphical front-end package Wafe.

Chapter 6

Henry B. Wolfe has been an active computer professional for more than 40 years. He has earned a number of university degrees culminating with a Doctor of Philosophy from the University of Otago. The first ten years of his career was spent designing systems in a manufacturing environment. The next ten years of ever increasing responsibility was devoted to serving in the U.S. Federal Government rising to the position of Director of MIS for the Overseas Private Investment Corporation. After a short (and successful) foray into the oil and natural gas business Dr. Wolfe took up an academic post at the University of Otago and for the past fifteen or so years has specialized in computer security. During that period he has earned an international reputation in the field of computer virus defenses. Dr Wolfe occasionally writes about a wide range of security and privacy issues for Computers & Security, Network Security and the Computer Fraud & Security Bulletin (where he is also an Editorial Adviser).

Chapter 7

Dieter Gollmann was a scientific assistant at the University of Karlsruhe, Germany, where he was awarded the 'venia legendi' for computer science in 1991. At Royal Holloway, University of London) he worked as a Lecturer, Senior Lecturer, Reader, and finally as a Professor in Computer Science. He was a Visiting Professor at the Technical University of Graz in 1991 and an Adjunct Professor at the Information Security Research Centre, QUT, Brisbane, in 1995. He has been acting as a consultant for HP Laboratories (Bristol) and joined Microsoft Research in Cambridge in 1998. He has published a textbook on Computer Security and over 50 research papers on topics in cryptography and information security. He has served on the program committees of the major European conferences on computer security (ESORICS) and cryptography (EUROCRYPT), as well as other international conferences in these areas.

Chapter 8

Chris Mitchell received his B.Sc. (1975) and Ph.D. (1979) degrees in Mathematics from Westfield College, London University. Prior to his appointment in 1990 as Professor of Computer Science at Royal Holloway, University of London, he was a Project Manager in the Networks and Communications Laboratory of Hewlett-Packard Laboratories in Bristol, which he joined in June 1985. Between 1979 and 1985 he was at Racal-Comsec Ltd. (Salisbury, UK), latterly as Chief Mathematician. He has made contributions to a number of international collaborative projects, including two EU ACTS projects on security for third generation mobile telecommunications systems, and is currently convenor of Technical Panel

2 of BSI IST/33, dealing with Security Mechanisms and providing input to ISO/IEC JTC1/SC27 on which he currently serves as a UK Expert and as editor of two international security standards. He is academic editor of Computer and Communications Security Abstracts, and a member of the Editorial Advisory Board for the journals of the London Mathematical Society. He has published over 100 papers, mostly on security-related topics, and he continues to act as a consultant on a variety of topics in information security.

Chapter 9

Charles Prysby is a professor and head of the department of political science at the University of North Carolina at Greensboro. He received his Ph.D. from Michigan State University in 1973. His primary areas of research are in voting behavior, political parties, southern electoral politics, and contextual effects on political behavior. His articles have appeared in a number of journals and edited books, and he is the coauthor of *Political Behavior and the Local Context* (Praeger, 1991). He also is the coauthor of the computer-based instructional packages on voting behavior in presidential elections published by the American Political Science Association as part of the SETUPS series. For a number of years he has taught a graduate course on computer applications in public administration.

Nicole Prysby is an attorney with interests in the area of employment law. She received her J.D. with honors from the University of North Carolina School of Law in 1995. She is a contributing author for several publications in the employment and human resource law area, including the *State by State Guide to Human Resource Law*, and the *Multistate Payroll Guide*, and is a co-author of the *Multistate Guide to Benefits Law* (all Aspen/Panel). She currently is working in the field of environmental consulting, for Perrin Quarles, Associates, in Charlottesville, Virginia. From 1995-1997, she was an attorney in the Public Law Department at the National Legal Research Group, Charlottesville, Virginia.

Chapter 10

Gehan Gunasekara (BA,LLB *Wellington*, LLM (Hons) *Auckland)* is a lecturer in Information Technology Law at the University of Auckland. He teaches law subjects at the University's School of Business and Economics including undergraduate and post-graduate papers on privacy and data protection law. He has published articles in legal journals in both New Zealand and the United Kingdom and has contributed to several text books. His most recent and on-going research is a study of New Zealand's privacy legislation. Gehan is also interested in several other areas of commercial law. He is a Barristor and Solicitor of the High Court of New Zealand.

Index